SCALIA DISSENTS

SCALIA DISSENTS

Writings of the Supreme Court's
Wittiest, Most Outspoken Justice

Edited, and with an Introduction and Commentary
by Kevin A. Ring

Since 1947
REGNERY
PUBLISHING, INC.
An Eagle Publishing Company • Washington, DC

Library of Congress Cataloging-in-Publication Data
Scalia, Antonin.
    Scalia dissents : writings of the Supreme Court's wittiest, most outspoken justice / edited, and with an introduction and commentary, by Kevin A. Ring.
    p.   cm. Includes index.
   ISBN 0-89526-053-0 : (alk. paper)
  1. Scalia, Antonin. 2. Judicial opinions—United States. I. Ring, Kevin A.
II. Title.
   KF213.S32 2004 348.73'26—dc22

                                                                2004020794

Published in the United States by
Regnery Publishing, Inc.
An Eagle Publishing Company
One Massachusetts Avenue, NW
Washington, DC 20001
Visit us at www.regnery.com

Distributed to the trade by
National Book Network
4720-A Boston Way
Lanham, MD 20706

Printed on acid-free paper
Manufactured in the United States of America
10 9 8 7 6 5 4 3 2 1

Books are available in quantity for promotional or premium use. Write to Director of Special Sales, Regnery Publishing, Inc., One Massachusetts Avenue, NW, Washington, DC 20001, for information on discounts and terms or call (202) 216-0600.

For Kerrie

CONTENTS

INTRODUCTION

CALL IT A "SCALIA MOMENT." You are reading the latest opinion of Supreme Court Associate Justice Antonin Scalia and come across a witty line or turn of phrase that makes you laugh aloud, an insight or observation that makes you nod your head in agreement, or a caustic barb that makes you wince for the target. Since his appointment in 1986, Scalia has been the Court's premier conservative, intellectual gladiator, and chief wordsmith. More than anyone who has served on the High Court in recent history, Scalia has given life to Aristotle's injunction that "it is not enough to know what to say—one must know how to say it."[1]

His words can be pointed. "Today's opinion has no foundation in American constitutional law, and barely pretends to," he charged in one case.[2]

Scalia's opinions can also be witty and humorous. Explaining why he did not think the Court should try to create a standard for defining "literary or artistic value" in an obscenity case, Scalia said ". . . in my view it is quite impossible to come to an objective assessment of (at least) literary or artistic value, there being many accomplished people who found literature in Dada and art in the replication of a soup can."[3] In another decision, he explained why the Court could comfortably rely on the testimony of witnesses who saw the face of an alleged killer: "Facial features are the *primary means* by which human beings recognize one another. That is why police departments distribute "mug" shots of wanted felons, rather than Ivy-League-type posture pictures; it is why bank robbers wear stockings over their faces instead of floor-length capes over their shoulders; it is why the Lone Ranger wears a mask instead of a poncho; and it is why a criminal defense lawyer who seeks to destroy an identifying witness by asking 'You admit that you saw only the killer's face?' will be laughed out of the courtroom."[4]

His humor is often subtle. Consider his explanation of the proper meaning of the term, "modify." "'Modify,' in our view, connotes moderate change. It might be good English to say that the French Revolution 'modified' the status of the French nobility—but only because there is a figure of speech called understatement and a literary device known as sarcasm."[5]

Scalia can use words to create vivid images that help communicate his arguments. In one case, rather than simply admonish the Court for its selective use of the oft-criticized *Lemon* test, which was created to identify government action that violates the religious Establishment Clause (see chapter seven), Scalia wrote, "Like some ghoul in a late-night horror movie that repeatedly sits up in his grave and shuffles abroad, after being repeatedly killed and buried, *Lemon* stalks our Establishment Clause jurisprudence once again, frightening the little children and school attorneys of Center Moriches Union Free School District."[6]

Decrying the Court's refusal to reconsider its controversial decision in *Roe v. Wade* despite agreement among the majority of the Court that the decision was flawed, Scalia said, "It thus appears the mansion of constitutionalized abortion law, constructed overnight in *Roe v. Wade*, must be disassembled doorjamb by doorjamb, and never entirely brought down, no matter how wrong it might be."[7]

In addition, Scalia has a talent for putting complex arguments about fundamental principles in easy-to-understand terms. Slicing through the various First Amendment analyses that might be applied to determine the speech rights of the religious, Scalia concluded, "A priest has as much liberty to proselytize as a patriot."[8] In another case, while arguing for freedom of political parties to set their own rules of organization, Scalia wrote, "A freedom of political association that must await the Government's favorable response to a 'Mother, may I?' is not freedom of political association at all."[9]

Finally, as even casual followers of the Supreme Court know, Scalia's words can reveal his outrage at the decisions reached and lack of judicial restraint demonstrated by his colleagues on the High Court. Scalia concluded one opinion, "The Court must be living in another world. Day by day, case by case, it is busy designing a Constitution for a country I do not recognize."[10] And in another: "This Court seems incapable of admitting that some matters—*any* matters—are none of its business."[11]

Scalia's way with words is what makes this book possible. His opinions—though full of legal arguments and analyses only a lawyer could love—are highly readable. His entertaining writing style can make even the most mundane areas of the law interesting. It is no small feat.

The opinions chosen for this book are not necessarily Scalia's most important, but those that I believe are the most interesting to read. Moreover, *Scalia Dissents* is not a technically accurate title for this book; a reader will recognize that more than just dissenting opinions have been included. However, it is fitting because nearly every opinion reveals Scalia in strong disagreement with the reasoning, if not the conclusion, of a majority of the Court. These disagreements often prompt the justice to write his most passionate and memorable opinions.

The following writings show Scalia's judicial philosophy in practice, reveal his skill at argumentation, demonstrate his ability to foresee future controversies, and showcase his compelling writing style. In every opinion, a combination of these factors is at work. Before each opinion, I provide information to give the reader background on the case: the relevant text of the Constitution, its historical interpretation, Scalia's general view of the text, the Court's previous decisions in the area, the relevant facts that led to the case, and the opinions of the Court and other Justices.

For the sake of readability, I have eliminated many citations and almost all footnotes. Legal opinions are usually full of references to other cases or materials in order to support the arguments made therein. If a reader wishes to dig deeper into one or more opinions, he or she should consult an unedited version of the opinions.

A note about labels: After describing Scalia as the Court's "premier conservative," I spend some time arguing and include some cases to demonstrate that he is not always in step with political conservatives. The reason for the apparent conflict is that there is a difference between a "judicial conservative" and a "political conservative." By political conservative, I refer to an elected official or political activist who supports a set of policies, including smaller government, lower taxes, and traditional social values. By judicial conservative, I mean a judge who does not advance any political or policy preferences, but whose approach to constitutional and statutory interpretation involves fidelity to the text of the Constitution and adherence to the original

understanding of that document or to the intent of its drafters. A judicial conservative's approach will result in many politically conservative
outcomes, but it should not and will not always be the case.

Finally, it should be noted that this book is not a personal biogra-
phy of Justice Scalia. Though facts about his background are mentioned when relevant, I would like to merely share Scalia's most
compelling opinions and give readers, for the benefit of context, an
overview of his judicial philosophy.

Justice Scalia's way with words, his reasoning, and his vision—all
are showcased in the chapters that follow. Experience some of the
most noteworthy, colorful, and entertaining opinions ever written by
a United States Supreme Court Justice. And, finally, enjoy some classic "Scalia moments."

CHAPTER ONE

SCALIA'S PHILOSOPHY

J USTICE ANTONIN SCALIA is a verbal craftsman. His mastery of language and respect for words carry over into his judicial philosophy. That philosophy is fairly simple and straightforward, and he has explained and championed it in his opinions, public speeches, and even a book. As with his memorable opinions, the primary focus of Scalia's philosophy is *words*.

Scalia is a self-proclaimed "textualist." He believes laws—and especially that supreme law known as the Constitution of the United States—say what they mean and mean what they say. In short, when interpreting the Constitution, Scalia thinks judges should focus on the text. If someone claims he or she is being denied the exercise of a right or if the government asserts it has authority to take a given action, courts must make certain there is specific textual support for each assertion.

If the proper meaning of the text is clear, judges should then determine whether it provides support for the claimed individual right or governmental authority. If so, the claim is valid; if not, it should be rejected. The analysis is complete.

If the text is ambiguous or not dispositive, however, Scalia says courts should look to see if support for the claimed right or authority exists in the legal and social traditions of the United States. If an agency of government has been exercising a certain authority since the Constitution was adopted and it has been accepted by law or custom, it should stand. Conversely, if an asserted individual liberty has been prohibited by the states throughout history, the claim for constitutional protection should fail. Scalia has used the lack of textual and historical support to oppose recognition of, among others, the "right" to abortion (chapter five) and the "right" to die (see chapter twelve).

Scalia also advocates adoption and adherence to general and clear rules when interpreting the Constitution. For instance, with regard to the Fourth Amendment's prohibition on unreasonable searches and seizures, Scalia has noted that it is not always clear what constitutes a seizure[1]. Of course an individual has been seized if he has been physically forced into the back of a police car, but what if a suspect were being chased by police on foot? He certainly does not have freedom of movement at that point, but has he been seized for constitutional purposes? Scalia says that questions like this should be answered whenever possible with clear general rules. In a case involving these very facts, he joined an opinion that argued that police conduct does not constitute a seizure until it has had "a restraining effect." Such a rule, if adopted by the Court, would help to define what constitutes a seizure for all future related cases.

In Scalia's view, general rules are beneficial because they provide notice and certainty to the public that is expected to obey the law.[2] They also ensure that the American people will receive equal and consistent treatment, and not be subjected to the predilections of the current justices on the Court or to shifting popular opinion.

Consistent with his textualism and preference for clear lines, Scalia argues for a strict separation of powers between the executive, legislative, and judicial branches of the federal government. In his view, each branch of government has the authority granted to it by the Constitution. No more, no less. None of the branches can give up its power or exercise authority given to another branch, even if consent is explicit and the goal is more efficient government. Scalia contends the Constitution's structural designs—separation of powers (division of power among three federal branches) and federalism (division of power between federal government and states)—are more important to safeguarding individual liberties than the Bill of Rights (chapter three).[3]

Nevertheless, the Bill of Rights is not unimportant in Scalia's philosophy. He believes the freedoms enumerated in the Bill of Rights are nonnegotiable and deserve the highest level of protection, even when competing interests seem convincing. For example, the Confrontation Clause of the Sixth Amendment guarantees criminal defendants the right "to be confronted with the witnesses against him." The clause does not say defendants shall have that right "sometimes" or "often" and it does not cover "some" witnesses. All the time, all witnesses. Yet a majority of the Supreme Court has held that in light of modern psychology's concerns about the impact on youthful accusers and witnesses, especially those alleging sexual abuse, use of closed-circuit television does not abridge a defendant's confrontation right. Scalia opposed the Court's decision and said the Sixth Amendment should not be watered down to avoid potential harm to child witnesses.[4] The text is clear. The right is guaranteed.

These are the types of difficult cases, Scalia believes, for which the Framers designed a Constitution and gave the justices of the Supreme Court the benefit of life tenure—to prevent society from changing the law in ways that violate the enduring values the nation enshrined in the text of the Constitution. After all, Scalia argues, a democratic nation does not need a written constitution to reflect current values.[5] Elections do that. A written constitution is needed to protect values *against* prevailing wisdom.

For example, the First Amendment to the United States Constitution prohibits the suppression of free expression. The Framers wanted to create an environment in which all ideas would be heard and debated, and the best would prevail. They understood that for a self-governing people this freedom had to include the right to criticize the government.

Nearly two hundred years later, a substantial majority of the American public seemed willing to forfeit some of that freedom to curb a form of political protest that offended it: burning the American flag. The Congress, being a political body, responded by passing the Flag Protection Act of 1989. Scalia voted with four of his colleagues to strike down the law on the grounds that the act of burning the flag amounted to protected speech.[6] The value enshrined in the First Amendment—freedom of speech, especially political speech—must trump popular opinion, however strongly held, or the First Amendment's guarantee is meaningless (see chapter nine).

Scalia contends the nation's founding charter is flexible enough—as written—to deal with most challenges presented by modernity. The same guarantee of freedom of "the press," which covered early American printing presses, applies with equal force today to the online press, even though the Framers could not have foreseen computers, much less the Internet. When ruling on the legality of a police department's use of thermal imaging to search a suspected drug dealer's house for contraband without a warrant, Scalia did not find the Constitution lacking, even though it was written before sheriffs had cars, let alone thermal imaging technology. Scalia wrote for the Court's majority that the Fourth Amendment's prohibition against unreasonable searches protected Americans against this modern law enforcement practice.[7]

Finally, Scalia's fidelity to the Constitution does not lead him to conclude that the document cannot be changed. He simply argues it should only be amended according to the procedures set forth in the charter itself. The Constitution's amendment process was followed when the American people wanted to make structural changes to their government, as when they ratified the Seventeenth Amendment to provide for direct election of United States Senators. And, he has pointed out, it was used when Americans wished to create additional individual rights, such as when the Nineteenth Amendment was ratified to guarantee women the right to vote.[8]

Some might believe changes such as women's suffrage were long overdue and should have been incorporated into the Constitution by a more generous interpretation of another provision, such as the Equal Protection Clause. Yet the Supreme Court in those days did not feel empowered to establish new rights without textual or, at least, historical support. As important and overdue as the women's right to vote was, its legitimacy was established by its adoption—as required by the Constitution—by a two-thirds vote of the Congress and ratification by 75 percent of the states. This legitimacy stands in stark contrast to the way rights are added to the Constitution by activist judges today.

Scalia's judicial philosophy and methodology for constitutional interpretation are fairly simple to describe but not always easy to apply. Scalia admits as much.[9] But he says, adherence to his approach would help to steer judges clear of policymaking roles. Further, Scalia says you can't beat his methodology with no methodology[10]—and yet no other current justice of the Supreme Court is consistently applying an alternative theory of interpretation.

PHILOSOPHY IN PRACTICE

In applying his unique judicial philosophy, Scalia bucks some modern trends in constitutional interpretation. Chief among those theories is that of a "living" Constitution. The idea is that the document's meaning changes from age to age to accommodate the evolving values of the American people.[11] This view of constitutional interpretation, which is shared to some extent by nearly all liberal legal scholars, gives judges tremendous power. After all, it is the judge who gets to decide which rights and responsibilities are valued by the public and which ones can be discarded. The obvious danger in such an approach is that the rule of law becomes rule by lawyers.

In politically incorrect splendor, Scalia says he likes his Constitution "dead."[12] He argues that only a fixed and enduring charter can keep judges from reading new fads into the Constitution and less popular mandates out. He has pointed to the death penalty, ironically, as a good example of the dangers of a "living" Constitution.[13] Although the text of the Constitution specifically contemplates capital punishment, three members of the Supreme Court during the last twenty years have declared it unconstitutional in all situations (see chapter six). In their view, government-administered execution is no longer in synch with "evolving standards of decency." Still other judges have limited states' use of capital punishment against certain classes of convicted criminals after deciding, in their view, that it is now "cruel and unusual."

As breezily as advocates of a "living" Constitution write the death penalty out of the Constitution, they also read new rights into the nation's charter. Whether one believes a right to sodomy should or should not be protected, the Supreme Court decided in 1986 that it was not protected for the simple and obvious reasons that the Constitution does not mention it and because there is no history of protection for the liberty to engage in sodomy. Indeed, the opposite is true. Until 1961, every state across the country had prohibited it. The Supreme Court in 1986 did not argue that the states were correct to ban sodomy. Nor did it say, conversely, that states must ban sodomy. All it said was that because sodomy was not protected by an explicit provision of the Constitution or by a long-standing tradition of protecting the act, the voters of each state were free to decide whether or not to protect the practice within their borders.

Just seventeen years later, the Supreme Court in *Lawrence* v. *Texas* (2003) said quite simply, "that was then, this is now." Sodomy *is* a constitutional right. The "living" Constitution apparently "matured" between birthdays number 195 and 212 to the point that it now protects an individual's right to engage in sodomy and bars states from regulating it. For textualists like Scalia, the result does not change unless the law, that is, the text, changes. Thus, neither sodomy nor any other favored activity can become a constitutional right without passage of a constitutional amendment. But as Scalia wrote, for the advocates of the "living" Constitution every issue is open to new and changing interpretations.[14]

Though not to the degree it conflicts with the living Constitution theory, Scalia's approach also differs from a couple of modes of interpretation that are fashionable in conservative legal camps. While nearly all judicial conservatives agree that the text should control, they diverge over how to interpret ambiguous text or how to apply it to unforeseen circumstances. Some judicial conservatives suggest the proper interpretation can be discerned by examining the "original intent" of the Framers. They search the historical record in an attempt to figure out what James Madison or another drafter of the Constitution intended a particular provision—the Establishment Clause, for example—to accomplish. But this mode of interpretation suffers from its reliance on something that may be unknowable. To continue the example, if a search of the historical record revealed that James Madison intended the Establishment Clause to prevent only the declaration of a national religion, while every other Framer who supported its adoption intended the clause to prohibit any manifestation of government support for religion generally, whose intent should be determinative?

For this reason, among others, Scalia does not find intent authoritative. Instead, he searches for "original meaning," which he defines as the original understanding of the text at the time it was drafted and ratified. This theory of interpretation is known as originalism, as opposed to "original intent." To be sure, an originalist will look to many of the same historical sources that a proponent of original intent does; for example, the record of debates regarding the Constitution's ratification and the writings of the Framers. Scalia uses these sources not to determine the drafters' intent but to gain valuable insight into what the most informed people of the time understood the words of the Constitution to mean.

Scalia's reliance on context when interpreting the text of the Constitution also distinguishes him from those judicial conservatives, known as "strict constructionists," who believe all words should be interpreted narrowly. For example, where a strict constructionist might see the First Amendment as protecting "speech" and "press" and only activities that fit into one of those categories, Scalia says the First Amendment covers communication more generally. Thus, while a handwritten letter might not fall under "speech" or "press" for strict constructionists, he thinks such a letter is undoubtedly protected by the First Amendment.[15]

Scalia's textualism (informed by originalism) is a unique judicial philosophy. Moreover, Scalia is unique simply because he has articulated a coherent judicial philosophy that he applies to all cases. Some justices on the current Supreme Court seem to agree with parts of Scalia's methodology and disagree with others, but no other justice has put forward a comprehensive theory of constitutional interpretation to rival Scalia's.

The uniqueness of Scalia's philosophy—and the uniqueness in even articulating and adhering to a guiding philosophy—alone does not explain his near-cult-like following among many conservatives. After all, there have been other conservatives in government who have pressed the Right's view of the world. Even on the current Supreme Court, Chief Justice William Rehnquist and Justice Clarence Thomas have argued for greater fidelity to the Constitution and against judicial activism. What distinguishes Scalia is his ability to communicate the conservative judicial philosophy in a passionate, persuasive, and entertaining manner.

Scalia's unique communication skills are the product of what even liberal icons like Senator Ted Kennedy have described as a "brilliant" intellect.[16] Indeed, when first appointed to the Court, Scalia was considered to be an "intellectual lodestar who would pull the Court to the right by the force of his brilliance."[17] How bright is he? He graduated first in his high school class at Xavier Military Academy in Manhattan, first in his class at Georgetown University, and magna cum laude at Harvard Law School where he served as editor of the school's law review.[18] Scalia was so superior academically that one classmate said, "people just competed for second."[19]

Scalia's brilliance gives him a unique ability to foresee the logical (and often illogical) legal and policy consequences of the Court's decisions. Especially when in dissent, Scalia has used this ability to call attention to the flaws in the Court's reasoning, not only because of the result it produced in the case at hand but because of the results it is likely to produce in future cases. Illustrations abound.

In *Morrison* v. *Olson* (1988), the Supreme Court upheld the constitutionality of the law authorizing appointment of Independent Counsels. The law created a new office to prosecute alleged crimes of certain executive branch officials. In order to give the new prosecutor additional independence, the law limited the president's ability to appoint or terminate a counsel. Scalia wrote a memorable solo dissenting opinion in which he not only set forth the Constitution's structural incompatibility with the Independent Counsel law, he also foresaw the real-world problems the law posed (see chapter three). Scalia said that having a prosecutor who is not part of the executive branch (as the Constitution requires) will lead to unaccountable Inspector Javerts running wild in order to "get" someone.

Republicans acknowledged Scalia's prescience after watching Independent Counsel Lawrence Walsh announce the indictment of President George H. W. Bush's defense secretary a mere week before the 1992 election. Democrats did not appreciate Scalia's insight until Independent Counsel Kenneth Starr's investigation of President Bill Clinton culminated in his impeachment in 1998. Senate Democratic Whip Harry Reid, for one, took to the Senate floor to extol "the very articulate, brilliant Supreme Court Justice Antonin Scalia,"[20] who in his "visionary" *Morrison* dissent "predicted what we are now witnessing."[21] With each side's ox gored, Republicans and Democrats in the Congress both agreed to let the Independent Counsel statute expire in 1999.

In *Lee* v. *Weisman* (1992), the Supreme Court held that making students listen to nonecumenical invocations and benedictions at public high school graduation ceremonies amounted to coercion and breached the wall of separation between church and state required by the First Amendment's Establishment Clause. Scalia, in dissent, argued that whatever level of uneasiness nonbelieving adults feel when listening to prayers, it does not amount to an establishment of religion (see chapter seven). During the course of his argument, Scalia said if simply hearing a prayer amounts to impermissible coercion, then the Court was likely to find recitation of the Pledge of Allegiance at high school ceremonies unconstitutional. He noted that the Pledge had since 1954 included the words "under God." Scalia proved to be prophetic. In 2003, the Ninth Circuit Court of Appeals held that recitation of the Pledge in grade school classrooms violated the Establishment Clause. The Supreme Court in 2004 reversed the decision on procedural grounds, but the Pledge controversy is likely to return at some point in the future.

Finally, in *Lawrence* v. *Texas*, the 2003 Court decision declaring homosexual sodomy a constitutionally protected right, Scalia warned that the Court's reasoning would undermine state laws against same-sex marriages (see chapter eleven). Eight months later, the Massachusetts Supreme Judicial Court struck down the state ban on such marriages. Sooner than perhaps even he suspected, that issue will be before Scalia and the other justices of the Supreme Court.

THE CRITICS

While they concede he possesses a potent intellect, Scalia's critics have devoted a great deal of energy and ink to highlighting what they deem the flaws in his performance on the Court. Their criticism of Scalia almost always includes one of three points: (1) he does not apply his judicial philosophy consistently; (2) despite his complaints about activist judges, he himself is a judicial activist; and (3) he has failed to win majorities on the issues he cares about most deeply.

First, critics say that while Scalia loves to crow about his textualist methodology, he does not always apply it consistently. This criticism usually includes the charge that he deserts his methodology when it conflicts with a politically conservative agenda. His critics usually point to one or two of his several hundred opinions and argue that they are out of synch with one facet or another of his approach.

For example, a few critics have attacked Scalia's interpretation of the Equal Protection Clause of the Fourteenth Amendment as inconsistent with his professed allegiance to the Constitution's original meaning.[22] These critics argue that the Fourteenth Amendment was originally understood to benefit black Americans. They also make note of the historical evidence that affirmative action existed at the time the Equal Protection Clause was adopted. From these facts, they conclude that in using the Fourteenth Amendment to oppose affirmative action programs, Scalia ignores his originalist approach.

What this and related criticisms miss, however, is that Scalia is first and always a textualist. Originalism informs his understanding of the text, especially when the words are unclear, but the plain text is the law for Scalia. When he interprets the Equal Protection Clause of the Fourteenth Amendment—"no state . . . shall deny to any person within its jurisdiction the equal protection of the laws"—he reads "any person" to mean, as it says, any person. Black, white, brown—Americans of every color—deserve equal treatment according to the text. This interpretation of the Equal Protection Clause is not a case of Scalia ignoring his philosophy; it is a compelling example of his application of it.

The decisions and votes his critics do not point to are far more illuminating than the ones they do. For if his critics are right that Scalia disregards his philosophy when it leads to results that do not match his politically conservative ideology, it should be difficult to find in Scalia's jurisprudence examples that produced results diametrically opposed to the goals of a political conservative. Yet even a cursory review of his record reveals numerous such examples.

In *Employment Division of Oregon* v. *Smith* (1990), for example, Scalia wrote a majority opinion for the Court that was assailed almost universally by faith-driven conservatives for insufficiently protecting religious freedom. The case involved ceremonial use of peyote, an illegal drug in the State of Oregon, by Native Americans. Scalia, a strong proponent of legislative accommodation of religious exercise, said the Constitution only requires the courts to protect religion when its exercise is being attacked specifically by a government law or policy. Oregon's law, by contrast, prohibited any and all uses of peyote and did not target the Native Americans' rituals. Faithful to his philosophy, he refused to allow the Court to enter the business of crafting religious accommodations. That job should be left to the legislature, Scalia argued.

Scalia's commitment to textualism in some cases involving so-called substantive due process rights also produced results out of step with the political conservative agenda. He never accedes to the creation of "rights" favored by political conservatives (or liberals, for that matter).

In *Troxel* v. *Granville* (2000), for example, the issue of parental rights came before the Court (see chapter twelve). A plurality of the justices held that a mother had a constitutionally protected liberty to restrict the visitation privileges of her child's grandparents.

While it is hard to imagine that Scalia, father of nine children, is hostile to the idea that parents should have the freedom to raise their children as they see fit, he did not let any personal sympathy subordinate his view that rights not contained in the Constitution should not be added by judges. In his dissenting opinion, Scalia acknowledged that the Supreme Court in the 1920s created a constitutional right of parents "to direct the upbringing of their children." He argued, however, that this "right" had no basis in the text of the Constitution and thus should not be maintained, much less broadened. For Scalia, any issue not specifically addressed by the text or by tradition should be left to the American people to decide through democratic means.

Finally, Scalia provided the fifth and deciding vote to invalidate the aforementioned federal law prohibiting flag burning. Although later admitting in a speech that he does not care for "scruffy, bearded, sandal-wearing people who go around burning the United States flag,"[23] in *United States* v. *Eichman* (1990), Scalia agreed with a majority of the Court that an act of Congress criminalizing destruction of the American flag violated the Free Speech Clause of the First Amendment.

These and numerous other examples illustrate plainly that Scalia follows his philosophy and not his personal predilections. Some critics charge that these "contrarian" opinions are simply convenient props that allow Scalia to tout his neutral philosophy and record.[24] It is an impossible charge to rebut. Nor does one need to, since it serves only to endorse the original contention that Scalia's philosophy is not result-oriented.

Second, some critics assert that while Scalia decries judicial activism, he is an activist himself because he often votes to strike down laws and overturn Court precedents, especially when those laws and precedents conflict with what the critics believe to be his policy preferences.[25] These critics charge that while Scalia argues that judges should show restraint and yield to the informed judgment of legislatures, he is quick to overturn legislative enactments when they conflict with his notions of good policy.

There are really two parts to this charge. The first—Scalia is an activist because he votes to invalidate popular enacted laws and reverse Court precedents—seems premised on a mistaken understanding of the true vice of activism. Judicial activism is not considered objectionable simply because some Court precedents are overturned or popular laws are found unconstitutional; most Americans seem to accept that a major part of the Supreme Court's job, at least since *Marbury* v. *Madison* (1803), is to determine whether acts of Congress are faithful to the Constitution. Activism becomes problematic when the Court strikes down laws for reasons that have no grounding in the Constitution—as the Court did to FDR's New Deal programs in the 1930s, angering the Left, and then again when it invalidated state laws restricting abortion in the 1970s, provoking the Right.

Scalia is not a judicial activist, as that term is properly understood, because when he has voted to strike down acts of Congress, he has relied exclusively on the text and structure of the Constitution. Similarly, when he has ignored the doctrine of *stare decisis*—the following of Court precedent—he has done so because the Court's previous holdings had no foundation in constitutional text or American legal or social traditions. Thus, Scalia seeks to *deactivate* the Court's previous activism. That task will sometimes require reversing precedents as well as invalidating laws that rely on unconstitutional precedents.

The second part of the activist criticism is that Scalia is more apt to strike down laws and reverse prior rulings when they conflict with his personal policy preferences. This charge, however, resembles the first criticism—namely, that he jettisons his textualist philosophy when it conflicts with his personal ideology. The previous examples amply demonstrate otherwise. Still another decision reveals that Scalia refrains from substituting his notion of good policy even when doing so would *not* disrupt popularly enacted laws or long-standing precedents.

In *BMW* v. *Gore* (1996), the Supreme Court voted to overturn a state court's award of $2 million in punitive damages on grounds that it was "grossly excessive." The Court's decision fits nicely with the effort by many Republicans in Congress who have been trying to legislate curbs on the size of the verdicts juries can award—to some extent because they fear the impact of enormous awards on the economy, but also because the trial lawyers that take a cut of the awards help to bankroll the Democratic Party.

Scalia remained true to his principles and dissented from the Court's decision. He wrote that "no matter how much in need of correction" the system that produces excessive punitive damage awards may be, the Constitution does not give the federal government any authority to second-guess a state court's determination of what level of damages is "reasonable." If Scalia were truly an activist—no matter how that term is defined—it would be impossible to explain why he did not join the Court's decision (which merely overturned a state court award) to fix a broken system (whose political beneficiaries are not conservatives).

In reality, the essence of Scalia's philosophy for constitutional and statutory interpretation is a response to and repudiation of judicial activism. By urging courts to adhere to the text and its original meaning, Scalia seeks to box judges in so they are not tempted to impose their values through the law.

The final criticism frequently leveled at Scalia is that he has failed to have a significant influence on the Court, especially because of his inability to build majority support for his opinions.[26] It has been said in this regard that he has even disappointed conservatives who were hopeful he would be able to move the Court and the law rightward.[27] This is damning criticism. It is also sheer fiction. One would be hard-pressed to find a conservative who actually feels that way. Conservatives appreciate Scalia because he is unwilling to moderate his views in order to gain a majority. His defeats simply remind conservatives how much better off the Court would be with five Scalias rather than one.

To be sure, there have been justices who viewed their roles differently from Scalia. The late Justice William Brennan, the Court's leading liberal for many years, seemed to think the job of Supreme Court justice is similar to that of Senate majority leader. Brennan famously remarked, "You can do anything around here with five votes." Declare abortion a constitutional right? Terrific! Outlaw prayer at high school graduation ceremonies? Why not? Read the death penalty out of a Constitution that specifically references it? Good thinking! All of these things and more can be done with five votes. You need not even have support in the Constitution or the long-standing traditions of country. Alas, you also no longer have a rule of law or the constitutional framework established by the Framers.

More specifically, the charge that Scalia has failed to move the Court rightward is misguided for a few reasons. First, it is premised on the shaky assumption that having a discernible influence is likely, let alone possible. Yet whatever one thinks of the justices of the Supreme Court, they are not sheep. They arrive at the bench with their own views. If Justices Anthony Kennedy and David Souter truly believe the Constitution of the United States prohibits states from regulating an individual's "right to define" his or her own "concept of the universe, and of the mystery of the human life,"[28] Scalia's chances of seducing them with something as finite and terrestrial as the text of the Constitution is, at best, remote.

This criticism is supplemented with a more specific charge, which is that Scalia cannot attract a majority because his sharp pen and biting comments have alienated so many of his colleagues.[29] This is a dicey accusation for—if it is to have any meaning whatsoever—it implies that some of his benchmates vote against Scalia *even when they think he is right.* It accepts as fact that there are justices of the United States Supreme Court who are voting not in accordance with the Constitution, their conscience, or even the result of a coin flip, but out of anger or hurt feelings. Would proponents of this criticism dare name a specific justice or two who are so derelict in exercising their constitutional authority?

The focus on Scalia's "attacks" on his colleagues has earned him a reputation in some circles as something of a bully. Yet anyone who believes it is important to foster respect for the rule of law and for the Supreme Court as an institution, as Scalia assuredly does, should be able to appreciate the reasons for his frustration. He has set forth a comprehensive judicial philosophy and sought to apply it consistently in order to create a jurisprudence the American public can understand and follow. And yet during the same period the Court has zigged and zagged from one decision to the next without any discernible concern for the value of the rule of law and the need to have a guiding principle.

For example, when the Court votes to invalidate the laws of thirty states in order to extend an individual right that cannot be found in the text of the Constitution or traditions of the nation, Scalia is far from alone in his exasperation and even anger (see *Stenberg* v. *Carhart* (2000), chapter three). These are the same feelings shared by millions of Americans who wonder what guides the Supreme Court at times, other than the personal views of a majority of its justices.

Moreover, expressing one's sincere doubts about the wisdom or legitimacy of a majority's decision or the merits of a particular justice's arguments is not a Scalia invention or monopoly. It was Justice Harry Blackmun, the author of *Roe* v. *Wade*, who called a later majority's decision dealing with abortion "deceptive," "disingenuous," and full of "[b]ald assertion[s] masquerad[ing] as reasoning."[30] Likewise, the late Justice Thurgood Marshall, who served with Scalia for four years, routinely insinuated that colleagues who disagreed with his opinions on race-related cases were insensitive judicially if not personally to the Constitution's guarantee of equal treatment. It seems rather unfair to decry Scalia's caustic barbs while turning a deaf ear to Marshall's fighting words.

Scalia's philosophy, vision, and style have made him the subject of extensive academic inquiry and debate. To give just one barometer, a LexisNexis search revealed that Justice Scalia's name has appeared in the title of 113 law review articles since he joined the Court in 1986. By way of contrast, Justice Sandra Day O'Connor, who was confirmed five years *before* Scalia, has been mentioned in the title of law review essays forty times. This is revealing because Justice O'Connor is thought by many the most influential member of the Court in her role as the swing vote in many high-profile cases.

The comparison to Justice David Souter is even more revealing. Because he is a Republican nominee who has become the Court's second-most reliable liberal vote (after Justice John Paul Stevens), one might think Justice Souter's jurisprudence would have engendered more interest. But his name has appeared in the title of just five law review articles since he was elevated to the bench in 1990. If Scalia has been marginalized on the Court, we should all hope to be so marginalized in our chosen field of work.

In fact, Scalia's record of influence is significant—even if measured solely by votes with the majority or by majority opinions written in important cases. On vital constitutional debates, including the meaning of the First Amendment's Free Exercise Clause, the Fifth Amendment's Taking Clause (concerning private property rights), and the Eighth Amendment's Cruel and Unusual Clause, Scalia has been at the forefront of the Court's movement toward a jurisprudence in greater harmony with the Constitution.[31]

His impact appears even greater if the lens is widened beyond majority votes and opinions. Scalia's methodology for interpreting the Constitution has taken root in the Court. Although the justices do always accord the text its proper meaning, they now routinely begin their analysis with consideration of the textual provision at issue. This influence also holds true for statutory interpretation, an important development in light of the fact that interpreting federal statutes and regulations is the most frequent task of federal judges.

Ultimately, however, the true importance of a Supreme Court justice cannot be measured by the number of times he or she is on the winning side. To wit, Michael Jordan was rightly considered the world's best basketball player years before his team won its first championship. Scalia's importance, as two of his most thorough critics pegged it, "lies in the words and reasoning that constitute his vision, and that vision, when placed in the enduring form of a written opinion, has the potential to shape doctrines and decisions in the near and distant future."[32]

CHAPTER TWO

INTERPRETING LAWS

IT IS OFTEN SAID THAT THE UNITED STATES enjoys "a government of laws and not of men." Americans value the rule of law as the best alternative to arbitrary rule by individuals. If the rule of law is to have meaning, however, the public must understand what the law says.

Enter the judiciary. The Supreme Court in its famous decision in *Marbury* v. *Madison* (1803) said, "[I]t is emphatically the province and duty of the judicial department to say what the law is." Judges, we know, are given authority to interpret not only the Constitution but federal and state statutes and regulations as well. Some might think it is easy to know what the law is; just look it up in the codes of laws kept by the United States or individual states. Yet the task of determining the proper meaning of the law is not so simple.

Consider, for example, a case that reached the Supreme Court in 1993. Congress had passed a law imposing longer prison terms for those who "use" a firearm "during and in relation to" a drug trafficking crime. At issue was whether the tougher sentence should apply to a man who swapped his automatic rifle for cocaine. Six justices on the Court said the law applied because trading the weapon constituted a "use" of the weapon during a crime. Three justices, led by Scalia, said the law should not apply, arguing that to use an instrument means to use it for its intended purpose. Scalia wrote, "When someone asks, 'Do you use a cane?,' he is not inquiring whether you have your grandfather's silver-handled walking stick on display in the hall; he wants to know whether you walk with a cane."[1]

In cases like this, the debate among the justices focuses on figuring out what the words truly mean. Policy objectives do not seem to be in play. There are many cases, however, in which the Court seems to torture or ignore altogether the meaning of words in order to achieve a result it thinks Congress likely intended or that reflects, in the view of a majority of justices, good public policy.

In all cases of statutory interpretation, how should the Court figure out what the law is? Justice Scalia, unlike any other justice on the Supreme Court today, has developed a coherent methodology for approaching this issue.

Known as textualism, Scalia's methodology first directs judges to focus on the words of a statute or regulation. Unlike some conservative judges, Scalia says texts should not be construed "strictly." Nor should they be construed "liberally." Rather, Scalia says, words should be interpreted reasonably, that is, words should be accorded the ordinary meaning that would have made sense to the Congress (or state legislature) that passed the law and to the people who would have been subjected to it. At the same time, the Court should ensure the meaning makes sense within the context of the law or code of which it is a part. Where the meaning of a statute is not immediately clear, Scalia relies on some tools to find the right meaning. He often consults dictionaries from the period in which the law was passed. He will look to see if words are used elsewhere in the statute and, if so, will give them the same meaning.

Looking for original meaning, also known as originalism, is not the same as looking at the legislature's "intent" as evidenced by a statute's legislative history. Scalia objects to reliance on legislative intent for a couple of reasons. First, it is not usually ascertainable.[2] Members of Congress usually have many different reasons (or no reason at all) for voting for a bill, and thus there is no singular intent that can be attributed to the body passing the law. Second, even if intent can somehow be determined, it is an illegitimate source of meaning.[3] Scalia has written, "We are governed by laws, not the intention of legislators."[4] Statements on the floor of the House or Senate by the bill's sponsors, committee reports drafted by staff to explain the bill in greater detail—these, Scalia says, are not ratified by the Congress as a whole and thus do not reflect anything more than the desire of the person making the statement or writing the report.

Finally, Scalia says judges should allow even stupid laws to stand. "I do not think…the avoidance of unhappy consequences is adequate basis for interpreting a text," he wrote in one decision.[5] Unless confusion and uncertainty are traceable to scrivener's error, courts should give the law the meaning of its words. If that meaning is nonsensical and not what Congress intended, Congress can go back and change it. In Scalia's view, it is far better for Congress—elected by and accountable to the people—to make the law, rather than unelected, life-tenured judges.

Scalia has accused the Court of misusing its authority in order to rewrite the law on many occasions. One of his most memorable examples involved the case of golfer Casey Martin.

MARTIN v. PGA TOUR, INC. (2001)

This case involved a challenge to the professional golf association's rule prohibiting golfers from using motorized carts during tournaments. The challenge was brought by Casey Martin, a champion golfer. Martin has a
degenerative circulatory condition that resulted in the atrophy of his right
leg. By the end of his college career, he could no longer walk an 18-hole golf
course. He sought to compete in the PGA TOUR's qualifying school
(known as Q-school) in 1999 and petitioned to use a cart. The tour denied
his request. Martin sued, citing the Americans with Disability Act.

The Americans with Disability Act of 1990 (ADA) prohibits discrimination
against disabled individuals at places of public accommodation. As defined by
the Act, the law protects disabled individuals seeking "enjoyment of the goods,
services, facilities, privileges, advantages, or accommodations" at public establishments. The ADA specifically lists a "golf course" as an example of the type
of public accommodation at which a disabled person may "exercise or recreate." Businesses are required to make reasonable modifications of "policies,
practices, or procedures" as are necessary to ensure disabled individuals have
equal access to the same goods, services, and privileges others enjoy. But the
Act does not require places of public accommodation to make "modifications
[that] would fundamentally alter the nature" of the benefits sought.

In 2001, a seven-justice majority of the Supreme Court held that PGA
TOUR events fit within the Act's definition of "public accommodation" and
that Martin was likewise covered as an individual who deserved the "full and
equal enjoyment of the... privileges" of the courses used by the tour during its events. In response to the PGA TOUR's argument that the Act covers only "clients and customers" of the tour, the Court said Martin qualifies
as a customer because he paid a fee to compete in the qualifying school (Q-
School) as required. Finally, the Court said that allowing Martin to use a cart
would not "fundamentally alter" the game.

Scalia, joined by Justice Thomas, said the Court's decision reflected
"benevolent compassion" but was unfaithful to the text and meaning of the

ADA. He argued that "a professional sport" is not a place of public accommodation and that a professional athlete who plays a sport to provide entertainment for others is not a "customer." By torturing the text in these ways, Scalia said, the Court then is forced to answer the "incredibly difficult and incredibly silly question" of whether walking is essential to the game of golf. The Court's answer of "no" was unsatisfactory to Scalia and not simply, he said, because many consider walking to be "the central feature" of the game. Rather, he argued that because the rules of sports are entirely arbitrary, it is impossible to say that any are "essential."

Scalia admitted he was not convinced the PGA TOUR should not make an exception for Martin. But he said that decision belonged with the PGA TOUR, which could amend its rules, or with Congress, which could extend the Act to explicitly cover this and similar situations. The Court should not, according to Scalia, rewrite the law to promote "what this Court sententiously decrees to be 'decent, tolerant, [and] progressive.'"

JUSTICE SCALIA, WITH WHOM JUSTICE THOMAS JOINS, DISSENTING.

In my view today's opinion exercises a benevolent compassion that the law does not place it within our power to impose. The judgment distorts the text of Title III, the structure of the ADA, and common sense. I respectfully dissent.

I

The Court holds that a professional sport is a place of public accommodation and that respondent is a "custome[r]" of "competition" when he practices his profession. It finds that this strange conclusion is compelled by the "literal text" of Title III of the Americans with Disabilities Act of 1990 (ADA), by the "expansive purpose" of the ADA, and by the fact that Title II of the Civil Rights Act of 1964 has been applied to an amusement park and public golf courses. I disagree.

The ADA has three separate titles: Title I covers employment discrimination, Title II covers discrimination by government entities, and Title III covers discrimination by places of public accommodation. Title II is irrelevant to this case. Title I protects only "employees" of employers who have 15 or more employees. It does not protect independent contractors. Respondent claimed employment discrimination under Title I, but the District Court found him to be an independent contractor rather than an employee.

Respondent also claimed protection under §12182 of Title III. That section applies only to particular places and persons. The place must be a "place of public accommodation," and the person must be an "individual" seeking "enjoyment of the goods, services, facilities, privileges, advantages, or accommodations" of the covered place. Of course a court indiscriminately invoking the "sweeping" and "expansive" purposes of the ADA could argue that when a place of public accommodation denied *any* "individual," on the basis of his disability, *anything* that might be called a "privileg[e]," the individual has a valid Title III claim. On such an interpretation, the employees and independent contractors of every place of public accommodation come within Title III: The employee enjoys the "privilege" of employment, the contractor the "privilege" of the contract.

For many reasons, Title III will not bear such an interpretation. The provision of Title III at issue here (§12182, its principal provision) is a public-accommodation law, and it is the traditional understanding of public-accommodation laws that they provide rights for *customers.* "At common law, innkeepers, smiths, and others who made profession of a public employment, were prohibited from refusing, without good reason, to serve a customer." *Hurley* v. *Irish-American Gay, Lesbian and Bisexual Group of Boston, Inc.* (1995) (internal quotation marks omitted). This understanding is clearly reflected in the text of Title III itself. Section 12181(7) lists 12 specific types of entities that qualify as "public accommodations," with a follow-on expansion that makes it clear what the "enjoyment of the goods, services, etc." of those entities consists of—and it plainly envisions that the person "enjoying" the "public accommodation" will be a *customer.* For example, Title III is said to cover an "auditorium" or "other place of public gathering." Thus, "gathering" is the distinctive enjoyment derived from an auditorium; the persons "gathering" at an auditorium are presumably covered by Title III, but those contracting to clean the auditorium are not. Title III is said to cover a "zoo" or "other place of recreation." The persons "recreat[ing]" at a "zoo" are presumably covered, but the animal handlers bringing in the latest panda are not. The one place where Title III specifically addresses discrimination by places of public accommodation through "contractual" arrangements, it makes clear that discrimination against the other party to the contract is not covered, but only discrimination against "clients or customers of the covered public accommodation that enters into the contractual, licensing or other arrangement." And finally, the regulations promulgated by the Department of Justice reinforce the conclusion that Title III's protections extend only to customers. "The purpose of the ADA's public accommodations requirements," they say, "is to ensure accessibility to the goods offered by a public accommodation." Surely this has nothing to do with employees and independent contractors.

If there were any doubt left that §12182 covers only clients and customers of places of public accommodation, it is eliminated by the fact that a contrary interpretation would make a muddle of the ADA as a whole. The words of Title III must be read "in their context and with a view to their place in the overall statutory scheme." *Davis* v. *Michigan Dept. of Treasury* (1989). Congress expressly excluded employers of fewer than 15 employees from Title I. The mom-and-pop grocery store or laundromat need not worry about altering the nonpublic areas of its place of business to accommodate handicapped employees—or about the litigation that failure to do so will invite. Similarly, since independent contractors are not covered by Title I, the small business (or the large one, for that matter) need not worry about making special accommodations for the painters, electricians, and other independent workers whose services are contracted for from time to time. It is an entirely unreasonable interpretation of the statute to say that these exemptions so carefully crafted in Title I are entirely eliminated by Title III (for the many businesses that are places of public accommodation) because employees and independent contractors "enjoy" the employment and contracting that such places provide. The only *distinctive* feature of places of public accommodation is that they accommodate the *public*, and Congress could have no conceivable reason for according the employees and independent contractors of such businesses protections that employees and independent contractors of other businesses do not enjoy.

The United States apparently agrees that employee claims are not cognizable under Title III, but despite the implications of its own regulations, appears to believe (though it does not explicitly state) that claims of independent contractors are cognizable. In a discussion littered with entirely vague statements from the legislative history, the

United States argues that Congress presumably wanted independent contractors with private entities covered under Title III because independent contractors with governmental entities are covered by Title II—a line of reasoning that does not commend itself to the untutored intellect. But since the United States does not provide (and I cannot conceive of) any possible construction of the *terms* of Title III that will exclude employees while simultaneously covering independent contractors, its concession regarding employees effectively concedes independent contractors as well. Title III applies only to customers.

The Court, for its part, assumes that conclusion for the sake of argument, but pronounces respondent to be a "customer" of the PGA TOUR or of the golf courses on which it is played. That seems to me quite incredible. The PGA TOUR is a professional sporting event, staged for the entertainment of a live and TV audience, the receipts from whom (the TV audience's admission price is paid by advertisers) pay the expenses of the tour, including the cash prizes for the winning golfers. The professional golfers on the tour are no more "enjoying" (the statutory term) the entertainment that the tour provides, or the facilities of the golf courses on which it is held, than professional baseball players "enjoy" the baseball games in which they play or the facilities of Yankee Stadium. To be sure, professional ballplayers *participate* in the games, and *use* the ballfields, but no one in his right mind would think that they are *customers* of the American League or of Yankee Stadium. They are themselves the entertainment that the customers pay to watch. And professional golfers are no different. It makes not a bit of difference, insofar as their "customer" status is concerned, that the remuneration for their performance (unlike most of the remuneration for ballplayers) is not fixed but contingent—viz., the purses for the winners in the various events, and the compensation from product endorsements that consistent winners are assured. The compensation of *many* independent contractors is contingent upon their success—real estate brokers, for example, or insurance salesmen.

As the Court points out, the ADA specifically identifies golf courses as one of the covered places of public accommodation. See §12181(7)(L) ("a gymnasium, health spa, bowling alley, golf course, or other place of exercise or recreation"); and the distinctive "goo[d], servic[e], facilit[y], privileg[e], advantag[e], or accommodatio[n]" identified by that provision as distinctive to that category of place of public accommodation is "exercise or recreation." Respondent did not seek to "exercise" or "recreate" at the PGA TOUR events; he sought to make money (which is why he is called a *professional* golfer). He was not a customer *buying* recreation or entertainment; he was a professional athlete *selling* it. That is the reason (among others) the Court's reliance upon Civil Rights Act cases like *Daniel* v. *Paul* (1969) is misplaced. A professional golfer's practicing his profession is not comparable to John Q. Public's frequenting "a 232-acre amusement area with swimming, boating, sun bathing, picnicking, miniature golf, dancing facilities, and a snack bar."

The Court relies heavily upon the Q-School. It says that petitioner offers the golfing public the "privilege" of "competing in the Q-School and playing in the tours; indeed, the former is a privilege for which thousands of individuals from the general public pay, and the latter is one for which they vie." But the Q-School is no more a "privilege" offered for the general public's "enjoyment" than is the California Bar Exam. It is a competition for entry into the PGA TOUR—an open tryout, no different in principle from open casting for a movie or stage production, or walk-on tryouts for other professional sports, such as baseball. See, *e.g.*, Amateurs Join Pros for New Season of HBO's "Sopranos," *Detroit News*, Dec. 22, 2000, p. 2 (20,000 attend open casting for "The Sopranos"); Bill Zack, Atlanta Braves, *Sporting News*, Feb. 6, 1995 (1,300 would-be players attended an open tryout for the Atlanta Braves). It may well be that some amateur golfers enjoy trying to make the grade, just as some amateur actors may enjoy auditions, and amateur baseball players may enjoy open tryouts (I hesitate to say that amateur lawyers may enjoy taking the California Bar Exam). But the purpose of holding those tryouts is not to provide entertainment; it is to hire. At bottom, open tryouts for performances to be held at a place of public accommodation are no different from open bidding on contracts to cut the grass

> *But the Q[ualifying] School is no more a "privilege" offered for the general public's "enjoyment" than is the California Bar Exam. It is a competition for entry into the PGA TOUR.*

at a place of public accommodation, or open applications for any job at a place of public accommodation. Those bidding, those applying—and those trying out—are not converted into customers. By the Court's reasoning, a business exists not only to sell goods and services to the public, but to provide the "privilege" of employment to the public; wherefore it follows, like night the day, that everyone who seeks a job is a customer.

II

Having erroneously held that Title III applies to the "customers" of professional golf who consist of its practitioners, the Court then erroneously answers—or to be accurate simply ignores—a second question. The ADA requires covered businesses to make such reasonable modifications of "policies, practices, or procedures" as are necessary to "afford" goods, services, and privileges to individuals with disabilities; but it explicitly does not require "modifications [that] would fundamentally alter the nature" of the goods, services, and privileges. In other words, disabled individuals must be given *access* to the same goods, services, and privileges that others enjoy. The regulations state that Title III "does not require a public accommodation to alter its inventory to include accessible or special goods with accessibility features that are designed for, or facilitate use by, individuals with disabilities." As one Court of Appeals has explained:

> The common sense of the statute is that the content of the goods or services offered by a place of public accommodation is not regulated. A camera store may not refuse to sell cameras to a disabled person, but it is not required to stock cameras specially designed for such persons. Had Congress purposed to impose so enormous a burden on the retail sector of the economy and so vast a supervisory responsibility on the federal courts, we think it would have made its intention clearer and would at least have imposed some standards. It is hardly a feasible judicial function to decide whether shoestores should sell single shoes to one-legged persons and if so at what price, or how many Braille books the Borders or Barnes and Noble bookstore chains should stock in each of their stores.
>
> DOE v. MUTUAL OF OMAHA INS. CO. (CA7 1999)

Since this is so, even if respondent here is a consumer of the "privilege" of the PGA TOUR competition, I see no basis for considering whether the rules of that competition must be altered. It is as irrelevant to the PGA TOUR's compliance with the statute whether walking is essential to the game of golf as it is to the shoe store's compliance whether "pairness" is essential to the nature of shoes. If a shoe store wishes to sell shoes only in pairs it may; and if a golf tour (or a golf course) wishes to provide only walk-around golf, it may. The PGA TOUR cannot deny respondent *access* to that game because of his disability, but it need not provide him a game different (whether in its essentials or in its details) from that offered to everyone else.

Since it has held (or assumed) professional golfers to be customers "enjoying" the "privilege" that consists of PGA TOUR golf; and since it inexplicably regards the rules of PGA TOUR golf as merely "policies, practices, or procedures" by which access to PGA TOUR golf is provided, the Court must then confront the question whether respondent's requested modification of the supposed policy, practice, or procedure of walking would "fundamentally alter the nature" of the PGA TOUR game. The Court attacks this "fundamental alteration" analysis by asking two questions: first, whether the "essence" or an "essential aspect" of the sport of golf has been altered; and second, whether the change, even if not essential to the game, would give the disabled player an advantage over others and thereby "fundamentally alter the character of the competition." It answers no to both.

> *It is as irrelevant to the PGA TOUR's compliance with the statute whether walking is essential to the game of golf as it is to the shoe store's compliance whether "pairness" is essential to the nature of shoes. If a shoe store wishes to sell shoes only in pairs it may; and if a golf tour (or a golf course) wishes to provide only walk-around golf, it may.*

Before considering the Court's answer to the first question, it is worth pointing out that the assumption which underlies that question is false. Nowhere is it writ that PGA TOUR golf must be classic "essential" golf. Why cannot the PGA TOUR, if it wishes, promote a new game, with distinctive rules (much as the American League promotes a game of baseball in which the pitcher's turn at the plate can be taken by a "designated hitter")? If members of the public do not like the new rules—if they feel that these rules do not truly test the individual's skill at "real golf" (or the team's skill at "real baseball") they can withdraw their patronage. But the rules are the rules. They are (as in all games) entirely arbitrary, and there is no basis on which anyone—not even the Supreme Court of the United States—can pronounce one or another of them to be "nonessential" if the rulemaker (here the PGA TOUR) deems it to be essential.

If one assumes, however, that the PGA TOUR has some legal obligation to play classic, Platonic golf—and if one assumes the correctness of all the other wrong turns the Court has made to get to this point—then we Justices must confront what is indeed an awesome responsibility. It has been rendered the solemn duty of the Supreme Court of the United States, laid upon it by Congress in pursuance of the Federal Government's power "[t]o regulate Commerce with foreign Nations, and among the several States," U. S. Const., Art. I, §8, cl. 3, to decide What Is Golf. I am sure that the Framers of the Constitution, aware of the 1457 edict of King James II of Scotland prohibiting golf because it interfered with the practice of archery, fully expected that sooner or later the paths of golf and government, the law and the links, would once again cross, and that the judges of this august Court would some day have to wrestle with that age-old jurisprudential question, for which their years of study in the law have so well prepared them: Is someone riding around a golf course from shot to shot *really* a golfer? The answer, we learn, is yes. The Court ultimately concludes, and it will henceforth be the Law of the Land, that walking is not a "fundamental" aspect of golf.

Either out of humility or out of self-respect (one or the other) the Court should decline to answer this incredibly difficult and incredibly silly question. To say that something is "essential" is ordinarily to say that it is necessary to the achievement of a certain object. But since it is the very nature of a game to have no object except amusement (that is what distinguishes games from productive activity), it is quite impossible to say that any of a game's arbitrary rules is "essential." Eighteen-hole golf courses, 10-foot-high basketball hoops, 90-foot baselines, 100-yard football fields—all are arbitrary and none is essential. The only support for any of them is tradition and (in more modern times) insistence by what has come to be regarded as the ruling body of the sport—both of which factors support the PGA TOUR's position in the present case. (Many, indeed, consider walking to be *the central feature* of the game of golf—hence Mark Twain's classic criticism of the sport: "a good walk spoiled.") I suppose there is some point at which the rules of a well-known game are changed to such a degree that no reasonable person would call it the same game. If the PGA TOUR competitors were required to

I am sure that the Framers of the Constitution, aware of the 1457 edict of King James II of Scotland prohibiting golf because it interfered with the practice of archery, fully expected that sooner or later the paths of golf and government, the law and the links, would once again cross, and that the judges of this august Court would some day have to wrestle with that age-old jurisprudential question, for which their years of study in the law have so well prepared them: Is someone riding around a golf course from shot to shot really a golfer?

dribble a large, inflated ball and put it through a round hoop, the game could no longer reasonably be called golf. But this criterion—destroying recognizability as the same generic game—is surely not the test of "essentialness" or "fundamentalness" that the Court applies, since it apparently thinks that merely changing the diameter of the *cup* might "fundamentally alter" the game of golf.

Having concluded that dispensing with the walking rule would not violate federal-Platonic "golf" (and, implicitly, that it is federal-Platonic golf, and no other, that the PGA TOUR can insist upon) the Court moves on to the second part of its test: the competitive effects of waiving this nonessential rule. In this part of its analysis, the Court first finds that the effects of the change are "mitigated" by the fact that in the game of golf weather, a "lucky bounce," and "pure chance" provide different conditions for each competitor and individual ability may not "be the sole determinant of the outcome." I guess that is why those who follow professional golfing consider Jack Nicklaus the *luckiest* golfer of all time, only to be challenged of late by the phenomenal *luck* of Tiger Woods. The Court's empiricism is unpersuasive. "Pure chance" is randomly distributed among the players, but allowing respondent to use a cart gives him a "lucky" break every time he plays. Pure chance also only matters at the margin—a stroke here or there; the cart substantially improves this respondent's competitive prospects beyond a couple of strokes. But even granting that there are significant nonhuman variables affecting competition, that fact does not justify adding another variable that always favors one player.

In an apparent effort to make its opinion as narrow as possible, the Court relies upon the District Court's finding that even with a cart, respondent will be at least as fatigued as everyone else. This, the Court says, *proves* that competition will not be affected. Far from thinking that reliance on this finding cabins the effect of today's opinion, I think it will prove to be its most expansive and destructive feature. Because step one of the Court's two-part inquiry into whether a requested change in a sport will "fundamentally alter [its] nature" consists of an utterly unprincipled ontology of sports (pursuant to which the Court is not even sure whether golf's "essence" requires a 3-inch hole), there is every reason to think that in future cases involving requests for special treatment by would-be athletes the second step of the analysis will be determinative. In resolving that second step—determining whether waiver of the "nonessential" rule will have an impermissible "competitive effect"—by measuring the athletic capacity of the requesting individual, and asking whether the special dispensation would do no more than place him on a par (so to speak) with other competitors, the Court guarantees that future cases of this sort will have to be decided on the basis of individualized factual findings. Which means that future cases of this sort will be numerous, and a rich source of lucrative litigation. One can envision the parents of a Little League player with attention deficit disorder trying to convince a judge that their son's disability makes it at least 25% more difficult to hit a pitched ball. (If they are successful, the only thing that could prevent a court order giving the kid four strikes would be a judicial determination that, in baseball, three strikes are metaphysically necessary, which is quite absurd.)

One can envision the parents of a Little League player with attention deficit disorder trying to convince a judge that their son's disability makes it at least 25% more difficult to hit a pitched ball.

The statute, of course, provides no basis for this individualized analysis that is the Court's last step on a long and misguided journey.

The statute seeks to assure that a disabled person's disability will not deny him *equal access* to (among other things) competitive sporting events—not that his disability will not deny him an *equal chance to win* competitive sporting events. The latter is quite impossible, since the very *nature* of competitive sport is the measurement, by uniform rules, of unevenly distributed excellence. This unequal distribution is precisely what determines the winners and losers—and artificially to "even out" that distribution, by giving one or another player exemption from a rule that emphasizes his particular weakness, is to destroy the game. That is why the "handicaps" that are customary in social games of golf—which, by adding strokes to the scores of the good players and subtracting them from scores of the bad ones, "even out" the varying abilities—are *not* used in professional golf. In the Court's world, there is one set of rules that is "fair with respect to the able-bodied" but "individualized" rules, mandated by the ADA, for "talented but disabled athletes." The ADA mandates no such ridiculous thing. Agility, strength, speed, balance, quickness of mind, steadiness of nerves, intensity of concentration—these talents are not evenly distributed. No wild-eyed dreamer has ever suggested that the managing bodies of the competitive sports that test precisely these qualities should try to take account of the uneven distribution of God-given gifts when writing and enforcing the rules of competition. And I have no doubt Congress did not authorize misty-eyed judicial supervision of such a revolution.

My belief that today's judgment is clearly in error should not be mistaken for a belief that the PGA TOUR clearly *ought not* allow respondent to use a golf cart. *That* is a close question, on which even those who compete in the PGA TOUR are apparently divided; but it is a *different* question from the one before the Court. Just as it is a different question whether the Little League *ought* to give disabled young-sters a fourth strike, or some other waiver from the rules that makes up for their disabilities. In both cases, whether they *ought* to do so depends upon (1) how central to the game that they have organized (and over whose rules they are the master) they deem the waived provision to be, and (2) how competitive—how strict a test of raw athletic ability in all aspects of the competition—they want their game to be. But whether Congress has said they *must* do so depends upon the answers to the legal questions I have discussed above—not upon what this Court sen-tentiously decrees to be "decent, tolerant, [and] progressive."

And it should not be assumed that today's decent, tolerant, and pro-gressive judgment will, in the long run, accrue to the benefit of sports competitors with disabilities. Now that it is clear courts will review the rules of sports for "fundamentalness," organizations that value their autonomy have every incentive to defend vigorously the necessity of every regulation. They may still be second-guessed in the end as to the Platonic requirements of the sport, but they will *assuredly* lose if they have at all wavered in their enforcement. The lesson the PGA TOUR and other sports organizations should take from this case is to make sure that the same written rules are set forth for all levels of play, and never voluntarily to grant any modifications. The second lesson is to end open tryouts. I doubt that, in the long run, even disabled ath-letes will be well served by these incentives that the Court has created.

Complaints about this case are not "properly directed to Congress." They are properly directed to this Court's Kafkaesque determination that professional sports organizations, and the fields they rent for their exhibitions, are "places of public accommodation" to the competing athletes, and the athletes themselves "customers" of the organization that pays them; its Alice in Wonderland determination that there are such things as judicially determinable "essential" and "nonessential" rules of a made-up game; and its Animal Farm determination that fairness and the ADA mean that everyone gets to play by individualized rules which will assure that no one's lack of ability (or at least no one's lack of ability so pronounced that it amounts to a disability) will be a handicap. The year was 2001, and "everybody was finally equal." K. Vonnegut, Harrison Bergeron, in Animal Farm and Related Readings 129 (1997).

CHAPTER THREE

SEPARATION OF POWERS

THE CONSTITUTION OF THE UNITED STATES established three distinct branches of the federal government—the executive, the legislative, and the judicial. With this clear division of power between the branches in place, and fortified by the division of power between the federal government and states (a.k.a. federalism), "a double security arises," James Madison said, for the vital purpose of protecting "the rights of the people."[1] Far from serving as a simple housekeeping list of functions of the three branches, the Constitution's separation of powers is necessary to protect individual liberty by keeping the power of government in check.

Many judges today approach separation of powers questions from a practical standpoint. These judges, sometimes referred to as "functionalists," look at the overall balance of federal power before making a determination as to whether one branch has usurped too much power.[2] For example, the Court ruled in 1989 that creation of the U.S. Sentencing Commission—an entity in which federal judges are authorized to act in an executive policymaking capacity—did not violate the independent authority of the judiciary under Article III of the Constitution.[3]

Justice Scalia dissented from the Court's decision in that case and has squarely rejected the functional approach to separation-of-powers questions. Instead, he has tried to maintain clear lines. In his view, the Constitution does not allow for the branches to "share" authority specifically given to one branch. Not a little, not at all. His separation-of-powers opinions tend to be long and filled with references to the Framers' objectives in dividing power as they did, and sprinkled with pointed warnings about the harmful consequences of allowing power to be commingled.

Scalia's passionate views in this area do not seem to be fueled by a belief in the intrinsic good displayed by one or all of the branches; he is not, for example, adamantly opposed to the exercise of lawmaking power by executive agencies because he has high regard for the Congress. Rather, he believes first that the text of the Constitution demands clear separation (Article I grants "all" legislative power to Congress, not "some" or even "most"). Equally important to Scalia, it seems, are the practical reasons for dividing power cleanly and evenly; he recognizes and fears that any one of the branches, if not strictly limited, will seek greater power. To Scalia, as with Madison and the other Framers, the concentration of power in any one branch poses a threat to individual liberty.

Scalia believes the rigid separation of powers set forth in the Constitution is the most important bulwark against government tyranny, even more important than the Bill of Rights. For support, Scalia points to the fact that many foreign nations, including the former Soviet Union, established bills of rights patterned after and even more extensive than ours, but did not have a proper structure of government in place to protect them.[4] Moreover, Scalia notes that the original Constitution of the United States did not even contain a Bill of Rights. The

Framers thought liberty could be protected through a firm separation of powers that did not allow any single branch to grow too powerful.

Convinced of its ability to protect cherished liberties, and mindful of the tendency for power to be usurped gradually over time, Scalia seeks to maintain bright lines between the branches. He once wrote, "Separation of powers, a distinctively American political doctrine, profits from the advice authored by a distinctively American poet: Good fences make good neighbors."[5] Viewed in this context, it is easier to understand why seemingly arcane, structure-of-government cases prompt Scalia to write opinions as spirited and eloquent as one would expect to find in cases involving hot-button social issues, such as the death penalty or abortion.

MORRISON v. OLSON (1988)

In 1978, Congress passed the Ethics in Government Act. The new law provided for appointment of an independent counsel by a special court upon a recommendation by the U.S. attorney general. Up to that point, investigations into wrongdoing by executive officials had been carried out by special prosecutors appointed directly by the attorney general. In the wake of Watergate, however, where the attorney general himself was implicated in the cover-up, Congress thought an independent prosecutor was needed to restore public confidence. Unlike a special prosecutor, who was terminable at will, an independent counsel could only be removed by the Attorney General upon a showing of "good cause."

Article II, § 1 of the Constitution vests the executive power in the president of the United States. That power extends to the appointment and removal of "inferior Officers." Before *Morrison v. Olson*, the Supreme Court had reviewed the scope of the president's power to remove executive branch officials in order to determine whether the official exercised "purely executive" authority or if he or she also exercised "quasi-legislative" or "quasi-judicial" authority. Under this formalist approach, if an official exercised "purely executive" duties, the president had absolute authority to remove him or her. If the official exercised other powers, Congress could place restrictions on the president's removal authority.

In *Morrison*, the Court moved away from its formal approach and examined whether, on the whole, limiting his removal authority by requiring "good cause" impeded the president's ability to perform his constitutional duty. The Court concluded it did not. The majority found that the independent counsel was an "inferior" official with limited jurisdiction, tenure, and authority who could be terminated for misconduct. As a result, the president's control over the executive power was not unreasonably impaired by the new law and its creation of a new criminal prosecutor.

Justice Scalia, in a long solo dissenting opinion, strongly objected to the Court's adoption of a functional approach. By focusing on the "technical details" of the Appointments Clause and removal power rather than the Constitution's structural imperative to keep power strictly separated, Scalia said, the majority opinion missed the forest while staring at the trees. In his analysis, the independent counsel law had to be struck down because (1) criminal prosecution is an exercise of "purely executive power" and (2) the law deprived the president of "exclusive control" of that power.

What makes Scalia's opinion so noteworthy was his prediction as to how the independent counsel law might be abused in practice. He noted that normal prosecutions had a political brake in place; specifically, blame for the egregious conduct of an out-of-control Justice Department prosecutor could be put on the president that appointed or retained him. But no such protection existed against an independent counsel run amok under the law. Scalia wrote, "How frightening it must be to have your own independent counsel and staff appointed, with nothing else to do but to investigate you until investigation is no longer worthwhile."

Four years after the Court's decision in *Morrison*, many right-leaning Americans began to share Justice Scalia's concern about the dangers of a runaway independent counsel. Conservatives were outraged when Lawrence Walsh announced the re-indictment of former defense secretary Caspar Weinberger four days before the 1992 election on charges relating to the so-called Iran-Contra affair. Worse yet, they sensed dirty politics when Walsh's office leaked a note suggesting that President Bush, who was running for re-election, lied when he said he was "out of the loop" on Iran-Contra decisions.

Most left-leaning Americans did not appreciate Scalia's foresight until independent counsel Kenneth Starr and his staff spent more than four years and $40 million investigating President Bill Clinton's land deals and extra-marital relationships. Though Clinton was impeached by the House of Representatives, many thought the investigation was plagued by partisanship.

In his *Morrison* dissent, Scalia wrote, "I fear the Court has permanently encumbered the Republic with an institution that will do it great harm." Because so many came to share Scalia's fear, Congress let the law expire in 1999.

~∞∞~

JUSTICE SCALIA, DISSENTING.

It is the proud boast of our democracy that we have "a government of laws and not of men." Many Americans are familiar with that phrase; not many know its derivation. It comes from Part the First, Article XXX, of the Massachusetts Constitution of 1780, which reads in full as follows:

In the government of this Commonwealth, the legislative department shall never exercise the executive and judicial powers, or either of them: The executive shall never exercise the legislative and judicial powers, or either of them: The judicial shall never exercise the legislative and executive powers, or either of them: to the end it may be a government of laws and not of men.

The Framers of the Federal Constitution similarly viewed the principle of separation of powers as the absolutely central guarantee of a just Government. In No. 47 of The Federalist, Madison wrote that "[n]o political truth is certainly of greater intrinsic value, or is stamped with the authority of more enlightened patrons of liberty." The Federalist No. 47 (hereinafter Federalist). Without a secure structure of separated powers, our Bill of Rights would be worthless, as are the bills of rights of many nations of the world that have adopted, or even improved upon, the mere words of ours.

The principle of separation of powers is expressed in our Constitution in the first section of each of the first three Articles. Article I, 1, provides that "[a]ll legislative Powers herein granted shall be vested in a Congress of the United States, which shall consist of a Senate and House of Representatives." Article III, 1, provides that "[t]he judicial Power of the United States, shall be vested in one supreme Court, and in such inferior Courts as the Congress may from time to time ordain and establish." And the provision at issue here, Art. II, 1, cl. 1, provides that "[t]he executive Power shall be vested in a President of the United States of America."

But just as the mere words of a Bill of Rights are not self-effectuating, the Framers recognized "[t]he insufficiency of a mere parchment delineation of the boundaries" to achieve thej separation of powers. Federalist No. 73 (A. Hamilton). "[T]he great security," wrote Madison, "against a gradual concentration of the several powers in the same department consists in giving to those who administer each department the necessary constitutional means and personal motives to resist encroachments of the others. The provision for defense must in this, as in all other cases, be made commensurate to the danger of attack." Federalist No. 51. Madison continued:

> But it is not possible to give to each department an equal power of self-defense. In republican government, the legislative authority necessarily predominates. The remedy for this inconveniency is to divide the legislature into different branches; and to render them, by different modes of election and different principles of action, as little connected with each other as the nature of their common functions and their common dependence on the society will admit. . . . As the weight of the legislative authority requires that it should be thus divided, the weakness of the executive may require, on the other hand, that it should be fortified.

The major "fortification" provided, of course, was the veto power. But in addition to providing fortification, the Founders conspicuously and very consciously declined to sap the Executive's strength in the same way they had weakened the Legislature: by dividing the executive power. Proposals to have multiple executives, or a council of advisers with separate authority were rejected. See 1 M. Farrand, Records of the Federal Convention of 1787. Thus, while "[a]ll legislative Powers herein granted shall be vested in a Congress of the United States, which shall consist of a Senate *and* House of Representatives," U.S. Const., Art. I, 1 (emphasis added), "[t]he executive Power shall be vested in *a President of the United States*," Art. II, 1, cl. 1 (emphasis added).

That is what this suit is about. Power. The allocation of power among Congress, the President, and the courts in such fashion as to preserve the equilibrium the Constitution sought to establish—so that

Frequently an issue of this sort will come before the Court clad, so to speak, in sheep's cloth- ing. . . . But this wolf comes as a wolf.

"a gradual concentration of the several powers in the same department," Federalist No. 51 (J. Madison), can effectively be resisted. Frequently an issue of this sort will come before the Court clad, so to speak, in sheep's clothing: the poten- tial of the asserted principle to effect important change in the equilibrium of power is not immediately evident, and must be discerned by a careful and perceptive analysis. But this wolf comes as a wolf.

I

The present case began when the Legislative and Executive Branches became "embroiled in a dispute concerning the scope of the con- gressional investigatory power," *United States* v. *House of Representatives of United States* (DC 1983), which—as is often the case with such interbranch conflicts—became quite acrimonious. In the course of oversight hearings into the administration of the Superfund by the Environmental Protection Agency (EPA), two Subcommittees of the House of Representatives requested and then subpoenaed numerous internal EPA documents. The President responded by personally directing the EPA Administrator not to turn over certain of the doc- uments and by having the Attorney General notify the congressional Subcommittees of this assertion of executive privilege. In his decision to assert executive privilege, the President was counseled by appellee Olson, who was then Assistant Attorney General of the Department of Justice for the Office of Legal Counsel, a post that has traditionally had responsibility for providing legal advice to the President (subject to approval of the Attorney General). The House's response was to pass a resolution citing the EPA Administrator, who had possession of the documents, for contempt. Contempt of Congress is a criminal offense. The United States Attorney, however, a member of the Executive Branch, initially took no steps to prosecute the contempt citation. Instead, the Executive Branch sought the immediate assistance of the Third Branch by filing a civil action asking the District Court to declare that the EPA Administrator had acted lawfully in withholding the documents under a claim of executive privilege. The District Court declined (in my view correctly) to get involved in the controversy, and urged the other two branches to try "[c]ompromise and cooperation, rather than confrontation." After further haggling, the two branches eventually reached an agreement giving the House Subcommittees limited access to the contested documents.

Congress did not, however, leave things there. Certain Members of the House remained angered by the confrontation, particularly by the role played by the Department of Justice. Specifically, the Judiciary Committee remained disturbed by the possibility that the Department had persuaded the President to assert executive privilege despite reservations by the EPA; that the Department had "deliberately and unnecessarily precipitated a constitutional confrontation with Congress"; that the Department had not properly reviewed and selected the documents as to which executive privilege was asserted; that the Department had directed the United States Attorney not to present the contempt certification involving the EPA Administrator to a grand jury for prosecution; that the Department had made the decision to sue the House of Representatives; and that the Department had not adequately advised and represented the President, the EPA, and the EPA Administrator. Accordingly, staff counsel of the House Judiciary Committee were commissioned (apparently without the knowledge of many of the Committee's members) to investigate the Justice Department's role in the controversy. That investigation lasted 2½ years, and produced a 3,000-page report issued by the Committee over the vigorous dissent of all but one of its minority-party members. That report, which among other charges questioned the truthfulness of certain statements made by Assistant Attorney General Olson during testimony in front of the Committee during the early stages of its investigation, was sent to the Attorney General along with a formal request that he appoint an independent counsel to investigate Mr. Olson and others.

As a general matter, the Act before us here requires the Attorney General to apply for the appointment of an independent counsel within 90 days after receiving a request to do so, unless he determines within that period that "there are no reasonable grounds to believe that further investigation or prosecution is warranted." As a practical matter, it would be surprising if the Attorney General had any choice (assuming this statute is constitutional) but to seek appointment of an independent counsel to pursue the charges against the principal object of the congressional request, Mr. Olson. Merely the political consequences (to him and the President) of seeming to break the law by refusing to do so would have been substantial. How could it not be, the public would ask, that a 3,000-page indictment drawn by our representatives over 2½ years does not even establish "reasonable grounds to believe" that further investigation or prosecution is warranted with respect to at least the principal alleged culprit? But the Act establishes more than just practical compulsion. Although the Court's opinion asserts that the Attorney General had "no duty to comply with the [congressional] request" that is not entirely accurate. He had a duty to comply unless he could conclude that there were "*no reasonable grounds to believe*," not that prosecution was warranted, but merely that "*further investigation*" was war-ranted (emphasis added) after a 90-day investi-gation in which he was prohibited from using such routine investigative techniques as grand juries, plea bargaining, grants of immunity, or even subpoenas. The Court also makes much of

> *The context of this statute is acrid with the smell of threatened impeachment.*

the fact that "the courts are specifically prevented from reviewing the Attorney General's decision not to seek appointment, 592(f)." Yes, but Congress is not prevented from reviewing it. The context of this statute is acrid with the smell of threatened impeachment. Where, as here, a request for appointment of an independent counsel has come from the Judiciary Committee of either House of Congress, the Attorney General must, if he decides not to seek appointment, explain to that Committee why.

Thus, by the application of this statute in the present case, Congress has effectively compelled a criminal investigation of a high-level appointee of the President in connection with his actions arising out of a bitter power dispute between the President and the Legislative Branch. Mr. Olson may or may not be guilty of a crime; we do not know. But we do know that the investigation of him has been com-menced, not necessarily because the President or his authorized sub-ordinates believe it is in the interest of the United States, in the sense that it warrants the diversion of resources from other efforts, and is worth the cost in money and in possible damage to other govern-mental interests; and not even, leaving aside those normally considered

factors, because the President or his authorized subordinates necessar-
·ily believe that an investigation is likely to unearth a violation worth
prosecuting; but only because the Attorney General cannot affirm, as
Congress demands, that there are no reasonable grounds to believe that
further investigation is warranted. The decisions regarding the scope
of that further investigation, its duration, and, finally, whether or not
prosecution should ensue, are likewise beyond the control of the President and his subordinates.

II

If to describe this case is not to decide it, the concept of a government of separate and coordinate powers no longer has meaning. The
Court devotes most of its attention to such relatively technical details
as the Appointments Clause and the removal power, addressing briefly
and only at the end of its opinion the separation of powers. As my
prologue suggests, I think that has it backwards. Our opinions are full
of the recognition that it is the principle of separation of powers, and
the inseparable corollary that each department's "defense must . . . be
made commensurate to the danger of attack," Federalist No. 51 (J.
Madison), which gives comprehensible content to the Appointments
Clause, and determines the appropriate scope of the removal power.
Thus, while I will subsequently discuss why our appointments and
removal jurisprudence does not support today's holding, I begin with
a consideration of the fountainhead of that jurisprudence, the separation and equilibration of powers.

First, however, I think it well to call to mind an important and
unusual premise that underlies our deliberations, a premise not expressly
contradicted by the Court's opinion, but in my view not faithfully
observed. It is rare in a case dealing, as this one does, with the consti-

tutionality of a statute passed by the Congress of the United States, not to find anywhere in the Court's opinion the usual, almost formulary caution that we owe great deference to Congress' view that what it has done is constitutional and that we will decline to apply the statute only if the presumption of constitutionality can be overcome. That caution is not recited by the Court in the present case because it does not apply. Where a private citizen challenges action of the Government on grounds unrelated to separation of powers, harmonious functioning of the system demands that we ordinarily give some deference, or a presumption of validity, to the actions of the political branches in what is agreed, between themselves at least, to be within their respective spheres. But where the issue pertains to separation of powers, and the political branches are (as here) in disagreement, neither can be presumed correct. The reason is stated concisely by Madison: "The several departments being perfectly co-ordinate by the terms of their common commission, neither of them, it is evident, can pretend to an exclusive or superior right of settling the boundaries between their respective powers. . . ." Federalist No. 49. The playing field for the present case, in other words, is a level one. As one of the interested and coordinate parties to the underlying constitutional dispute, Congress, no more than the President, is entitled to the benefit of the doubt. To repeat, Article II, 1, cl. 1, of the Constitution provides:

The executive Power shall be vested in a President of the United States.

As I described at the outset of this opinion, this does not mean some of the executive power, but all of the executive power. It seems to me, therefore, that the decision of the Court of Appeals invalidating the present statute must be upheld on fundamental separation-of-powers principles if the following two questions are answered affirmatively: (1) Is the conduct of a criminal prosecution (and of an investigation to decide whether to prosecute) the exercise of purely executive power? (2) Does the statute deprive the President of the United States of exclusive control over the exercise of that power? Surprising to say, the Court appears to concede an affirmative answer to both questions, but seeks to avoid the inevitable conclusion that since the statute vests some purely executive power in a person who is not the President of the United States it is void.

The Court concedes that "[t]here is no real dispute that the functions performed by the independent counsel are 'executive'," though it qualifies that concession by adding "in the sense that they are law enforcement functions that typically have been undertaken by officials within the Executive Branch." The qualifier adds nothing but atmosphere. In what other sense can one identify "the executive Power" that is supposed to be vested in the President (unless it includes everything the Executive Branch is given to do) except by reference to what has always and everywhere—if conducted by government at all—been conducted never by the legislature, never by the courts, and always by the executive. There is no possible doubt that the independent counsel's functions fit this description. She is vested with the "full power and independent authority to exercise all *investigative and prosecutorial* functions and powers of the Department of Justice [and] the Attorney General." (emphasis added). Governmental investigation and prosecution of crimes is a quintessentially executive function.

As for the second question, whether the statute before us deprives the President of exclusive control over that quintessentially executive activity: The Court does not, and could not possibly, assert that it does not. That is indeed the whole object of the statute. Instead, the Court points out that the President, through his Attorney General, has at least some control. That concession is alone enough to invalidate the statute, but I cannot refrain from pointing out that the Court greatly exaggerates the extent of that "some" Presidential control. "Most importan[t]" among these controls, the Court asserts, is the Attorney General's "power to remove the counsel for 'good cause.'" This is somewhat like referring to shackles as an effective means of locomotion. As we recognized in *Humphrey's Executor* v. *United States* (1935)—indeed, what *Humphrey's Executor* was all about—limiting removal power to "good cause" is an impediment to, not an effective grant of, Presidential control. We said that limitation was necessary with respect to members of the Federal Trade Commission, which we found to be "an agency of the legislative and judicial departments," and "wholly disconnected from the executive department" because "it is quite evident that one who holds his office only during the pleasure of another, cannot be depended upon to maintain an attitude of independence against the latter's will." What we in *Humphrey's Executor* found to be a means of eliminating Presidential control, the Court today considers the "most importan[t]" means of assuring Presidential control. Congress, of course, operated under no such illusion when it enacted this statute, describing the "good cause" limitation as "protecting the independent counsel's ability to act independently of the President's direct control" since it permits removal only for "misconduct."

Moving on to the presumably "less important" controls that the President retains, the Court notes that no independent counsel may be appointed without a specific request from the Attorney General. As I have discussed above, the condition that renders such a request mandatory (inability to find "no reasonable grounds to believe" that further investigation is warranted) is so insubstantial that the Attorney General's discretion is severely confined. And once the referral is made, it is for the Special Division to determine the scope and duration of the investigation. And in any event, the limited power over referral is irrelevant to the question whether, once appointed, the independent counsel exercises executive power free from the President's control. Finally, the Court points out that the Act directs the independent counsel to abide by general Justice Department policy, except when not "possible." The exception alone shows this to be an empty promise. Even without that, however, one would be hard put to come up with many investigative or prosecutorial "policies" (other than those imposed by the Constitution or by Congress through law) that are absolute. Almost all investigative and prosecutorial decisions—including the ultimate decision whether, after a technical violation of the law has been found, prosecution is warranted—involve the balancing of innumerable legal and practical considerations. Indeed, even political considerations (in the nonpartisan sense) must be considered, as exemplified by the recent decision of an independent counsel to subpoena the former Ambassador of Canada, producing considerable tension in our relations with that country. Another pre-eminently political decision is whether getting a conviction in a particular case is worth the disclosure of national security information that would be necessary. The Justice Department and our intelligence agencies are often in disagreement on this point, and the Justice Department does not always win. The present Act even goes so far as specifically to take the resolution of that dispute away from the President and give it to the independent counsel. In sum, the balancing of various legal, practical, and political considerations, none of which is absolute, is the very essence of prosecutorial discretion. To take this away is to remove the core of the prosecutorial function, and not merely "some" Presidential control.

As I have said, however, it is ultimately irrelevant how much the statute reduces Presidential control. The case is over when the Court acknowledges, as it must, that "[i]t is undeniable that the Act reduces the amount of control or supervision that the Attorney General and, through him, the President exercises over the investigation and prosecution of a certain class of alleged criminal activity." It effects a revolution in our constitutional jurisprudence for the Court, once it has determined that (1) purely executive functions are at issue here, and (2) those functions have been given to a person whose actions are not fully within the supervision and control of the President, nonetheless to proceed further to sit in judgment of whether "the President's need to control the exercise of [the independent counsel's] discretion is *so central* to the functioning of the Executive Branch" as to require complete control (emphasis added), whether the conferral of his powers upon someone else "*sufficiently* deprives the President of control over the independent counsel to interfere impermissibly with [his] constitutional obligation to ensure the faithful execution of the laws" (emphasis added), and whether "the Act give[s] the Executive Branch *sufficient* control over the independent counsel to ensure that the President is able to perform his constitutionally assigned duties" (emphasis added). It is not for us to determine, and we have never presumed to determine, how much of the purely executive powers of government must be within the full control of the President. The Constitution prescribes that they all are.

The utter incompatibility of the Court's approach with our constitutional traditions can be made more clear, perhaps, by applying it to the powers of the other two branches. Is it conceivable that if Congress passed a statute depriving itself of less than full and entire control over some insignificant area of legislation, we would inquire whether the matter was "so central to the functioning of the Legislative Branch" as really to require complete control, or whether the statute gives Congress "sufficient control over the surrogate legislator to ensure that Congress is able to perform its constitutionally assigned duties"? Of course we would have none of that. Once we determined that a purely legislative power was at issue we would require it to be exercised, wholly and entirely, by Congress. Or to bring the point closer to home, consider a statute giving to non–Article III judges just a tiny bit of purely judicial power in a relatively insignificant field, with substantial control, though not total control, in the courts—perhaps "clear error" review, which would be a fair judicial equivalent of the Attorney General's "for cause" removal power here. Is there any doubt that we would not pause to inquire whether the matter was "so central to the functioning of the Judicial Branch" as really to require complete control, or whether we retained "sufficient control over the matters to be decided that we are able to perform our constitutionally assigned duties"? We would say that our "constitutionally assigned duties" include complete control over all exercises of the judicial power—or, as the plurality opinion said in *Northern Pipeline Construction Co.* v. *Marathon Pipe Line Co.* (1982): "The inexorable command of [Article III] is clear and definite: The judicial power of the United States must be exercised by courts having the attributes prescribed in Art. III." We should say here that the President's constitutionally assigned duties include complete control over investigation and prosecution of violations of the law, and that the inexorable command of Article II is clear and definite: the executive power must be vested in the President of the United States.

Is it unthinkable that the President should have such exclusive power, even when alleged crimes by him or his close associates are at issue? No more so than that Congress should have the exclusive power of legislation, even when what is at issue is its own exemption from the burdens of certain laws. See Civil Rights Act of 1964, Title VII, 42 U.S.C. 2000e et seq. (prohibiting "employers," not defined to include the United States, from discriminating on the basis of race, color, religion, sex, or national origin). No more so than that this Court should have the exclusive power to pronounce the final decision on justiciable cases and controversies, even those pertaining to the constitutionality of a statute reducing the salaries of the Justices. A system of separate and coordinate powers necessarily involves an acceptance of exclusive power that can theoretically be abused. As we reiterate this very day, "[i]t is a truism that constitutional protections have costs." *Coy v. Iowa* (1988). While the separation of powers may prevent us from righting every wrong, it does so in order to ensure that we do not lose liberty. The checks against any branch's abuse of its exclusive powers are twofold: First, retaliation by one of the other branch's use of its exclusive powers: Congress, for example, can impeach the executive who willfully fails to enforce the laws; the executive can decline to prosecute under unconstitutional statutes; and the courts can dismiss malicious prosecutions. Second, and ultimately, there is the political check that the people will replace those in the political branches (the branches more "dangerous to the political rights of the Constitution," Federalist No. 78) who are guilty of abuse. Political pressures produced special prosecutors—for Teapot Dome and for Watergate, for example—long before this statute created the independent counsel.

The Court has, nonetheless, replaced the clear constitutional prescription that the executive power belongs to the President with a "balancing test." What are the standards to determine how the balance is to be struck, that is, how much removal of Presidential power is too much? Many countries of the world get along with an executive that is much weaker than ours—in fact, entirely dependent upon the continued support of the legislature. Once we depart from the text of the Constitution, just where short of that do we stop? The most amazing feature of the Court's opinion is that it does not even purport to give an answer. It simply announces, with no analysis, that the ability to control the decision whether to investigate and prosecute the President's closest advisers, and indeed the President himself, is not "so central to the functioning of the Executive Branch" as to be constitutionally required to be within the President's control. Apparently that is so because we say it is so. Having abandoned as the basis for our decisionmaking the text of Article II that "the executive Power" must be vested in the President, the Court does not even attempt to craft a substitute criterion—a "justiciable standard," however remote from the Constitution—that today governs, and in the future will govern, the decision of such questions. Evidently, the governing standard is to be what might be called the unfettered wisdom of a majority of this Court, revealed to an obedient people on a case-by-case basis. This is not only not the government of laws that the Constitution established; it is not a government of laws at all.

> *Evidently, the governing standard is to be what might be called the unfettered wisdom of a majority of this Court, revealed to an obedient people on a case-by-case basis.*

In my view, moreover, even as an ad hoc, standardless judgment the Court's conclusion must be wrong. Before this statute was passed, the President, in taking action disagreeable to the Congress, or an executive officer giving advice to the President or testifying before Congress concerning one of those many matters on which the two branches are from time to time at odds, could be assured that his acts and motives would be adjudged—insofar as the decision whether to conduct a criminal investigation and to prosecute is concerned—in the Executive Branch, that is, in a forum attuned to the interests and the policies of the Presidency. That was one of the natural advantages the Constitution gave to the Presidency, just as it gave members of Congress (and their staffs) the advantage of not being prosecutable for anything said or done in their legislative capacities. It is the very object of this legislation to eliminate that assurance of a sympathetic forum. Unless it can honestly be said that there are "no reasonable grounds to believe" that further investigation is warranted, further investigation must ensure; and the conduct of the investigation, and determination of whether to prosecute, will be given to a person neither selected by nor subject to the control of the President—who will in turn assemble a staff by finding out, presumably, who is willing to put aside whatever else they are doing, for an indeterminate period of time, in order to investigate and prosecute the President or a particular named individual in his administration. The prospect is frightening (as I will discuss at some greater length at the conclusion of this opinion) even outside the context of a bitter, interbranch political dispute. Perhaps the boldness of the President himself will not be affected—though I am not even sure of that. (How much easier it is for Congress, instead of accepting the political damage attendant to the commencement of impeachment proceedings against the President on trivial grounds—or, for that matter, how easy it is for one of the President's political foes outside of Congress—simply to trigger a debilitating criminal investigation of the Chief Executive under this law.) But as for the

President's high-level assistants, who typically have no political base of support, it is as utterly unrealistic to think that they will not be intimidated by this prospect, and that their advice to him and their advocacy of his interests before a hostile Congress will not be affected, as it would be to think that the Members of Congress and their staffs would be unaffected by replacing the Speech or Debate Clause with a similar provision. It deeply wounds the President, by substantially reducing the President's ability to protect himself and his staff. That is the whole object of the law, of course, and I cannot imagine why the Court believes it does not succeed.

Besides weakening the Presidency by reducing the zeal of his staff, it must also be obvious that the institution of the independent counsel enfeebles him more directly in his constant confrontations with Congress, by eroding his public support. Nothing is so politically effective as the ability to charge that one's opponent and his associates are not merely wrongheaded, naive, ineffective, but, in all probability, "crooks." And nothing so effectively gives an appearance of validity to such charges as a Justice Department investigation and, even better, prosecution. The present statute provides ample means for that sort of attack, assuring that massive and lengthy investigations will occur, not merely when the Justice Department in the application of its usual standards believes they are called for, but whenever it cannot be said that there are "no reasonable grounds to believe" they are called for. The statute's highly visible procedures assure, moreover, that unlike most investigations these will be widely known and prominently displayed. Thus, in the 10 years since the institution of the independent counsel was established by law, there have been nine highly publicized investigations, a source of constant political damage to two administrations. That they could not remotely be described as merely the application of "normal" investigatory and prosecutory standards is demonstrated by, in addition to the language of the statute ("no reasonable grounds to believe"), the following facts: Congress appropriates approximately $50 million annually for general legal activities, salaries, and expenses of the Criminal Division of the Department of Justice. This money is used to support "[f]ederal appellate activity," "[o]rganized crime prosecution," "[p]ublic integrity" and "[f]raud" matters, "[n]arcotic & dangerous drug prosecution," "[i]nternal security," "[g]eneral litigation and legal advice," "special investigations," "[p]rosecution support," "[o]rganized crime drug enforcement," and "[m]anagement & administration." By comparison, between May 1986 and August 1987, four independent counsels (not all of whom were operating for that entire period of time) spent almost $5 million (one-tenth of the amount annually appropriated to the entire Criminal Division), spending almost $1 million in the month of August 1987 alone. For fiscal year 1989, the Department of Justice has requested $52 million for the entire Criminal Division and $7 million to support the activities of independent counsel.

Nothing is so politically effective as the ability to charge that one's opponent and his associates are not merely wrongheaded, naive, ineffective, but, in all probability, "crooks."

In sum, this statute does deprive the President of substantial control over the prosecutory functions performed by the independent counsel, and it does substantially affect the balance of powers. That the Court could possibly conclude otherwise demonstrates both the wisdom of our former constitutional system, in which the degree of reduced control and political impairment were irrelevant, since all purely executive power had to be in the President; and the folly of the new system of standardless judicial allocation of powers we adopt today.

III

As I indicated earlier, the basic separation-of-powers principles I have discussed are what give life and content to our jurisprudence concerning the President's power to appoint and remove officers. The same result of unconstitutionality is therefore plainly indicated by our case law in these areas.

Article II, 2, cl. 2, of the Constitution provides as follows:

[The President] shall nominate, and by and with the Advice and Consent of the the Senate, shall appoint Ambassadors, other public Ministers and Consuls, Judges of the supreme Court, and all other Officers of the United States, whose Appointments are not herein otherwise provided for, and which shall be established by Law: but the Congress may by Law vest the Appointment of such inferior Officers, as they think proper, in the President alone, in the Courts of Law, or in the Heads of Departments.

Because appellant (who all parties and the Court agree is an officer of the United States) was not appointed by the President with the advice and consent of the Senate, but rather by the Special Division of the United States Court of Appeals, her appointment is constitutional only if (1) she is an "inferior" officer within the meaning of the above Clause, and (2) Congress may vest her appointment in a court of law.

As to the first of these inquiries, the Court does not attempt to "decide exactly" what establishes the line between principal and "inferior" officers, but is confident that, whatever the line may be, appellant "clearly falls on the 'inferior officer' side" of it. The Court gives three reasons: First, she "is subject to removal by a higher Executive Branch official," namely, the Attorney General. Second, she is "empowered by the Act to perform only certain, limited duties." Third, her office is "limited in jurisdiction" and "limited in tenure."

The first of these lends no support to the view that appellant is an inferior officer. Appellant is removable only for "good cause" or physical or mental incapacity. By contrast, most (if not all) principal officers in the Executive Branch may be removed by the President at will. I fail to see how the fact that appellant is more difficult to remove than most principal officers helps to establish that she is an inferior officer. And I do not see how it could possibly make any difference to her superior or inferior status that the President's limited power to remove her must be exercised through the Attorney General. If she were removable at will by the Attorney General, then she would be subordinate to him and thus properly designated as inferior; but the Court essentially admits that she is not subordinate. If it were common usage to refer to someone as "inferior" who is subject to removal for cause by another, then one would say that the President is "inferior" to Congress.

The second reason offered by the Court—that appellant performs only certain, limited duties—may be relevant to whether she is an inferior officer, but it mischaracterizes the extent of her powers. As the Court states: "Admittedly, the Act delegates to appellant [the] *'full power and independent authority to exercise all investigative and prosecutorial functions and powers of the Department of Justice.'* " (emphasis added). Moreover, in addition to this general grant of power she is given a broad range of specifically enumerated powers, including a power not even the Attorney General possesses: to "contes[t] in court...any claim of privilege or attempt to withhold evidence on grounds of national security." Once all of this is "admitted," it seems to me impossible to maintain that appellant's authority is so "limited" as to render her an inferior officer. The Court seeks to brush this away by asserting that the independent counsel's power does not include any authority to "formulate policy for the Government or the Executive Branch." But the same could be said for all officers of the Government, with the single exception of the President. All of them only formulate policy within their respective spheres of responsibility—as does the independent counsel, who must comply with the policies of the Department of Justice only to the extent possible.

The final set of reasons given by the Court for why the independent counsel clearly is an inferior officer emphasizes the limited nature of her jurisdiction and tenure. Taking the latter first, I find nothing unusually limited about the independent counsel's tenure. To the contrary, unlike most high ranking Executive Branch officials, she continues to serve until she (or the Special Division) decides that her work is substantially completed. This particular independent prosecutor has already served more than two years, which is at least as long as many Cabinet officials. As to the scope of her jurisdiction, there can be no doubt that is small (though far from unimportant). But within it she exercises more than the full power of the Attorney General. The Ambassador to Luxembourg is not anything less than a principal officer, simply because Luxembourg is small. And the federal judge who sits in a small district is not for that reason "inferior in rank and authority." If the mere fragmentation of executive responsibilities into small compartments suffices to render the heads of each of those compartments inferior officers, then Congress could deprive the President of the right to appoint his chief law enforcement officer by dividing up the Attorney General's responsibilities among a number of "lesser" functionaries.

More fundamentally, however, it is not clear from the Court's opinion why the factors it discusses—even if applied correctly to the facts of this case—are determinative of the question of inferior officer status. The apparent source of these factors is a statement in *United States* v. *Germaine* (1879) (discussing *United States* v. *Hartwell* (1868)), that "the term [officer] embraces the ideas of tenure, duration, emolument, and duties." Besides the fact that this was dictum, it was dictum in a case where the distinguishing characteristics of inferior officers versus superior officers were in no way relevant, but rather only the distinguishing characteristics of an "officer of the United States" (to which the criminal statute at issue applied) as opposed to a mere employee. Rather than erect a theory of who is an inferior officer on the foundation of such an irrelevancy, I think it preferable to look to the text of the Constitution and the division of power that it establishes. These demonstrate, I think, that the independent counsel is not an inferior officer because she is not subordinate to any officer in the Executive Branch (indeed, not even to the President). Dictionaries in use at the time of the Constitutional Convention gave the word "inferiour" two meanings which it still bears today: (1) "[l]ower in place, . . . station, . . . rank of life, . . . value or excellency," and (2) "[s]ubordinate." S. Johnson, Dictionary of the English Language (6th ed. 1785). In a document dealing with the structure (the constitution) of a government, one would naturally expect the word to bear the latter meaning— indeed, in such a context it would be unpardonably careless to use the word unless a relationship of subordination was intended. If what was meant was merely "lower in station or rank," one would use instead a term such as "lesser officers." At the only other point in the Constitution at which the word "inferior" appears, it plainly connotes a relationship of subordination. Article III vests the judicial power of the United States in "one supreme Court, and in such *inferior* Courts as the Congress may from time to time ordain and establish." U.S. Const., Art. III, 1 (emphasis added). In Federalist No. 81, Hamilton pauses to describe the "inferior" courts authorized by Article III as inferior in the sense that they are "subordinate" to the Supreme Court.

That "inferior" means "subordinate" is also consistent with what little we know about the evolution of the Appointments Clause. As originally reported to the Committee on Style, the Appointments Clause provided no "exception" from the standard manner of appointment (President with the advice and consent of the Senate) for inferior officers. 2 M. Farrand, Records of the Federal Convention of 1787 (rev. ed. 1966). On September 15, 1787, the last day of the Convention before the proposed Constitution was signed, in the midst of a host of minor changes that were being considered, Gouverneur Morris moved to add the exceptions clause. No great debate ensued; the only disagreement was over whether it was necessary at all. Nobody thought that it was a fundamental change, excluding from the President's appointment power and the Senate's confirmation power a category of officers who might function on their own, outside the supervision of those appointed in the more cumbersome fashion. And it is significant that in the very brief discussion Madison mentions (as in apparent contrast to the "inferior officers" covered by the provision) "Superior Officers." Of course one is not a "superior officer" without some supervisory responsibility, just as, I suggest, one is not an "inferior officer" within the meaning of the provision under discussion unless one is subject to supervision by a "superior officer." It is perfectly obvious, therefore, both from the relative brevity of the discussion this addition received, and from the content of that discussion, that it was intended merely to make clear (what Madison thought already was clear) that those officers appointed by the President with Senate approval could on their own appoint their subordinates, who would, of course, by chain of command still be under the direct control of the President....

To be sure, it is not a *sufficient* condition for "inferior" officer status that one be subordinate to a principal officer. Even an officer who is subordinate to a department head can be a principal officer. That is clear from the brief exchange following Gouverneur Morris' suggestion of the addition of the exceptions clause for inferior officers. Madison responded: "It does not go far enough if it be necessary at all—*Superior Officers below Heads of Departments* ought in some cases to have the appointment of the lesser offices." 2 M. Farrand, Records of the Federal Convention of 1787 (emphasis added).

But it is surely a *necessary* condition for inferior officer status that the officer be subordinate to another officer.

The independent counsel is not even subordinate to the President. The Court essentially admits as much, noting that "appellant may not be 'subordinate' to the Attorney General (and the President) insofar as she possesses a degree of independent discretion to exercise the powers delegated to her under the Act." In fact, there is no doubt about it. As noted earlier, the Act specifically grants her the "full power and independent authority to exercise all investigative and prosecutorial functions of the Department of Justice" and makes her removable only for "good cause," a limitation specifically intended to ensure that she be independent of, not subordinate to, the President and the Attorney General.

Because appellant is not subordinate to another officer, she is not an "inferior" officer and her appointment other than by the President with the advice and consent of the Senate is unconstitutional.

IV

I will not discuss at any length why the restrictions upon the removal of the independent counsel also violate our established precedent dealing with that specific subject. For most of it, I simply refer the reader to the scholarly opinion of Judge Silberman for the Court of Appeals below. I cannot avoid commenting, however, about the essence of what the Court has done to our removal jurisprudence today.

There is, of course, no provision in the Constitution stating who may remove executive officers, except the provisions for removal by impeachment. Before the present decision it was established, however, (1) that the President's power to remove principal officers who exercise purely executive powers could not be restricted, and (2) that his power to remove inferior officers who exercise purely executive powers, and whose appointment Congress had removed from the usual procedure of Presidential appointment with Senate consent, could be restricted, at least where the appointment had been made by an officer of the Executive Branch.

The Court could have resolved the removal power issue in this case by simply relying upon its erroneous conclusion that the independent counsel was an inferior officer, and then extending our holding that the removal of inferior officers appointed by the Executive can be restricted, to a new holding that even the removal of inferior officers appointed by the courts can be restricted. That would in my view be a considerable and unjustified extension, giving the Executive full discretion in neither the selection nor the removal of a purely executive officer. The course the Court has chosen, however, is even worse.

Since our 1935 decision in Humphrey's *Executor* v. *United States*—which was considered by many at the time the product of an activist, anti-New Deal Court bent on reducing the power of President Franklin Roosevelt—it has been established that the line of permissible restriction upon removal of principal officers lies at the point at which the powers exercised by those officers are no longer purely executive. Thus, removal restrictions have been generally regarded as lawful for so-called "independent regulatory agencies," such as the Federal Trade Commission, the Interstate Commerce Commission, and the Consumer Product Safety Commission, which engage substantially in what has been called the "quasi-legislative activity" of rulemaking, and for members of Article I courts, such as the Court of Military Appeals, who engage in the "quasi-judicial" function of adjudication. It has often been observed, correctly in my view, that the line between "purely executive" functions and "quasi-legislative" or "quasi-judicial" functions is not a clear one or even a rational one. But at least it permitted the identification of certain officers, and certain agencies, whose functions were entirely within the control of the President. Congress had to be aware of that restriction in its legislation. Today, however, *Humphrey's Executor* is swept into the dustbin of repudiated constitutional principles. "[O]ur present considered view," the Court says, "is that the determination of whether the Constitution allows Congress to impose a 'good cause'–type restriction on the President's power to remove an official cannot be made to turn on whether or not that official is classified as 'purely executive.'" What *Humphrey's Executor* (and presumably *Myers*) really means, we are now told, is not that there are any "rigid categories of those officials who may or may not be removed at will by the President," but simply that Congress cannot "interfere with the President's exercise of the 'executive power' and his constitutionally appointed duty to 'take care that the laws be faithfully executed.'"

One can hardly grieve for the shoddy treatment given today to *Humphrey's Executor*, which, after all, accorded the same indignity (with much less justification) to Chief Justice Taft's opinion 10 years earlier in *Myers* v. *United States* (1926)—gutting, in six quick pages devoid of textual or historical precedent for the novel principle it set forth, a carefully researched and reasoned 70-page opinion. It is in fact comforting to witness the reality that he who lives by the ipse dixit dies by the ipse dixit. But one must grieve for the Constitution. *Humphrey's Executor* at least had the decency formally to observe the constitutional principle that the President had to be the repository of all executive power, which, as *Myers* carefully explained, necessarily means that he must be able to discharge those who do not perform executive functions according to his liking. As we noted in *Bowsher*, once an officer is appointed "'it is only the authority that can remove him, and not the authority that appointed him, that he must fear and, in the performance of his functions, obey.'" By contrast, "our present considered view" is simply that any executive officer's removal can be restricted, so long as the President remains "able to accomplish his constitutional role." There are now no lines. If the removal of a prosecutor, the virtual embodiment of the power to "take care that the laws be faithfully executed," can be restricted, what officer's removal cannot? This is an open invitation for Congress to experiment. What

> *It is in fact comforting to witness the reality that he who lives by the ipse dixit dies by the ipse dixit. But one must grieve for the Constitution.*

about a special Assistant Secretary of State, with responsibility for one very narrow area of foreign policy, who would not only have to be confirmed by the Senate but could also be removed only pursuant to certain carefully designed restrictions? Could this possibly render the President "[un]able to accomplish his constitutional role"? Or a special Assistant Secretary of Defense for Procurement? The possibilities are endless, and the Court does not understand what the separation of powers, what "[a]mbition . . . counteract[ing] ambition." Federalist No. 51 (Madison), is all about, if it does not expect Congress to try them. As far as I can discern from the Court's opinion, it is now open season upon the President's removal power for all executive officers, with not even the superficially principled restriction of *Humphrey's Executor* as cover. The Court essentially says to the President: "Trust us. We will make sure that you are able to accomplish your constitutional role." I think the Constitution gives the President—and the people—more protection than that.

V

The purpose of the separation and equilibration of powers in general, and of the unitary Executive in particular, was not merely to assure effective government but to preserve individual freedom. Those who hold or have held offices covered by the Ethics in Government Act are entitled to that protection as much as the rest of us, and I conclude my discussion by considering the effect of the Act upon the fairness of the process they receive.

Only someone who has worked in the field of law enforcement can fully appreciate the vast power and the immense discretion that are placed in the hands of a prosecutor with respect to the objects of his investigation. Justice Robert Jackson, when he was Attorney General under President Franklin Roosevelt, described it in a memorable speech to United States Attorneys, as follows:

> There is a most important reason why the prosecutor should have, as nearly as possible, a detached and impartial view of all groups in his community. Law enforcement is not automatic. It isn't blind. One of the greatest difficulties of the position of prosecutor is that he must pick his cases, because no prosecutor can even investigate all of the cases in which he receives complaints. If the Department of Justice were to make even a pretense of reaching every probable violation of federal law, ten times its present staff will be inadequate. We know that no local police force can strictly enforce the traffic laws, or it would arrest half the driving population on any given morning. What every prosecutor is practically required to do is to select the cases for prosecution and to select those in which the offense is the most flagrant, the public harm the greatest, and the proof the most certain.
>
> If the prosecutor is obliged to choose his case, it follows that he can choose his defendants. Therein is the most dangerous power of the prosecutor: that he will pick people that he thinks he should get, rather than cases that need to be prosecuted. With the law books filled with a great assortment of crimes, a prosecutor stands a fair chance of finding at least a technical violation of some act on the part of almost anyone. In such a case, it is not a question of discovering the commission of a crime and then looking for the man who has committed it, it is a question of picking the man and then searching the law books, or putting investigators to work, to pin some offense on him. It is in this

realm—in which the prosecutor picks some person whom he dislikes or desires to embarrass, or selects some group of unpopular persons and then looks for an offense, that the greatest danger of abuse of prosecuting power lies. It is here that law enforcement becomes personal, and the real crime becomes that of being unpopular with the predominant or governing group, being attached to the wrong political views, or being personally obnoxious to or in the way of the prosecutor himself.

R. Jackson, The Federal Prosecutor

Address Delivered at the Second Annual Conference

of United States Attorneys, April 1, 1940

Under our system of government, the primary check against prosecutorial abuse is a political one. The prosecutors who exercise this awesome discretion are selected and can be removed by a President, whom the people have trusted enough to elect. Moreover, when crimes are not investigated and prosecuted fairly, nonselectively, with a reasonable sense of proportion, the President pays the cost in political damage to his administration. If federal prosecutors "pick people that [they] thin[k] [they] should get, rather than cases that need to be prosecuted," if they amass many more resources against a particular prominent individual, or against a particular class of political protesters, or against members of a particular political party, than the gravity of the alleged offenses or the record of successful prosecutions seems to warrant, the unfairness will come home to roost in the Oval Office. I leave it to the reader to recall the examples of this in recent years. That result, of course, was precisely what the Founders had in mind when they provided that all executive powers would be exercised by a single Chief Executive. As Hamilton put it, "[t]he ingredients which constitute safety in the republican sense are a due dependence on the people, and a due responsibility." Federalist No. 70. The President is directly dependent on the people, and since there is only one President, he is responsible. The people know whom to blame, whereas "one of the weightiest objections to a plurality in the executive . . . is that it tends to conceal faults and destroy responsibility."

That is the system of justice the rest of us are entitled to, but what of that select class consisting of present or former high-level Executive Branch officials? If an allegation is made against them of any violation of any federal criminal law (except Class B or C misdemeanors or infractions) the Attorney General must give it his attention. That in itself is not objectionable. But if, after a 90-day investigation without the benefit of normal investigatory tools, the Attorney General is unable to say that there are "no reasonable grounds to believe" that further investigation is warranted, a process is set in motion that is not in the full control of persons "dependent on the people," and whose flaws cannot be blamed on the President. An independent counsel is selected, and the scope of his or her authority prescribed, by a panel of judges. What if they are politically partisan, as judges have been known to be, and select a prosecutor antagonistic to the administration, or even to the particular individual who has been selected for this special treatment? There is no remedy for that, not even a political one. Judges, after all, have life tenure, and appointing a surefire enthusiastic prosecutor could hardly be considered an impeachable offense. So if there is anything wrong with the selection, there is effectively no one to blame. The independent counsel thus selected proceeds to assemble a staff. As I observed earlier, in the nature of things this has to be done by finding lawyers who are willing to lay aside their current careers for an indeterminate amount of time, to take on a job that has no prospect of permanence and little prospect for promotion. One thing is certain, however: it involves investigating and perhaps prosecuting a particular individual. Can one imagine a less equitable manner of fulfilling the executive responsibility to investigate and prosecute? What would be the reaction if, in an area not covered by this statute, the Justice Department posted a public notice inviting applicants to assist in an investigation and possible prosecution of a certain prominent person? Does this not invite what Justice Jackson described as "picking the man and then searching the law books, or putting investigators to work, to pin some offense on him"? To be sure, the investigation must relate to the area of criminal offense specified by the life-tenured judges. But that has often been (and nothing prevents it from being) very broad—and should the independent counsel or his or her staff come up with something beyond that scope, nothing prevents him or her from asking the judges to expand his or her authority or, if that does not work, referring it to the Attorney General, whereupon the whole process would recommence and, if there was "reasonable basis to believe" that further investigation was warranted, that new offense would be referred to the Special Division, which would in all likelihood assign it to the same independent counsel. It seems to me not conducive to fairness. But even if it were entirely evident that unfairness was in fact the result— the judges hostile to the administration, the independent counsel an old foe of the President, the staff refugees from the recently defeated administration—there would be no one accountable to the public to whom the blame could be assigned.

I do not mean to suggest that anything of this sort (other than the inevitable self-selection of the prosecutory staff) occurred in the present case. I know and have the highest regard for the judges on the

Special Division, and the independent counsel herself is a woman of accomplishment, impartiality, and integrity. But the fairness of a process must be adjudged on the basis of what it permits to happen, not what it produced in a particular case. It is true, of course, that a similar list of horribles could be attributed to an ordinary Justice Department prosecution—a vindictive prosecutor, an antagonistic staff, etc. But the difference is the difference that the Founders envisioned when they established a single Chief Executive accountable to the people: the blame can be assigned to someone who can be punished.

The above described possibilities of irresponsible conduct must, as I say, be considered in judging the constitutional acceptability of this process. But they will rarely occur, and in the average case the threat to fairness is quite different. As described in the brief filed on behalf of three ex–Attorneys General from each of the last three administrations:

> The problem is less spectacular but much more worrisome. It is that the institutional environment of the Independent Counsel—specifically, her isolation from the Executive Branch and the internal checks and balances it supplies—is designed to heighten, not to check, all of the occupational hazards of the dedicated prosecutor; the danger of too narrow a focus, of the loss of perspective, of preoccupation with the pursuit of one alleged suspect to the exclusion of other interests.
>
> BRIEF FOR EDWARD H. LEVI, GRIFFIN B. BELL, AND
> WILLIAM FRENCH SMITH AS AMICI CURIAE

It is, in other words, an additional advantage of the unitary Executive that it can achieve a more uniform application of the law. Perhaps that is not always achieved, but the mechanism to achieve it is there. The mini-Executive that is the independent counsel, however, operating in an area where so little is law and so much is discretion, is intentionally cut off from the unifying influence of the Justice Department, and from the perspective that multiple responsibilities provide. What would normally be regarded as a technical violation (there are no rules defining such things), may in his or her small world assume the proportions of an indictable offense. What would normally be regarded as an investigation that has reached the level of pursuing such picayune matters that it should be concluded, may to him or her be an investigation that ought to go on for another year. How frightening it must be to have your own independent counsel and staff appointed, with nothing else to do but to investigate you until investigation is no longer worthwhile—with whether it is worthwhile not depending upon what such judgments usually hinge on, competing responsibilities. And to have that counsel and staff decide, with no basis for comparison, whether what you have done is bad enough, willful enough, and provable enough, to warrant an

How frightening it must be to have your own independent counsel and staff appointed, with nothing else to do but to investigate you until investigation is no longer worthwhile.

indictment. How admirable the constitutional system that provides the means to avoid such a distortion. And how unfortunate the judicial decision that has permitted it.

The notion that every violation of law should be prosecuted, including—indeed, especially—every violation by those in high places, is an attractive one, and it would be risky to argue in an election campaign that that is not an absolutely overriding value. *Fiat justitia, ruat coelum.* Let justice be done, though the heavens may fall. The reality is, however, that it is not an absolutely overriding value, and it was with the hope that we would be able to acknowledge and apply such realities that the Constitution spared us, by life tenure, the necessity of election campaigns. I cannot imagine that there are not many thoughtful men and women in Congress who realize that the benefits of this legislation are far outweighed by its harmful effect upon our system of government, and even upon the nature of justice received by those men and women who agree to serve in the Executive Branch. But it is difficult to vote not to enact, and even more difficult to vote to repeal, a statute called, appropriately enough, the Ethics in Government Act. If Congress is controlled by the party other than the one to which the President belongs, it has little incentive to repeal it; if it is controlled by the same party, it dare not. By its shortsighted action today, I fear the Court has permanently encumbered the Republic with an institution that will do it great harm.

Worse than what it has done, however, is the manner in which it has done it. A government of laws means a government of rules. Today's decision on the basic issue of fragmentation of executive power is ungoverned by rule, and hence ungoverned by law. It extends into the very heart of our most significant constitutional function the "totality of the circumstances" mode of analysis that this Court has in recent years become fond of. Taking all things into account, we conclude that the power taken away from the President here is not really too much. The next time executive power is assigned to someone other than the President we may conclude, taking all things into account, that it is too much. That opinion, like this one, will not be confined by any rule. We will describe, as we have today (though I hope more accurately) the effects of the provision in question, and will authoritatively announce: "The President's need to control the exercise of the [subject officer's] discretion is so central to the functioning of the Executive Branch as to require complete control." This is not analysis; it is ad hoc judgment. And it fails to explain why it is not true that—as the text of the Constitution seems to require, as the Founders seemed to expect, and as our past cases have uniformly assumed—all purely executive power must be under the control of the President.

The ad hoc approach to constitutional adjudication has real attraction, even apart from its work-saving potential. It is guaranteed to produce a result, in every case, that will make a majority of the Court happy with the law. The law is, by definition, precisely what the majority thinks, taking all things into account, it ought to be. I prefer to rely upon the judgment of the wise men who constructed our system, and of the people who approved it, and of two centuries of history that have shown it to be sound. Like it or not, that judgment says, quite plainly, that "[t]he executive Power shall be vested in a President of the United States."

RACE

T HE FOURTEENTH AMENDMENT to the Constitution states that "[n]o State shall make or enforce any law which shall . . . deny any person within its jurisdiction the equal protection of the laws." The amendment was ratified after the Civil War with the purpose of ensuring equal treatment of ex-slaves by the states. But it has been interpreted by the Supreme Court over the years to protect women, ethnic minorities, homosexuals, and other classes of people.

While the Fourteenth Amendment speaks only of the states, the Supreme Court has held since 1954 that the federal government is subject to the same duty of nondiscrimination (under the Due Process Clause of the Fifth Amendment).[1] Thus, although the Court has struggled with the issue, the current analysis for determining whether a class of individuals has suffered from unequal treatment is the same regardless of whether it is an act of Congress or of a particular state.

The Equal Protection guarantee is commonly invoked when an individual or group is treated differently because of an identifiable trait, for example, race, age, and sexuality. Not all classifications give

rise to constitutional violations. In most cases, the states have wide latitude to treat groups differently so long as they have a "rational basis"
for doing so. In cases involving legislative classifications based on race
and national origin, however, courts will require the government to
demonstrate that the classification is narrowly tailored to achieve a
compelling government interest. This very demanding level of
review—known as strict scrutiny—usually results in the courts invalidating the law making the classification. That is why the standard is
sometimes called "strict in theory, but fatal in fact."[2]

When Justice Scalia joined the Supreme Court in 1986, the Court
had held that legislative classifications designed to overcome past racial
discrimination by favoring minorities were permissible and not subject to strict scrutiny under the Equal Protection Clause. The prevailing wisdom was that Congress and the states had the authority to take
concrete steps to rectify any inequities caused by racial prejudice and
bigotry. In short, they were free to try to "level the playing field."

Justice Scalia argued that such "benign" racial classifications were
no more constitutional than distinctions rooted in prejudice. In *Richmond* v. *J.A. Croson Co.* (1989), the Court agreed with Scalia and held
that all racial classifications would thereafter be subject to strict
scrutiny. To Justice Scalia, application of this new standard meant the
end was near for any and all government-sponsored racial distinctions.
In his view, the government simply never has a compelling interest in
discriminating based on race.

Specifically, he has argued that the Equal Protection Clause applies
to individuals and therefore government cannot unfairly discriminate
against any individual in order to give an advantage to an individual
who is a member of a group that was historically disadvantaged. His
opinions on race have been brief, but eloquent.

RICHMOND v. J.A. CROSON CO. (1989)

The City of Richmond, Virginia, enacted a plan to help minority-owned businesses by requiring that prime contractors on city construction projects subcontract at least 30 percent of the contract to one or more minority business enterprises. To be considered a minority business enterprise, a business had to be at least 51 percent owned by minority group members. The City Council designed the plan to overcome the effects of past discrimination against African Americans in the Richmond area. As such, it was deemed a modest remedial effort to right past wrongs.

The Supreme Court deemed the Richmond plan unconstitutional because the city did not provide direct evidence of prior discrimination against minorities in the construction business, nor did the city show that race-neutral plans could not have helped the city to achieve its objective of increasing minority-business participation. The opinion marked the first time that the Supreme Court applied "strict scrutiny" review to a racial classification designed to benefit minorities. This new application of the strict scrutiny standard angered the Court's liberal members, who believed the government should be free to take steps to undo the effects of past racism. The majority argued that application of the tougher standard of review would not doom all government efforts to eradicate racism. Writing for the Court, Justice O'Connor said cities such as Richmond had a compelling interest in reversing the effects of past racism and were free to do so as long as they proved that racism had indeed existed and that their use of reverse discrimination was necessary to remedy the harmful effects or the past racism.

Writing separately, Justice Scalia agreed with the majority that courts should apply strict scrutiny to any attempt by the government to use racial classifications. But he disagreed with the majority's assertion that government can use "benign" racial discrimination in favor of a race that has been the subject of discrimination in the past. Scalia advised that the government must be especially vigilant about combating discrimination at the local level, since the smaller numbers needed to create a ruling majority there increased the incidence of discrimination. Finally, Scalia argued that the government has options for ameliorating the effects of past discrimination without resorting to further race-based classifications. For example, it can enact laws that provide government assistance to disadvantaged individuals (including blacks) rather than to blacks (some of whom might be disadvantaged).

~∞❀∞~

JUSTICE SCALIA, CONCURRING IN THE JUDGMENT.

I agree with much of the Court's opinion, and, in particular, with Justice O'Connor's conclusion that strict scrutiny must be applied to all governmental classification by race, whether or not its asserted purpose is "remedial" or "benign." I do not agree, however, with Justice O'Connor's dictum suggesting that, despite the Fourteenth Amendment, state and local governments may in some circumstances discriminate on the basis of race in order (in a broad sense) "to ameliorate the effects of past discrimination." The benign purpose of compensating for social disadvantages, whether they have been acquired by reason of prior discrimination or otherwise, can no more be pursued by the illegitimate means of racial discrimination than can other assertedly benign purposes we have repeatedly rejected. The difficulty of overcoming the effects of past discrimination is as nothing compared with the difficulty of eradicating from our society the source of those effects, which is the tendency—fatal to a Nation such as ours—to classify and judge men and women on the basis of their country of origin or the color of their skin. A solution to the first problem that aggravates the second is no solution at all. I share the view expressed by Alexander Bickel that "[t]he lesson of the great decisions of the Supreme Court and the lesson of contemporary history have been the same for at least a generation: discrimination on the basis of race is illegal, immoral, unconstitutional, inherently wrong, and destructive of democratic society." A. Bickel, *The Morality of Consent* (1975). At least where state or local action is at issue, only a social emergency rising to the level of imminent danger to life and limb—for example, a prison race riot, requiring temporary segregation of inmates—can justify an exception to the principle embodied in the Fourteenth Amendment that "[o]ur Constitution is colorblind, and neither knows nor tolerates classes among citizens," *Plessy* v. *Ferguson* (1896) (Harlan, J., dissenting).

We have in some contexts approved the use of racial classifications by the Federal Government to remedy the effects of past discrimination. I do not believe that we must or should extend those holdings to the States. In *Fullilove* v. *Klutznick* (1980), we upheld legislative action by Congress similar in its asserted purpose to that at issue here. And we have permitted federal courts to prescribe quite severe, race-conscious remedies when confronted with egregious and persistent unlawful discrimination. As Justice O'Connor acknowledges, however, it is one thing to permit racially based conduct by the Federal Government—whose legislative powers concerning matters of race were explicitly enhanced by the Fourteenth Amendment—and quite another to permit it by the precise entities against whose conduct in matters of race that Amendment was specifically directed. As we said in *Ex parte Virginia*, the Civil War Amendments were designed to "take away all possibility of oppression by law because of race or color" and "to be . . . limitations on the power of the States and enlargements of the power of Congress." Thus, without revisiting what we held in *Fullilove* (or trying to derive a rationale from the three separate opinions supporting the judgment, none of which commanded more than three votes), I do not believe our decision in that case controls the one before us here.

A sound distinction between federal and state (or local) action based on race rests not only upon the substance of the Civil War Amendments, but upon social reality and governmental theory. It is a simple fact that what Justice Stewart described in *Fullilove* as "the dispassionate objectivity [and] the flexibility that are needed to mold a race-conscious remedy around the single objective of eliminating the effects of past or present discrimination"—political qualities already to be doubted in a national legislature—are substantially less likely to exist at the state or local level. The struggle for racial justice has historically been a struggle by the national society against oppression in the individual States. And the struggle retains that character in modern times. Not all of that struggle has involved discrimination against blacks and not all of it has been in the Old South. What the record shows, in other words, is that racial discrimination against any group finds a more ready expression at the state and local than at the federal level. To the children of the Founding Fathers, this should come as no surprise. An acute awareness of the heightened danger of oppression from political factions in small, rather than large, political units dates to the very beginning of our national history. As James Madison observed in support of the proposed Constitution's enhancement of national powers:

> The smaller the society, the fewer probably will be the distinct parties and interests composing it; the fewer the distinct parties and interests, the more frequently will a majority be found of the same party; and the smaller the number of individuals composing a majority, and the smaller the compass within which they are placed, the more easily will they concert and execute their

plan of oppression. Extend the sphere and you take in a greater variety of parties and interests; you make it less probable that a majority of the whole will have a common motive to invade the rights of other citizens; or if such a common motive exists, it will be more difficult for all who feel it to discover their own strength and to act in unison with each other.

THE FEDERALIST NO. 10

The prophe[c]y of these words came to fruition in Richmond in the enactment of a set-aside clearly and directly beneficial to the dominant political group, which happens also to be the dominant racial group. The same thing has no doubt happened before in other cities (though the racial basis of the preference has rarely been made textually explicit)—and blacks have often been on the receiving end of the injustice. Where injustice is the game, however, turnabout is not fair play.

> *Where injustice is the game, however, turnabout is not fair play.*

In my view there is only one circumstance in which the States may act by race to "undo the effects of past discrimination": where that is necessary to eliminate their own maintenance of a system of unlawful racial classification. If, for example, a state agency has a discriminatory pay scale compensating black employees in all positions at 20% less than their nonblack counterparts, it may assuredly promulgate an order raising the salaries of "all black employees" to eliminate the differential. This distinction explains our school desegregation cases, in which we have made plain that States and localities sometimes have an obligation to adopt race-conscious remedies. While there is no doubt that those cases have taken into account the continuing "effects" of previously mandated racial school assignment, we have held those effects to justify a race-conscious remedy only because we have concluded, in that context, that they perpetuate a "dual school system." We have stressed each school district's constitutional "duty to dismantle its dual system," and have found that "[e]ach instance of a failure or refusal to fulfill this affirmative duty *continues the violation* of the Fourteenth Amendment." *Columbus Board of Education* v. *Penick* (1979) (emphasis added). Concluding in this context that race-neutral efforts at "dismantling the state-imposed dual system" were so ineffective that they might "indicate a lack of good faith," *Green* v. *New Kent County School Board* (1968), we have permitted, as part of the local authorities'"affirmative duty to disestablish the dual school system[s]," such voluntary (that is, noncourt-ordered) measures as attendance zones drawn to achieve greater racial balance, and out-of-zone assignment by race for the same purpose. While thus permitting the use of race to declassify racially classified students, teachers, and educational resources, however, we have also made it clear that the remedial power extends no further than the scope of the continuing constitutional violation. And it is implicit in our cases that after the dual school system has been completely disestablished, the States may no longer assign students by race.

Our analysis in *Bazemore* v. *Friday* reflected our unwillingness to conclude, outside the context of school assignment, that the continuing effects of prior discrimination can be equated with state maintenance of a discriminatory system. There we found both that the government's adoption of "wholly neutral admissions" policies for 4-H and Homemaker Clubs sufficed to remedy its prior constitutional violation of maintaining segregated admissions, and that there was no further obligation to use racial reassignments to eliminate continuing effects—that is, any remaining all-black and all-white clubs. "[H]owever sound *Green [v. New Kent County School Board]* may have been in the context of the public schools," we said, "it has no application to this wholly different milieu." The same is so here.

A State can, of course, act "to undo the effects of past discrimination" in many permissible ways that do not involve classification by race. In the particular field of state contracting, for example, it may adopt a preference for small businesses, or even for new businesses— which would make it easier for those previously excluded by discrimination to enter the field. Such programs may well have racially disproportionate impact, but they are not based on race. And, of course, a State may "undo the effects of past discrimination" in the sense of giving the identified victim of state discrimination that which it wrongfully denied him—for example, giving to a previously rejected black applicant the job that, by reason of discrimination, had been awarded to a white applicant, even if this means terminating the latter's employment. In such a context, the white jobholder is not being selected for disadvantageous treatment because of his race, but because he was wrongfully awarded a job to which another is entitled. That is worlds apart from the system here, in which those to be disadvantaged are identified solely by race.

I agree with the Court's dictum that a fundamental distinction must be drawn between the effects of "societal" discrimination and the effects of "identified" discrimination, and that the situation would be different if Richmond's plan were "tailored" to identify those particular bidders who "suffered from the effects of past discrimination by the city or prime contractors." In my view, however, the reason that would make a difference is not, as the Court states, that it would justify race-conscious action ... but rather that it would enable race-neutral remediation. Nothing prevents Richmond from according a contracting preference to identified victims of discrimination. While most of the beneficiaries might be black, neither the beneficiaries nor those disadvantaged by the preference would be identified on the basis of their race. In other words, far from justifying racial classification, identification of actual victims of discrimination makes it less supportable than ever, because more obviously unneeded.

In this final book, Professor Bickel wrote:

[A] racial quota derogates the human dignity and individuality of all to whom it is applied; it is invidious in principle as well as in practice. Moreover, it can easily be turned against those it purports to help. The history of the racial quota is a history of subjugation, not beneficence. Its evil lies not in its name, but in its effects: a quota is a divider of society, a creator of castes, and it is all the worse for its racial base, especially in a society desperately striving for an equality that will make race irrelevant.

BICKEL, *THE MORALITY OF CONSENT*

Those statements are true and increasingly prophetic. Apart from their societal effects, however, which are "in the aggregate disastrous," *id.*, it is important not to lose sight of the fact that even "benign" racial quotas have individual victims, whose very real injustice we ignore whenever we deny them enforcement of their right not to be disadvantaged on the basis of race. As Justice Douglas observed: "A DeFunis who is white is entitled to no advantage by virtue of that fact; nor is he subject to any disability, no matter what his race or color. Whatever his race, he had a constitutional right to have his application considered on its individual merits in a racially neutral manner." *DeFunis v. Odegaard* (1974) (dissenting opinion). When we depart from this

American principle we play with fire, and much more than an occasional DeFunis, Johnson, or Croson burns.

It is plainly true that in our society blacks have suffered discrimination immeasurably greater than any directed at other racial groups. But those who believe that racial preferences can help to "even the score" display, and reinforce, a manner of thinking by race that was the source of the injustice and that will, if it endures within our society, be the source of more injustice still. The relevant proposition is not that it was blacks, or Jews, or Irish who were discriminated against, but that it was individual men and women, "created equal," who were discriminated against. And the relevant resolve is that that should never happen again. Racial preferences appear to "even the score" (in some small degree) only if one embraces the proposition that our society is appropriately viewed as divided into races, making it right that an injustice rendered in the past to a black man should be compensated for by discriminating against a white. Nothing is worth that embrace. Since blacks have been disproportionately disadvantaged by racial discrimination, any race-neutral remedial program aimed at the disadvantaged as such will have a disproportionately beneficial impact on blacks. Only such a program, and not one that operates on the basis of race, is in accord with the letter and the spirit of our Constitution.

Those who believe that racial preferences can help to "even the score" display, and reinforce, a manner of thinking by race that was the source of the injustice and that will, if it endures within our society, be the source of more injustice still.

Since I believe that the appellee here had a constitutional right to have its bid succeed or fail under a decisionmaking process uninfected with racial bias, I concur in the judgment of the Court.

ADARAND CONSTRUCTORS, INC. v. PENA (1995)

Six years after *Croson*, the Supreme Court extended its decision to apply strict scrutiny to federal affirmative action plans. At issue in *Adarand* was a federal program to provide financial incentives to government contractors who hired small businesses controlled by "socially and economically disadvantaged" individuals. Lower courts upheld the program, but a closely divided Supreme Court sent the case back for review with instruction to apply strict scrutiny to the federal contracting program.

Justice Scalia filed a very short opinion agreeing with the Court's decision. In a concise manner, Scalia explained that the Constitution's guarantee of equal protection applies to individuals, not races.

~∽⊚⟡⊚∽~

JUSTICE SCALIA, CONCURRING IN
PART AND CONCURRING IN THE JUDGMENT.

I join the opinion of the Court... except insofar as it may be inconsistent with the following: In my view, government can never have a "compelling interest" in discriminating on the basis of race in order to "make up" for past racial discrimination in the opposite direction. Individuals who have been wronged by unlawful racial discrimination should be made whole; but under our Constitution there can be no such thing as either a creditor or a debtor race. That concept is alien to the Constitution's focus upon the individual, see Amdt. 14, §1 ("[N]or shall any State... deny to *any person*" the equal protection of the laws) (emphasis added), and its rejection of dispositions based on race, see Amdt. 15, §1 (prohibiting abridgment of the right to vote "on account of race"), or based on blood, see Art. III, §3 ("[N]o Attainder of Treason shall work Corruption of Blood"); Art. I, §9 ("No Title of Nobility shall be granted by the United States"). To pursue the concept of racial entitlement—even for the most admirable and benign of purposes—is to reinforce and preserve for future mischief the way of thinking that produced race slavery, race privilege and race hatred. In the eyes of government, we are just one race here. It is American.

> *Under our Constitution there can be no such thing as either a creditor or a debtor race. . . . In the eyes of government, we are just one race here. It is American.*

It is unlikely, if not impossible, that the challenged program would survive under this understanding of strict scrutiny, but I am content to leave that to be decided on remand.

GRUTTER V. BOLLINGER (2003)

In 2003, the Supreme Court heard two affirmative action cases involving admissions policies at the University of Michigan. In *Grutter* v. *Bollinger,* the Court was asked to decide if the University of Michigan Law School's admissions policy violated the Equal Protection Clause of the Fourteenth Amendment. The controversy arose after a white applicant with high test scores was denied admission. She claimed her denial was due to the reverse discrimination she suffered as a result of the law school's race-conscious admissions policy.

The law school admitted to using race as a factor in assessing applicants but justified its practice on the ground that "achieving diversity among the student body" is a compelling government interest. Specifically, the school said it sought to attain a "critical mass" of underrepresented minority students in order to produce "educational benefits" such as "cross-racial understanding" and breaking down of racial stereotypes. The school contended the scheme did not amount to an unlawful quota system as demonstrated by the fact that minority population fluctuated from year to year. The policy was "narrowly tailored," the school argued, to meet its goal of diversity since no other means existed to advance its interest without reducing the academic quality of the school.

In a 5–4 decision written by Justice O'Connor, the Court upheld the law school's admissions policy. The Court not only agreed with the school that obtaining a diverse student body was a compelling government interest, but it held that its program of considering race along with many other factors that may contribute to diversity was an appropriately narrow way to further that interest.

In the other University of Michigan affirmative action case decided that day, the Supreme Court in *Gratz* v. *Bollinger* struck down the undergraduate school's admissions program. The undergraduate school attempted to increase diversity on campus by granting twenty points, or one-fifth of the points needed to gain admission, to every "underrepresented minority" applicant. The Court ruled that, although diversity might represent a compelling government interest, the awarding of points based solely on race was not narrowly tailored to achieving the asserted interest in fostering diversity.

Justice Scalia voted against both affirmative action programs. In *Gutter*, Scalia wrote an opinion in which he reiterated his argument that government can never have a compelling interest in classifying people on the basis of race. Scalia then questioned the importance of the "educational benefits" the law school alleged would flow from a racially diverse student body. Finally, he predicted that rather than settling the issue of affirmative action on America's campuses, the Court's unprincipled "split doubleheader"—upholding the law school's race-conscious policy, while striking down the undergraduate school's program—would precipitate more lawsuits.

JUSTICE SCALIA, WITH WHOM JUSTICE THOMAS JOINS, CONCURRING IN PART AND DISSENTING IN PART.

I join the opinion of The Chief Justice. As he demonstrates, the University of Michigan Law School's mystical "critical mass" justification for its discrimination by race challenges even the most gullible mind. The admissions statistics show it to be a sham to cover a scheme of racially proportionate admissions.

I also join Parts I through VII of Justice Thomas's opinion. I find particularly unanswerable his central point: that the allegedly "compelling state interest" at issue here is not the incremental "educational benefit" that emanates from the fabled "critical mass" of minority students, but rather Michigan's interest in maintaining a "prestige" law school whose normal admissions standards disproportionately exclude blacks and other minorities. If that is a compelling state interest, everything is.

I add the following: The "educational benefit" that the University of Michigan seeks to achieve by racial discrimination consists, according to the Court, of "'cross-racial understanding'" and "'better prepar[ation of] students for an increasingly diverse workforce and society,'" all of which is necessary not only for work, but also for good "citizenship." This is not, of course, an "educational benefit" on which students will be graded on their Law School transcript (Works and Plays Well with Others: B$^+$) or tested by the bar examiners (Q: Describe in 500 words or less your cross-racial understanding). For it is a lesson of life rather than law—essentially the same lesson taught to (or rather learned by, for it cannot be "taught" in the usual sense) people three feet shorter and twenty years younger than the full-grown adults at the University of Michigan Law School, in institutions ranging from Boy Scout troops to public-school kindergartens. If properly considered an "educational benefit" at all, it is surely not one that is either uniquely relevant to law school or uniquely "teachable" in a formal educational setting. *And therefore:* If it is appropriate for the University of Michigan Law School to use racial discrimination for the purpose of putting together a "critical mass" that will convey generic lessons in socialization and good citizenship, surely it is no less appropriate—indeed, *particularly* appropriate—for the civil service system of the State of Michigan to do so. There, also, those exposed to "critical masses" of certain races will presumably become better Americans, better Michiganders, better civil servants. And surely private employers cannot be criticized—indeed, should be praised—if they also "teach" good citizenship to their adult employees through a patriotic, all-American system of racial discrimination in hiring. The nonminority individuals who are deprived of a legal education, a civil service job, or any job at all by reason of their skin color will surely understand.

> *This is not an "educational benefit" on which students will be graded on their Law School transcript (Works and Plays Well with Others: B⁺) or tested by the bar examiners (Q: Describe in 500 words or less your cross-racial understanding).*

Unlike a clear constitutional holding that racial preferences in state educational institutions are impermissible, or even a clear anticonstitutional holding that racial preferences in state educational institutions are OK, today's *Grutter-Gratz* split double header seems perversely designed to prolong the controversy and the litigation. Some future lawsuits will presumably focus on whether the discriminatory scheme in question contains enough evaluation of the applicant "as an individual" and sufficiently avoids "separate admissions tracks" to fall under *Grutter* rather than *Gratz*. Some will focus on whether a university has gone beyond the bounds of a " 'good faith effort' " and has so zealously pursued its "critical mass" as to make it an unconstitutional *de facto* quota system, rather than merely " 'a permissible goal.' " Other lawsuits may focus on whether, in the particular setting at issue, any educational benefits flow from racial diversity. (That issue was not contested in *Grutter*; and while the opinion accords "a degree of deference to a university's academic decisions," "deference does not imply abandonment or abdication of judicial review," *Miller-El* v. *Cockrell* (2003).) Still other suits may challenge the bona fides of the institution's expressed commitment to the educational benefits of diversity that immunize the discriminatory scheme in *Grutter*. (Tempting targets, one would suppose, will be those universities that talk the talk of multiculturalism and racial diversity in the courts but walk the walk of tribalism and racial segregation on their campuses—through minority-only student organizations, separate minority housing opportunities, separate minority student centers, even separate minority-only graduation ceremonies.) And still other suits may claim that the institution's racial preferences have gone below or above the mystical *Grutter*-approved "critical mass."

Tempting targets, one would suppose, will be those universities that talk the talk of multiculturalism and racial diversity in the courts but walk the walk of tribalism and racial segregation on their campuses.

Finally, litigation can be expected on behalf of minority groups intentionally short changed in the institution's composition of its generic minority "critical mass." I do not look forward to any of these cases. The Constitution proscribes government discrimination on the basis of race, and state-provided education is no exception.

CHAPTER FIVE

ABORTION

T HE CONSTITUTION OF THE UNITED STATES does not contain a
provision stating: "Congress shall make no law abridging the
right of privacy." Nor does it mention the word "abortion." During
the past fifty years, however, the Supreme Court has decreed that certain "private" activities, including abortion, should be considered "fundamental rights" under the Constitution. These newly discovered
rights receive the same high level of constitutional protection as those
in the Bill of Rights, including the freedoms of speech and religion.

The theory that the Court relies upon to protect these "rights" is
called substantive due process. Under this theory, the Fourteenth
Amendment's protection of "liberty" includes substantive rights that
one will not find anywhere in the Constitution. For example, in 1965,
the Court found married individuals had a fundamental right to use
contraceptives.[1] In 1966, the right was extended to all individuals,
married or not.[2] And then, in its 1973 decision in *Roe* v. *Wade*, the
Court declared abortion a constitutional right.

Since his appointment to the High Court, Justice Scalia has been the
most passionate and persistent critic of the view that the Constitution

contains a right to end the natural development of an unborn child. He does not believe judges should have free reign to create rights as they see fit; instead, he believes they should employ a standard that is rooted in the Constitution and American history and that cannot be altered or manipulated by future court majorities. First, the Court should look to the text of the Constitution to determine if there is specific language justifying protection for the claimed right. If there is no such text, the Court should inquire whether there exists a long-standing social history in the United States for protecting the asserted right. If neither of these conditions is met, no fundamental right can be said to exist.

Scalia has pointed out in several opinions that the text of the Constitution is completely and undeniably silent on the subject of abortion. In addition, procurement of an abortion is not protected by any long-standing tradition since many states enacted laws limiting abortion before *Roe* v. *Wade*. Therefore, abortion cannot be considered a "fundamental right" worthy of constitutional protection.

In the absence of text and tradition, Scalia maintains the Supreme Court has nothing to guide its decisions in the abortion area. The result, he argues, is constant confusion and inconsistency. In a 1990 case involving Minnesota's law requiring minors to obtain parental consent before having an abortion,[3] Justice Scalia noted that at the time, the justices on the Court had applied various legal standards (and even applied the same standards differently) to state abortion restrictions. Scalia concluded, "The random and unpredictable results of our consequently unchanneled individual views make it increasingly evident, term after term, that the tools for this job are not to be found in the lawyer's—and hence not in the judge's—work-box. I continue to dissent from this enterprise of devising an Abortion Code, and from the illusion that we have authority to do so."[4]

Instead, Justice Scalia contends that issues involving the circumstances in which a state can lawfully regulate abortion are policy questions. They should be resolved by legislatures, in which the majority of citizens can express their will through their elected representatives. In advocating that the Court get out of what he calls the "abortion-umpiring" business, Scalia does not suggest that abortion will (or even should) become illegal. Rather, as with all issues not addressed by the Constitution, he believes that the matter should be decided by the people. Thus, while abortion might be outlawed or severely restricted in some states, it would likely maintain strong legal protection in many other states.

Finally, Justice Scalia has expressed great concern that the Court's continued involvement in the abortion issue has undermined its credibility as a neutral interpreter of laws. By creating a right to abortion without textual support and then constantly shifting the standards it uses to decide abortion-related cases, the Court, Scalia says, is guilty of swapping its judicial role for policymaking and, as a result, inviting political lobbying efforts designed to influence not only its abortion decisions, but also who should be nominated and confirmed to serve on the Supreme Court. He bemoans the fact that our nation's highest court—set up by our Founders to be insulated from public persuasion—has become a magnet for mass public demonstration every time a case involving abortion goes before the Court.

WEBSTER v. REPRODUCTIVE HEALTH SERVICES (1989)

In 1986, Missouri passed a law requiring doctors perform certain medical tests before performing an abortion on any fetus they believe to be at least twenty weeks old to determine whether the fetus is "viable." The statute also prohibited the use of public funds to perform or assist abortions that are not necessary to save the life of the mother. Finally, the law barred use of state funds for encouraging or counseling a woman to have an abortion unless the abortion was deemed necessary to save the life of the mother.

At the time of the decision, *Roe* v. *Wade* was still the law of the land. Thus, judges considering the constitutionality of legislative proposals to regulate abortion had to use the *Roe* Court's trimester analysis to determine whether a regulation was too restrictive. In short, the Court in *Roe* said that women had an unrestricted right to choose abortion during the first three months of pregnancy. In the second trimester, the government could regulate abortion if it was doing so to protect the health of the mother. In the final trimester of pregnancy, the *Roe* majority ruled that the government's interest in protecting the potential life of the unborn child was great enough to warrant significant restrictions on abortion.

Several post-*Roe* decisions upheld legislative attempts to regulate abortion. For example, the Supreme Court in 1980 declared constitutional federal legislation prohibiting the use of Medicaid funds to pay for nontherapeutic abortions. But strict constructionists and antiabortion advocates never accepted the *Roe* decision as legitimate and hoped a future Court would have the opportunity to overturn it. In 1989, after President Reagan had added Justices Sandra Day O'Connor, Scalia, and Anthony Kennedy to the high court, *Roe's* critics sensed such an opportunity had arrived in the form of the *Webster* case.

To the clear disappointment of Justice Scalia, Justice O'Connor demurred. She filed a separate opinion agreeing with the plurality to uphold the Missouri law's restrictions on abortion, but declining to reexamine *Roe*. O'Connor said she did not believe the viability testing requirement conflicted with *Roe* or any other abortion-related decision. The Court had a practice of not deciding a constitutional question unless it was absolutely essential to resolving the case before it. Applying that practice in this case, she said, *Roe* need not be reconsidered because the case could be decided without doing so.

O'Connor agreed with the Court that Missouri's restrictions did not violate the Constitution. In order to make that determination, she employed a standard that asked whether the state regulations imposed an "undue burden" on a woman's decision to seek an abortion. O'Connor had used the "undue burden" language in a dissent she had written six years earlier, in which she said the "*Roe* framework . . . is clearly on a collision course with itself."[5] In *Webster,* she found that none of the Missouri restrictions constituted an undue burden.

Scalia's frustration at Justice O'Connor's decision to sidestep *Roe* was at full boil. In a separate concurrence, he attacked nearly every point of her opinion. Whereas O'Connor cautioned against devising a broader rule of constitutional law than she felt was required to decide the case, Justice Scalia cited prior cases from the very same Court term in which O'Connor authored or joined opinions that did exactly that. He then dismissed the "undue burden" for providing no guidance to the Court on how to resolve abortion-related questions. Finally, Scalia charged that, by ducking *Roe* altogether, the Court made the "least responsible" decision.

⊰⊙⊱

JUSTICE SCALIA, CONCURRING IN
PART AND CONCURRING IN THE JUDGMENT.

. . . As to Part II-D [regarding viability testing], I share Justice Blackmun's view that it effectively would overrule *Roe* v. *Wade.* I think that should be done, but would do it more explicitly. Since today we contrive to avoid doing it, and indeed avoid almost any decision of national import, I need not set forth my reasons, some of which have been well recited in dissents of my colleagues in other cases.

The outcome of today's case will doubtless be heralded as a triumph of judicial statesmanship. It is not that, unless it is statesmanlike needlessly to prolong this Court's self-awarded sovereignty over a field where it has little proper business since the answers to most of the cruel questions posed are political and not juridicial—a sovereignty which therefore quite properly, but to the great damage of the Court, makes it the object of the sort of organized public pressure that political institutions in a democracy ought to receive.

Justice O'Connor's assertion, that a "fundamental rule of judicial restraint" requires us to avoid reconsidering *Roe*, cannot be taken seriously. By finessing *Roe* we do not, as she suggests, adhere to the strict and venerable rule that we should avoid "decid[ing] questions of a constitutional nature." We have not disposed of this case on some statutory or procedural ground, but have decided, and could not avoid deciding, whether the Missouri statute meets the requirements of the United States Constitution. The only choice available is whether, in deciding that constitutional question, we should use *Roe* v. *Wade* as the benchmark, or something else. What is involved, therefore, is not the rule of avoiding constitutional questions where possible, but the quite separate principle that we will not "'formulate a rule of constitutional law broader than is required by the precise facts to which it is applied.'" The latter is a sound general principle, but one often departed from when good reason exists. Just this Term, for example, in an opinion authored by Justice O'Connor, despite the fact that we had already held a racially based set-aside unconstitutional because unsupported by evidence of identified discrimination, which was all that was needed to decide the case, we went on to outline the criteria for properly tailoring race-based remedies in cases where such evidence is present. Also this Term, in an opinion joined by Justice O'Connor, we announced the constitutional rule that deprivation of the right to confer with counsel during trial violates the Sixth Amendment even if no prejudice can be shown, despite our finding that there had been no such deprivation on the facts before us—which was all that was needed to decide that case....

It would be wrong, in any decision, to ignore the reality that our policy not to "formulate a rule of constitutional law broader than is required by the precise facts" has a frequently applied good-cause exception. But it seems particularly perverse to convert the policy into an absolute in the present case, in order to place beyond reach the inexpressibly "broader-than-was-required-by-the-precise-facts" structure established by *Roe v. Wade*.

The real question, then, is whether there are valid reasons to go beyond the most stingy possible holding today. It seems to me there are not only valid but compelling ones. Ordinarily, speaking no more broadly than is absolutely required avoids throwing settled law into confusion; doing so today preserves a chaos that is evident to anyone who can read and count. Alone sufficient to justify a broad holding is the fact that our retaining control, through *Roe*, of what I believe to be, and many of our citizens recognize to be, a political issue, continuously distorts the public perception of the role of this Court. We can now look forward to at least another Term with carts full of mail from the public, and the streets full of demonstrators, urging us—their unelected and life-tenured judges who have been awarded those extraordinary, undemocratic characteristics precisely in order that we might follow the law despite popular will—to follow the popular will. Indeed, I expect we can look forward to even more

> *We can now look forward to at least another term with carts full of mail from the public, and the streets full of demonstrators, urging us—their unelected and life-tenured judges who have been awarded those extraordinary, undemocratic characteristics precisely in order that we might follow the law despite popular will—to follow the popular will.*

of that than before, given our indecisive decision today. And if these reasons for taking the unexceptional course of reaching a broader holding are not enough, then consider the nature of the constitutional question we avoid: In most cases, we do not harm by not speaking more broadly than the decision requires. Anyone affected by the conduct that the avoided holding would have prohibited will be able to challenge it himself and have his day in court to make the argument. Not so with respect to the harm that many States believed, pre-*Roe*, and many may continue to believe, is caused by largely unrestricted abortion. That will continue to occur if the States have the constitutional power to prohibit it, and would do so, but we skillfully avoid telling them so. Perhaps those abortions cannot constitutionally be proscribed. That is surely an arguable question, the question that reconsideration of *Roe* v. *Wade* entails. But what is not at all arguable, it seems to me, is that we should decide now and not insist that we be run into a corner before we grudgingly yield up our judgment. The only sound reason for the latter course is to prevent a change in the law—but to think that desirable begs the question to be decided.

It was an arguable question today whether...the Missouri law contravened this Court's understanding of *Roe* v. *Wade*, and I would have examined *Roe* rather than examining this contravention. Given the Court's newly contracted abstemiousness, what will it take, one must wonder, to permit us to reach that fundamental question? The result of our vote today is that will not reconsider that prior opinion, even if most of the Justices think it is wrong, unless we have a statute before us that in fact contradicts it—and even then (under our newly discovered "no-broader-then-necessary" requirement) only minor problematic aspects of *Roe* will be reconsidered, unless one expects state legislatures to adopt provisions whose compliance with *Roe* cannot even be argued with a straight face. It thus appears that the mansion of constitutionalized abortion law, constructed overnight in *Roe* v. *Wade*, must be disassembled doorjamb by doorjamb, and never entirely brought down, no matter how wrong it might be. . . .

> *It thus appears that the mansion of constitutionalized abortion law, constructed overnight in Roe v. Wade, must be disassembled doorjamb by doorjamb, and never entirely brought down, no matter how wrong it might be.*

[Footnote] . . . Justice O'Connor would nevertheless uphold the law because it "does not impose an undue burden on a woman's abortion decision." This conclusion is supported by the observation that the required tests impose only a marginal cost on the abortion procedure, far less of an increase than the cost–doubling hospitalization requirement invalidated in *Akron* v. *Akron Center for Reproductive Health, Inc.* The fact that the challenged regulation is less costly than what we struck down in *Akron* tells us only that we cannot decide the present case on the basis of that earlier decision. It does not tell us whether the present requirement is an "undue burden," and I know of no basis for determining that this particular burden (or any other for that matter) is "due." One could with equal justification conclude that it is not. To avoid the question of *Roe* v. *Wade*'s validity, with the attendant costs that this will have for the Court and for the principles of self-governance, on the basis of a standard that offers "no guide but the Court's own discretion" merely adds to the irrationality of what we do today.

Similarly irrational is the new concept that Justice O'Connor introduces into the law in order to achieve her result, the notion of a State's "interest in potential life when viability is possible." Since "viability" means the mere possibility (not the certainty) of survivability outside the womb, "possible viability" must mean the possibility of a possibility of survivability outside the womb. Perhaps our next opinion will expand the third trimester into the second even further, by approving state action designed to take account of "the chance of possible viability."

Of the four courses we might have chosen today—to reaffirm *Roe*, to overrule it explicitly, to overrule it sub silentio, or to avoid the question—the last is the least responsible. On the question of the constitutionality of §188.029 [viability testing requirement], I concur in the judgment of the Court and strongly dissent from the manner in which it has been reached.

PLANNED PARENTHOOD OF SOUTHEASTERN PENNSYLVANIA v. CASEY (1992)

Three years after *Webster*, the Court was asked to determine the constitutionality of five provisions of Pennsylvania's abortion law. These provisions required a woman seeking an abortion to give her informed consent; mandated the consent of one parent for a minor seeking an abortion (with provision for judicial approval where parental consent could not be obtained); required a woman to obtain the written approval of her husband before seeking an abortion (with exceptions); imposed certain reporting requirements on facilities that perform abortions; and, finally, set forth a definition of "medical emergency" that would alleviate the need to comply with the other requirements.

The Court's decision was not noteworthy because it upheld four of the five restrictions (only the spousal consent law was struck down). Rather, it was important—and controversial—because the Court threw aside the trimester analysis yet preserved *Roe*'s "central holding" that abortion is a constitutionally protected right.

Since its *Webster* decision, the composition of the Court had changed with the addition of Justices David Souter and Clarence Thomas who were selected by Republican President George H. W. Bush. Souter and Thomas gave antiabortion forces renewed hope that *Roe* v. *Wade* might be overturned, a fanciful thought in hindsight as Souter quickly emerged as one of the Court's most reliably liberal votes.

Souter joined Justices O'Connor and Kennedy to draft the Court's main opinion in *Casey*. Although public opinion polls at the time showed the country almost evenly divided on abortion, the three Republican president-appointed justices chose to preserve *Roe* on the grounds that its creation of a constitutional right to abortion had established a rule of law that was accepted by most Americans. The plurality said that *stare decisis*—the practice of adhering to precedent—was especially important in this case because the issue was divisive and because so many people had come to rely on the legality of abortion. According to the joint opinion, the Court's legitimacy was at stake and any decision to overturn *Roe* would be perceived as succumbing to political pressure. Thus, the Justices wrote that, notwithstanding the doubts they had about *Roe*, it was important to preserve its central holding. The opinion did not rely solely on the Justices' concern for the Court's legitimacy. In often grandiloquent language, the joint authors reaffirmed abortion's protection within the fundamental right to privacy. In trying to define this right, the Justices wrote, "At the heart of liberty is the right to define one's own concept of existence, of meaning, of the universe, and of the mystery of human life."

The joint opinion—long on lofty rhetoric about things such as the "mystery of human life" and short on traditional constitutional interpretation—prompted Justice Scalia to pen one of the most caustic opinions ever written by a Justice of the Supreme Court. At the outset, Scalia set forth in very clear

terms the standard he uses to determine whether a right deserves constitutional protection before finding that abortion falls short of this standard. He
expressed contempt for the joint opinion authors' reliance on *stare decisis* to
overcome their admitted reservations about *Roe*, concluding, "The notion
that we would decide a case differently from the way we otherwise would
have in order to show that we can stand firm against public disapproval is
frightening." He also chastised the three Justices for adopting the "undue burden" standard, which he derided "as doubtful in its application as it is unprincipled in its origin." Scalia also took the joint opinion authors to task for
pretending to save *Roe* when, in fact, they abandoned the trimester analysis—
the only thing most people remember about that decision.

Lastly, Scalia challenged the joint opinion for claiming that *Roe* helped
to settle the "national controversy" over abortion. He observed that the
abortion debate grew even more intense in the wake of *Roe* as the question was elevated from a state to a national level. Scalia concluded the joint
opinion would only further provoke greater passion on both sides of the
abortion divide.

⚬⚬⚬

JUSTICE SCALIA, WITH WHOM THE CHIEF JUSTICE, JUSTICE WHITE, AND JUSTICE THOMAS JOIN, CONCURRING IN THE JUDGMENT IN PART AND DISSENTING IN PART.

My views on this matter are unchanged from those I set forth in my
separate opinions in *Webster* v. *Reproductive Health Services* and *Ohio*
v. *Akron Center for Reproductive Health*. The States may, if they wish,
permit abortion on demand, but the Constitution does not *require*
them to do so. The permissibility of abortion, and the limitations
upon it, are to be resolved like most important questions in our

democracy: by citizens trying to persuade one another and then voting. As the Court acknowledges, "where reasonable people disagree
the government can adopt one position or the other." The Court is
correct in adding the qualification that this "assumes a state of affairs
in which the choice does not intrude upon a protected liberty," but
the crucial part of that qualification is the penultimate word. A State's
choice between two positions on which reasonable people can disagree is constitutional even when (as is often the case) it intrudes
upon a "liberty" in the absolute sense. Laws against bigamy, for example—with which entire societies of reasonable people disagree—
intrude upon men and women's liberty to marry and live with one
another. But bigamy happens not to be a liberty specially "protected"
by the Constitution.

That is, quite simply, the issue in this case: not whether the power
of a woman to abort her unborn child is a "liberty" in the absolute
sense; or even whether it is a liberty of great importance to many
women. Of course it is both. The issue is whether it is a liberty protected by the Constitution of the United States. I am sure it is not. I
reach that conclusion not because of anything so exalted as my views
concerning the "concept of existence, of meaning, of the universe, and
of the mystery of human life." Rather, I reach it for the same reason I
reach the conclusion that bigamy is not constitutionally protected—
because of two simple facts: (1) the Constitution says absolutely nothing about it, and (2) the long-standing traditions of American society
have permitted it to be legally proscribed.

The Court destroys the proposition, evidently meant to represent
my position, that "liberty" includes "only those practices, defined at
the most specific level, that were protected against government interference by other rules of law when the Fourteenth Amendment was

ratified" (citing *Michael H.* v. *Gerald D.* (1989)). That is not, however, what *Michael H.* says; it merely observes that, in defining "liberty," we may not disregard a specific, "relevant tradition protecting, or denying protection to, the asserted right." But the Court does not wish to be fettered by any such limitations on its preferences. The Court's statement that it is "tempting" to acknowledge the authoritativeness of tradition in order to "cur[b] the discretion of federal judges" is, of course, rhetoric rather than reality; no government official is "tempted" to place restraints upon his own freedom of action, which is why Lord Acton did not say "Power tends to purify." The Court's temptation is in the quite opposite and more natural direction—towards systematically eliminating checks upon its own power; and it succumbs.

> *No government official is "tempted" to place restraints upon his own freedom of action, which is why Lord Acton did not say "Power tends to purify."*

Beyond that brief summary of the essence of my position, I will not swell the United States Reports with repetition of what I have said before; and applying the rational basis test, I would uphold the Pennsylvania statute in its entirety. I must, however, respond to a few of the more outrageous arguments in today's opinion, which it is beyond human nature to leave unanswered. I shall discuss each of them under a quotation from the Court's opinion to which they pertain.

The inescapable fact is that adjudication of substantive due process claims may call upon the Court, in interpreting the Constitution, to exercise that same capacity which, by tradition, courts always have exercised: reasoned judgment.

Assuming that the question before us is to be resolved at such a level of philosophical abstraction, in such isolation from the traditions of American society, as by simply applying "reasoned judgment," I do not see how that could possibly have produced the answer the Court arrived at in *Roe* v. *Wade*. Today's opinion describes the methodology of *Roe,* quite accurately, as weighing against the woman's interest the State's "'important and legitimate interest in protecting the potentiality of human life.'" (quoting *Roe*). But "reasoned judgment" does not begin by begging the question, as *Roe* and subsequent cases unquestionably did by assuming that what the State is protecting is the mere "potentiality of human life." The whole argument of abortion opponents is that what the Court calls the fetus and what others call the unborn child *is a human life*. Thus, whatever answer *Roe* came up with after conducting its "balancing" is bound to be wrong, unless it is correct that the human fetus is in some critical sense merely potentially human. There is of course no way to determine that as a legal matter; it is, in fact, a value judgment. Some societies have considered newborn children not yet human, or the incompetent elderly no longer so.

The authors of the joint opinion, of course, do not squarely contend that *Roe* v. *Wade* was a *correct* application of "reasoned judgment"; merely that it must be followed, because of *stare decisis.* But in their exhaustive discussion of all the factors that go into the determination of when *stare decisis* should be observed and when disregarded, they never mention "how wrong was the decision on its face?" Surely, if "[t]he Court's power lies . . . in its legitimacy, a product of substance and perception," the "substance" part of the equation demands that plain error be acknowledged and eliminated. *Roe* was plainly wrong—even on the Court's methodology of "reasoned judgment," and even more so (of course) if the proper criteria of text and tradition are applied.

The emptiness of the "reasoned judgment" that produced *Roe* is displayed in plain view by the fact that, after more than 19 years of effort by some of the brightest (and most determined) legal minds in the country, after more than 10 cases upholding abortion rights in this Court, and after dozens upon dozens of *amicus* briefs submitted in this and other cases, the best the Court can do to explain how it is that the word "liberty" *must* be thought to include the right to destroy human fetuses is to rattle off a collection of adjectives that simply decorate a value judgment and conceal a political choice. The right to abort, we are told, inheres in "liberty" because it is among "a person's most basic decisions"; it involves a "most intimate and personal choic[e]"; it is "central to personal dignity and autonomy"; it "originate[s] within the zone of conscience and belief"; it is "too intimate and personal" for state interference; it reflects "intimate views" of a "deep, personal character"; it involves "intimate relationships" and notions of "personal autonomy and bodily integrity"; and it concerns a particularly "'important decisio[n].'" But it is obvious to anyone applying "reasoned judgment" that the same adjectives can be applied to many forms of conduct that this Court (including one of the Justices in today's majority) has held are *not* entitled to constitutional protection—because, like abortion, they are forms of conduct that have long been criminalized in American society. Those adjectives might

> *The best the Court can do to explain how it is that the word "liberty" must be thought to include the right to destroy human fetuses is to rattle off a collection of adjectives that simply decorate a value judgment and conceal a political choice.*

be applied, for example, to homosexual sodomy, polygamy, adult incest, and suicide, all of which are equally "intimate" and "deep[ly] personal" decisions involving "personal autonomy and bodily integrity," and all of which can constitutionally be proscribed because it is our unquestionable constitutional tradition that they are proscribable. It is not reasoned judgment that supports the Court's decision; only personal predilection. Justice Curtis' warning is as timely today as it was 135 years ago:

> [W]hen a strict interpretation of the Constitution, according to the fixed rules which govern the interpretation of laws, is abandoned, and the theoretical opinions of individuals are allowed to control its meaning, we have no longer a Constitution; we are under the government of individual men, who for the time being have power to declare what the Constitution is, according to their own views of what it ought to mean.
>
> DRED SCOTT v. SANDFORD, (1857)

Liberty finds no refuge in a jurisprudence of doubt.

One might have feared to encounter this august and sonorous phrase in an opinion defending the real *Roe* v. *Wade,* rather than the revised version fabricated today by the authors of the joint opinion. The shortcomings of *Roe* did not include lack of clarity: virtually all regulation of abortion before the third trimester was invalid. But to come across this phrase in the joint opinion—which calls upon federal district judges to apply an "undue burden" standard as doubtful in application as it is unprincipled in origin—is really more than one should have to bear.

The joint opinion frankly concedes that the amorphous concept of "undue burden" has been inconsistently applied by the Members of this Court in the few brief years since that "test" was first explicitly propounded by Justice O'Connor in her dissent in *Akron I*. Because the three Justices now wish to "set forth a standard of general application," the joint opinion announces that "it is important to clarify what is meant by an undue burden." I certainly agree with that, but I do not agree that the joint opinion succeeds in the announced endeavor. To the contrary, its efforts at clarification make clear only that the standard is inherently manipulable, and will prove hopelessly unworkable in practice.

The joint opinion explains that a state regulation imposes an "undue burden" if it "has the purpose or effect of placing a substantial obstacle in the path of a woman seeking an abortion of a nonviable fetus." An obstacle is "substantial," we are told, if it is "calculated[,] [not] to inform the woman's free choice, [but to] hinder it." This latter statement cannot possibly mean what it says. *Any* regulation of abortion that is intended to advance what the joint opinion concedes is the State's "substantial" interest in protecting unborn life will be "calculated [to] hinder" a decision to have an abortion. It thus seems more accurate to say that the joint opinion would uphold abortion regulations only if they do not *unduly* hinder the woman's decision. That, of course, brings us right back to square one: Defining an "undue burden" as an "undue hindrance" (or a "substantial obstacle") hardly "clarifies" the test. Consciously or not, the joint opinion's verbal shell game will conceal raw judicial policy choices concerning what is "appropriate" abortion legislation.

The ultimately standardless nature of the "undue burden" inquiry is a reflection of the underlying fact that the concept has no principled or coherent legal basis. As The Chief Justice points out, *Roe*'s strict scrutiny-standard "at least had a recognized basis in constitutional law at the time *Roe* was decided," while "[t]he same cannot be said for the 'undue burden' standard, which is created largely out of whole cloth by the authors of the joint opinion." The joint opinion is flatly wrong in asserting that "our jurisprudence relating to all liberties save perhaps abortion has recognized" the permissibility of laws that do not impose an "undue burden." It argues that the abortion right is similar to other rights in that a law "not designed to strike at the right itself, [but which] has the incidental effect of making it more difficult or more expensive to [exercise the right,]" is not invalid. I agree, indeed I have forcefully urged, that a law of general applicability which places only an incidental burden on a fundamental right does not infringe that right, but that principle does not establish the quite different (and quite dangerous) proposition that a law which *directly* regulates a fundamental right will not be found to violate the Constitution unless it imposes an "undue burden." It is that, of course, which is at issue here: Pennsylvania has *consciously and directly* regulated conduct that our cases have held is constitutionally protected. The appropriate analogy, therefore, is that of a state law requiring purchasers of religious books to endure a 24-hour waiting period, or to pay a nominal additional tax of 1¢. The joint opinion cannot possibly be correct in suggesting that we would uphold such legislation on the ground that it does not impose a "substantial obstacle" to the exercise of First Amendment rights. The "undue burden" standard is not at all the generally applicable principle the joint opinion pretends it to be; rather, it is a unique concept created specially for this case, to preserve some judicial foothold in this ill-gotten territory. In claiming otherwise, the three Justices show their willingness to place all constitutional rights at risk in an effort to preserve what they deem the "central holding in *Roe*."

The rootless nature of the "undue burden" standard, a phrase plucked out of context from our earlier abortion decisions, is further reflected in the fact that the joint opinion finds it necessary expressly to repudiate the more narrow formulations used in Justice O'Connor's earlier opinions. Those opinions stated that a statute imposes an "undue burden" if it imposes "*absolute* obstacles or *severe* limitations on the abortion decision," *Akron I* (dissenting opinion) (emphasis added). Those strong adjectives are conspicuously missing from the joint opinion, whose authors have for some unexplained reason now determined that a burden is "undue" if it merely imposes a "substantial" obstacle to abortion decisions. Justice O'Connor has also abandoned (again without explanation) the view she expressed in *Planned Parenthood Assn. of Kansas City, Mo., Inc.* v. *Ashcroft* that a medical regulation which imposes an "undue burden" could nevertheless be upheld if it "reasonably relate[s] to the preservation and protection of maternal health." In today's version, even health measures will be upheld only "*if they do not constitute an undue burden*" (emphasis added). Gone too is Justice O'Connor's statement that "the State possesses *compelling* interests in the protection of potential human life . . . throughout pregnancy," *Akron I* (emphasis added); instead, the State's interest in unborn human life is stealthily downgraded to a merely "substantial" or "profound" interest.

> *It is difficult to maintain the illusion that we are interpreting a Constitution rather than inventing one, when we amend its provisions so breezily.*

(That had to be done, of course, since designating the interest as "compelling" throughout pregnancy would have been, shall we say, a "substantial obstacle" to the joint opinion's determined effort to reaffirm what it views as the "central holding" of *Roe*.) And "viability" is no longer the "arbitrary" dividing line previously decried by Justice O'Connor in *Akron I*; the Court now announces that "the attainment of viability may continue to serve as the critical fact." It is difficult to maintain the illusion that we are interpreting a Constitution rather than inventing one, when we amend its provisions so breezily.

Because the portion of the joint opinion adopting and describing the undue burden test provides no more useful guidance than the empty phrases discussed above, one must turn to the 23 pages applying that standard to the present facts for further guidance. In evaluating Pennsylvania's abortion law, the joint opinion relies extensively on the factual findings of the District Court, and repeatedly qualifies its conclusions by noting that they are contingent upon the record developed in these cases. Thus, the joint opinion would uphold the 24-hour waiting period contained in the Pennsylvania statute's informed consent provision because "the record evidence shows that, in the vast majority of cases, a 24-hour delay does not create any appreciable health risk." The three Justices therefore conclude that, "on the record before us, . . . we are not convinced that the 24-hour waiting period constitutes an undue burden." The requirement that a doctor provide the information pertinent to informed consent would also be upheld because "there is no evidence on this record that [this requirement] would amount in practical terms to a substantial obstacle to a woman seeking an abortion." Similarly, the joint opinion would uphold the reporting requirements of the Act because "there is no . . . showing on the record before us" that these requirements constitute a "substantial obstacle" to abortion decisions. But at the same time the opinion pointedly observes that these reporting requirements may increase the costs of abortions, and that "at some point, [that fact] could become a substantial obstacle." Most significantly, the joint opinion's conclusion that the spousal notice requirement of the Act imposes an "undue burden" is based in large measure on the District Court's "detailed findings of fact," which the joint opinion sets out at great length.

I do not, of course, have any objection to the notion that, in applying legal principles, one should rely only upon the facts that are contained in the record or that are properly subject to judicial notice. But what is remarkable about the joint opinion's fact-intensive analysis is that it does not result in any measurable clarification of the "undue burden" standard. Rather, the approach of the joint opinion is, for the most part, simply to highlight certain facts in the record that apparently strike the three Justices as particularly significant in establishing (or refuting) the existence of an undue burden; after describing these facts, the opinion then simply announces that the provision either does or does not impose a "substantial obstacle" or an "undue burden." We do not know whether the same conclusions could have been reached on a different record, or in what respects the record would have had to differ before an opposite conclusion would have been appropriate. The inherently standardless nature of this inquiry invites the district judge to give effect to his personal preferences about abortion. By finding and relying upon the right facts, he can invalidate, it would seem, almost any abortion restriction that strikes him as "undue"—subject, of course, to the possibility of being reversed by a court of appeals or Supreme Court that is as unconstrained in reviewing his decision as he was in making it.

To the extent I can discern *any* meaningful content in the "undue burden" standard as applied in the joint opinion, it appears to be that a State may not regulate abortion in such a way as to reduce significantly its incidence. The joint opinion repeatedly emphasizes that an important factor in the "undue burden" analysis is whether the regulation "prevent[s] a significant number of women from obtaining an abortion;" whether a "significant number of women . . . are likely to be deterred from procuring an abortion" and whether the regulation often "deters" women from seeking abortions. We are not told, however, what forms of "deterrence" are impermissible or what degree of success in deterrence is too much to be tolerated. If, for example, a State required a woman to read a pamphlet describing, with illustrations, the facts of fetal development before she could obtain an abortion, the effect of such legislation might be to "deter" a "significant number of women" from procuring abortions, thereby seemingly allowing a district judge to invalidate it as an undue burden. Thus, despite flowery rhetoric about the State's "substantial" and "profound" interest in "potential human life," and criticism of *Roe* for undervaluing that interest, the joint opinion permits the State to pursue that interest only so long as it is not too successful. As Justice Blackmun recognizes (with evident hope), the "undue burden" standard may ultimately require the invalidation of each provision upheld today if it can be shown, on a better record, that the State is too effectively "express[ing] a preference for childbirth over abortion." Reason finds no refuge in this jurisprudence of confusion.

> While we appreciate the weight of the arguments . . . that *Roe* should be overruled, the reservations any of us may have in reaffirming the central holding of *Roe* are outweighed by the explication of individual liberty we have given combined with the force of *stare decisis.*

The Court's reliance upon *stare decisis* can best be described as contrived. It insists upon the necessity of adhering not to all of *Roe,* but only to what it calls the "central holding." It seems to me that *stare decisis* ought to be applied even to the doctrine of *stare decisis,* and I confess never to have heard of this new, keep-what-you-want-and-throw-away-the-rest version. I wonder whether, as applied to *Marbury v. Madison,* for example, the new version of *stare decisis* would be satisfied if we allowed courts to review the constitutionality of only those statutes that (like the one in *Marbury*) pertain to the jurisdiction of the courts.

> *It seems to me that stare decisis ought to be applied even to the doctrine of stare decisis, and I confess never to have heard of this new, keep-what-you-want-and-throw-away-the-rest version.*

I am certainly not in a good position to dispute that the Court *has saved* the "central holding" of *Roe* since to do that effectively I would have to know what the Court has saved, which in turn would require me to understand (as I do not) what the "undue burden" test means. I must confess, however, that I have always thought, and I think a lot of other people have always thought, that the arbitrary trimester framework, which the Court today discards, was quite as central to *Roe* as the arbitrary viability test, which the Court today retains. It seems particularly ungrateful to carve the trimester framework out of the core of *Roe,* since its very rigidity (in sharp contrast to the utter indeterminability of the "undue burden" test) is probably the only reason the Court is able to say, in urging *stare decisis,* that *Roe* "has in no sense proven 'unworkable.'" I suppose the Court is entitled to call a "central holding" whatever it wants to call a "central holding"—which is, come to think of it, perhaps one of the difficulties with this modified version of *stare decisis.* I thought I might note, however, that the following portions of *Roe* have not been saved:

— Under *Roe,* requiring that a woman seeking an abortion be provided truthful information about abortion before giving informed written consent is unconstitutional if the information is designed to influence her choice. Under the joint opinion's "undue burden" regime (as applied today, at least) such a requirement is constitutional.

— Under *Roe,* requiring that information be provided by a doctor, rather than by nonphysician counselors, is unconstitutional. Under the "undue burden" regime (as applied today, at least) it is not.

— Under *Roe,* requiring a 24-hour waiting period between the time the woman gives her informed consent and the time of the abortion is unconstitutional. Under the "undue burden" regime (as applied today, at least) it is not.

— Under *Roe,* requiring detailed reports that include demographic data about each woman who seeks an abortion and various information about each abortion is unconstitutional. Under the "undue burden" regime (as applied today, at least) it generally is not.

Where, in the performance of its judicial duties, the Court decides a case in such a way as to resolve the sort of intensely divisive controversy reflected in *Roe* . . . its decision has a dimension that the resolution of the normal case does not carry. It is the dimension present whenever the Court's interpretation of the Constitution calls the contending sides of a national controversy to end their national division by accepting a common mandate rooted in the Constitution.

The Court's description of the place of *Roe* in the social history of the United States is unrecognizable. Not only did *Roe* not, as the Court suggests, *resolve* the deeply divisive issue of abortion; it did more than anything else to nourish it, by elevating it to the national level, where it is infinitely more difficult to resolve. National politics were not plagued by abortion protests, national abortion lobbying, or abortion marches on Congress, before *Roe* v. *Wade* was decided. Profound disagreement existed among our citizens over the issue—as it does over other issues, such as the death penalty—but that disagreement was being worked out at the state level. As with many other issues, the division of sentiment within each State was not as closely balanced as it was among the population of the Nation as a whole, meaning not only that more people would be satisfied with the results of state-by-state resolution, but also that those results would be more stable. Pre-*Roe,* moreover, political compromise was possible.

To portray Roe as the statesmanlike "settlement" of a divisive issue, a jurisprudential Peace of Westphalia that is worth preserving, is nothing less than Orwellian.

Roe's mandate for abortion on demand destroyed the compromises of the past, rendered compromise impossible for the future, and required the entire issue to be resolved uniformly, at the national level. At the same time, *Roe* created a vast new class of abortion consumers and abortion proponents by eliminating the moral opprobrium that had attached to the act. ("If the Constitution *guarantees* abortion, how can it be bad?"—not an accurate line of thought, but a natural one.) Many favor all of those developments, and it is not for me to say that they are wrong. But to portray Roe as the statesmanlike "settlement" of a divisive issue, a jurisprudential Peace of Westphalia that is worth preserving, is nothing less than Orwellian. *Roe* fanned into life an issue that has inflamed our national politics in general, and has obscured with its smoke the selection of Justices to this Court, in particular, ever since. And by keeping us in the abortion-umpiring business, it is the perpetuation of that disruption, rather than of any *Pax Roeana* that the Court's new majority decrees.

> [T]o overrule under fire...would subvert the Court's legitimacy....
>
> ...To all those who will be...tested by following, the Court implicitly undertakes to remain steadfast....The promise of constancy, once given, binds its maker for as long as the power to stand by the decision survives and...the commitment [is not] obsolete....
>
> [The American people's] belief in themselves as...a people [who aspire to live according to the rule of law] is not readily separable from their understanding of the Court invested with the authority to decide their constitutional cases and speak before all others for their constitutional ideals. If the Court's legitimacy should be undermined, then so would the country be in its very ability to see itself through its constitutional ideals.

The Imperial Judiciary lives. It is instructive to compare this Nietzschean vision of us unelected, life-tenured judges—leading a Volk who will be "tested by following," and whose very "belief in themselves" is mystically bound up in their "understanding" of a Court that "speak[s] before all others for their constitutional ideals"—with the somewhat more modest role envisioned for these lawyers by the Founders.

> The judiciary... has... no direction either of the strength or of the wealth of the society, and can take no active resolution whatever. It may truly be said to have neither Force nor Will, but merely judgment....
>
> THE FEDERALIST NO. 78

Or, again, to compare this ecstasy of a Supreme Court in which there is, especially on controversial matters, no shadow of change or hint of alteration ("There is a limit to the amount of error that can plausibly be imputed to prior courts"), with the more democratic views of a more humble man:

> [T]he candid citizen must confess that if the policy of the Government upon vital questions affecting the whole people is to be irrevocably fixed by decisions of the Supreme Court,... the people will have ceased to be their own rulers, having to that extent practically resigned their Government into the hands of that eminent tribunal.
>
> A. LINCOLN, FIRST INAUGURAL ADDRESS (MAR. 4, 1861)

It is particularly difficult, in the circumstances of the present decision, to sit still for the Court's lengthy lecture upon the virtues of "constancy," of "remain[ing] steadfast," and adhering to "principle." Among the five Justices who purportedly adhere to *Roe,* at most three agree upon the *principle* that constitutes adherence (the joint opinion's "undue burden" standard)—and that principle is inconsistent with *Roe.* To make matters worse, two of the three, in order thus to remain steadfast, had to abandon previously stated positions. It is beyond me how the Court expects these accommodations to be accepted "as grounded truly in principle, not as compromises with social and political pressures having, as such, no bearing on the principled choices that the Court is obliged to make." The only principle the Court "adheres" to, it seems to me, is the principle that the Court must be seen as standing by *Roe.* That is not a principle of law (which is what I thought the Court was talking about), but a principle of *Realpolitik*— and a wrong one at that.

I cannot agree with, indeed I am appalled by, the Court's suggestion that the decision whether to stand by an erroneous constitutional decision must be strongly influenced—*against* overruling, no less—by the substantial and continuing public opposition the decision has generated. The Court's judgment that any other course would "subvert the Court's legitimacy" must be another consequence of reading the error-filled history book that described the deeply divided country brought together by *Roe.* In my history book, the Court was covered with dishonor and deprived of legitimacy by *Dred Scott* v. *Sandford,* an erroneous (and widely opposed) opinion that it did not abandon, rather than by *West Coast Hotel Co.* v. *Parrish,* which produced the famous "switch in time" from the Court's erroneous (and widely opposed) constitutional opposition to the social measures of the New Deal. (Both *Dred Scott* and one line of the cases resisting the New Deal rested upon the concept of "substantive due process" that the Court praises and employs today....)

But whether it would "subvert the Court's legitimacy" or not, the notion that we would decide a case differently from the way we otherwise would have in order to show that we can stand firm against public disapproval is frightening. It is a bad enough idea, even in the head of someone like me, who believes that the text of the Constitution, and our traditions, say what they say and there is no fiddling with them. But when it is in the mind of a Court that believes the Constitution has an evolving meaning; that the Ninth Amendment's reference to "othe[r]" rights is not a disclaimer, but a charter for action; and that the function of this Court is to "speak before all others for [the people's] constitutional ideals" unrestrained by meaningful text or tradition—then the notion that the Court must adhere to a decision for as long as the decision faces "great opposition" and the Court is "under fire" acquires a character of almost czarist arrogance. We are offended by these marchers who descend upon us, every year on the anniversary of *Roe,* to protest our saying that the Constitution requires what our society has never thought the Constitution requires. These people who refuse to be "tested by following" must be taught a lesson. We have no Cossacks, but at least we can stubbornly refuse to abandon an erroneous opinion that we might otherwise change—to show how little they intimidate us.

Of course, as The Chief Justice points out, we have been subjected to what the Court calls "political pressure" by *both* sides of this issue. Maybe today's decision *not* to overrule *Roe* will be seen as buckling to pressure from *that* direction. Instead of engaging in the hopeless task of predicting public perception—a job not for lawyers but for political campaign managers—the Justices should do what is legally right by asking two questions: (1) Was *Roe* correctly decided? (2) Has *Roe* succeeded in producing a settled body of law? If the answer to both questions is no, *Roe* should undoubtedly be overruled.

In truth, I am as distressed as the Court is—and expressed my distress several years ago—about the "political pressure" directed to the Court: the marches, the mail, the protests aimed at inducing us to change our opinions. How upsetting it is, that so many of our citizens (good people, not lawless ones, on both sides of this abortion issue, and on various sides of other issues as well) think that we Justices should properly take into account their views, as though we were engaged not in ascertaining an objective law, but in determining some kind of social consensus. The Court would profit, I think, from giving less attention to the *fact* of this distressing phenomenon, and more attention to the *cause* of it. That cause permeates today's opinion: a new mode of constitutional adjudication that relies not upon text and traditional practice to determine the law, but upon what the Court calls "reasoned judgment," which turns out to be nothing but philosophical predilection and moral intuition. All manner of "liberties," the Court tells us, inhere in the Constitution and are enforceable by this Court—not just those mentioned in the text or established in the traditions of our society. Why even the Ninth Amendment—which says only that "[t]he enumeration in the Constitution, of certain rights, shall not be construed to deny or disparage others retained by the people"—is, despite our contrary understanding for almost 200 years, a literally boundless source of additional, unnamed, unhinted-at "rights," definable and enforceable by us, through "reasoned judgment."

What makes all this relevant to the bothersome application of "political pressure" against the Court are the twin facts that the American people love democracy and the American people are not fools. As long as this Court thought (and the people thought) that we Justices were doing essentially lawyers' work up here—reading text and discerning our society's traditional understanding of that text—the public pretty much left us alone. Texts and traditions are facts to study, not convictions to demonstrate about. But if in reality our process of constitutional adjudication consists primarily of making *value judgments;* if we can ignore a long and clear tradition clarifying an ambiguous text, as we did, for example, five days ago in declaring unconstitutional invocations and benedictions at public high school graduation ceremonies; if, as I say, our pronouncement of constitutional law rests primarily on value judgments, then a free and intelligent people's attitude towards us can be expected to be (*ought* to be) quite different. The people know that their value judgments are quite as good as those taught in any law school—maybe better. If, indeed, the "liberties" protected by the Constitution are, as the Court says, undefined and unbounded, then the people *should* demonstrate, to protest that we do not implement *their* values instead of *ours.* Not only that, but the confirmation hearings for new Justices *should* deteriorate into question-and-answer sessions in which Senators go through a list of their constituents' most favored and most disfavored alleged constitutional rights, and seek the nominee's commitment to support or oppose them. Value judgments, after all, should be voted on, not dictated; and if our Constitution has somehow accidentally committed them to the Supreme Court, at least we can have a sort of plebiscite each time a new nominee to that body is put forward. . . .

There is a poignant aspect to today's opinion. Its length, and what might be called its epic tone, suggest that its authors believe they are bringing to an end a troublesome era in the history of our Nation, and of our Court. "It is the dimension" of authority, they say, to "cal[l] the contending sides of national controversy to end their national division by accepting a common mandate rooted in the Constitution."

There comes vividly to mind a portrait by Emanuel Leutze that hangs in the Harvard Law School: Roger Brooke Taney, painted in 1859, the 82nd year of his life, the 24th of his Chief Justiceship, the second after his opinion in *Dred Scott*. He is all in black, sitting in a shadowed red armchair, left hand resting upon a pad of paper in his lap, right hand hanging limply, almost lifelessly, beside the inner arm of the chair. He sits facing the viewer, and staring straight out. There seems to be on his face, and in his deep-set eyes, an expression of profound sadness and disillusionment. Perhaps he always looked that way, even when dwelling upon the happiest of thoughts. But those of us who know how the lustre of his great Chief Justiceship came to be eclipsed by *Dred Scott* cannot help believing that he had that case—its already apparent consequences for the Court, and its soon-to-be-played-out consequences for the Nation—burning on his mind. I expect that two years earlier he, too, had thought himself "call[ing] the contending sides of national controversy to end their national division by accepting a common mandate rooted in the Constitution."

It is no more realistic for us in this litigation than it was for him in that, to think that an issue of the sort they both involved—an issue involving life and death, freedom and subjugation—can be "speedily and finally settled" by the Supreme Court, as President James Buchanan, in his inaugural address, said the issue of slavery in the territories would be. Quite to the contrary, by foreclosing all democratic outlet for the deep passions this issue arouses, by banishing the issue from the political forum that gives all participants, even the losers, the satisfaction of a fair hearing and an honest fight, by continuing the imposition of a rigid national rule instead of allowing for regional differences, the Court merely prolongs and intensifies the anguish.

We should get out of this area, where we have no right to be, and where we do neither ourselves nor the country any good by remaining.

STENBERG v. CARHART (2000)

In the mid-1990s, many Americans were shocked to learn of an abortion procedure known as "partial-birth abortion." The procedure is used to abort fetuses in women who are twenty to thirty-two weeks pregnant. Guided by ultrasound, the doctor reaches into the uterus, grabs the unborn baby's legs with forceps, and pulls the baby into the birth canal, except for the head, which is deliberately kept just inside the womb. The doctor then forces scissors into the back of the baby's skull and spreads the tips of the scissors apart to enlarge the wound. After removing the scissors, a suction catheter is inserted into the skull and the baby's brain is sucked out.

The procedure was so gruesome that many traditionally prochoice legislators—along with upwards of 70 percent of Americans—supported a ban on the practice. The U.S. Congress passed legislation to prohibit doctors from performing the procedure. The ban was vetoed by President Bill Clinton, but a nearly identical version was later signed by President George W. Bush.

Many states, including Nebraska, also passed legislative bans. The Nebraska law stated, "No partial-birth abortion shall be performed in this state, unless such procedure is necessary to save the life of the mother whose life is endangered by a physical disorder, physical illness, or physical injury, including a life-endangering physical condition caused by or arising from the pregnancy itself."

The statute defined partial-birth abortion as "an abortion procedure in which the person performing the abortion partially delivers vaginally a living unborn child before killing the unborn child and completing the delivery. The law further defined the phrase "partially delivers vaginally a living unborn child before killing the unborn child" as "deliberately and intentionally delivering into the vagina a living unborn child, or a substantial portion thereof, for the purpose of performing a procedure that the person performing such procedure knows will kill the unborn child and does kill the unborn child."

Writing for the majority of the Court, Justice Stephen Breyer said that the statute violated the Constitution because it did not allow an exception for the preservation of the health of the mother and because it eliminated this procedure as a choice for a woman, "thereby unduly burdening the right to choose abortion itself."

Scalia did nothing to hide his disdain for the Court's opinion, comparing it to the two decisions many legal scholars consider among the worst in Supreme Court history: *Korematsu* v. *United States* (1944), which upheld the internment of Japanese Americans during World War II, and *Dred Scott* (1856), the slave case that precipitated the Civil War. The impassioned language notwithstanding, Scalia wrote that he did not originally intend to deliver a separate dissenting opinion. Rather, he planned to let Justice Clarence Thomas's and Justice Anthony Kennedy's dissenting opinions expose what he viewed as the flaws in the majority's decision. He said, however, he was afraid their opinions might make it seem as though the Court's decision was an aberration. In Scalia's mind, the *Stenberg* case was the foreseeable—albeit regrettable—product of the Court's recent abortion decisions, especially *Casey*. Scalia, in a highly unusual move for any Justice, directly implored the Court to overturn *Casey*.

⊱∞◊∞⊰

JUSTICE SCALIA, DISSENTING.

I am optimistic enough to believe that, one day, *Stenberg* v. *Carhart* will be assigned its rightful place in the history of this Court's jurisprudence beside *Korematsu* and *Dred Scott*. The method of killing a human child—one cannot even accurately say an entirely unborn human child—proscribed by this statute is so horrible that the most clinical description of it evokes a shudder of revulsion. And the Court must know (as most state legislatures banning this procedure have concluded) that demanding a "health exception"—which requires the abortionist to assure himself that, in his expert medical judgment, this method is, in the case at hand, marginally safer than others (how can one prove the contrary beyond a reasonable doubt?)—is to give live-birth abortion free rein. The notion that the Constitution of the United States, designed, among other things, "to establish Justice, insure domestic Tranquility, . . . and secure the Blessings of Liberty to ourselves and our Posterity," prohibits the States from simply banning this visibly brutal means of eliminating our half-born posterity is quite simply absurd. . . .

It would be unfortunate, however, if those who disagree with the result were induced to regard it as merely a regrettable misapplication of *Casey*. It is not that, but is *Casey*'s logical and entirely predictable consequence. To be sure, the Court's construction of this statute so as to make it include procedures other than live-birth abortion involves not only a disregard of fair meaning, but an abandonment of the principle that even ambiguous statutes should be interpreted in such a fashion as to render them valid rather than void. *Casey* does not permit that jurisprudential novelty—which must

> *The notion that the Constitution of the United States, designed, among other things, "to establish Justice, insure domestic Tranquility, . . . and secure the Blessings of Liberty to ourselves and our Posterity," prohibits the States from simply banning this visibly brutal means of eliminating our half-born posterity is quite simply absurd.*

be chalked up to the Court's inclination to bend the rules when any effort to limit abortion, or even to speak in opposition to abortion, is at issue. . . .

But the Court gives a second and independent reason for invalidating this humane (not to say antibarbarian) law: That it fails to allow an exception for the situation in which the abortionist believes that the live-birth method of destroying the child might be safer for the woman. (As pointed out by Justice Thomas, and elaborated upon by Justice Kennedy, there is no good reason to believe this is ever the case, but—who knows?—it sometime might be.)

I never put much stock in *Casey's* explication of the inexplicable. In the last analysis, my judgment that *Casey* does not support today's tragic result can be traced to the fact that what I consider to be an "undue burden'" is different from what the majority considers to be an "undue burden"—a conclusion that cannot be demonstrated true or false by factual inquiry or legal reasoning. It is a value judgment, dependent upon how much respects (or believes society ought to respect) the life of a partially delivered fetus, and how much one respects (or believes society ought to respect) the freedom of the woman who gave it life to kill it. Evidently, the five Justices in today's majority value the former less, or the latter more (or both), than the four of us in dissent. Case closed. There is no cause for anyone who believes in *Casey* to feel betrayed by this outcome. It has been arrived at by precisely the process *Casey* promised—a democratic vote by nine lawyers, not on the question whether the text of the Constitution has anything to say about this subject (it obviously does not); not even on the question (also appropriate for lawyers) whether the legal traditions of the American people would have sustained such a limitation upon abortion (they obviously would); but upon the pure policy question whether this limitation upon abortion is "undue"—i.e., goes too far.

In my dissent in *Casey*, I wrote that the "undue burden" test made law by the joint opinion created a standard that was "as doubtful in application as it is unprincipled in origin", "hopelessly unworkable in practice", "ultimately standardless." Today's decision is the proof. As long as we are debating the issue of necessity for a health-of-the-mother exception on the basis of *Casey*, it is really quite impossible for us dissenters to contend that the majority is wrong on the law—any more than it could be said that one is wrong in law to support or oppose the death penalty, or to support or oppose mandatory minimum sentences. The most that we can honestly say is that we disagree with the majority on their policy-judgment-couched-as-law. And those who believe that a 5-to-4 vote on a policy matter by unelected lawyers should not overcome the judgment of 30 state legislatures that have a problem, not with the *application* of *Casey*, but with its *existence*. *Casey* must be overruled.

> *The most that we can honestly say is that we disagree with the majority on their policy-judgment-couched-as-law.*

While I am in an I-told-you-so mood, I must recall my bemusement, in *Casey*, at the joint opinion's expressed belief that *Roe* v. *Wade* had "call[ed] the contending sides of a national controversy to end their national division by accepting a common mandate rooted in the Constitution," and that the decision in *Casey* would ratify that happy truce. It seemed to me, quite to the contrary, that "*Roe* fanned into life an issue that has inflamed our national politics in general, and has obscured with its smoke the selection of Justices to this Court in particular, ever since"; and that, "by keeping us in the abortion-umpiring business, it is the perpetuation of that disruption, rather than of any *Pax Roeana*, that the Court's new majority decrees." Today's decision, that the Constitution of the United States prevents the prohibition of a horrible mode of abortion, will be greeted by a firestorm of criticism—as well it should. I cannot understand why those who *acknowledge* that, in the opening words of Justice O'Connor's concurrence, "[t]he issue of abortion is one of the most contentious and controversial in contemporary American society," persist in the belief that this Court, armed with neither constitutional text nor accepted tradition, can resolve that contention and controversy rather than be consumed by it. If only for the sake of its own preservation, the Court should return this matter to the people—where the Constitution, by its silence on the subject, left it—and to let *them* decide, State by State, whether this practice should be allowed. *Casey* must be overruled.

CHAPTER SIX

DEATH PENALTY

THE CONSTITUTION OF THE UNITED STATES expressly refers to the
death penalty. The Due Process Clauses of the Fifth and Fourteenth Amendments state that no person shall be deprived of "life"
without due process of law. The Grand Jury Clause of the Fifth
Amendment ensures that no person shall be held for a "capital...
crime" without a grand jury indictment. These provisions make clear
that the constitution allows imposition of the death penalty with due
process and after indictment. Among historians, there is no serious
doubt as to whether the death penalty was an accepted form of punishment when the Constitution was adopted.

In 1972, however, the Supreme Court effectively suspended use of
capital punishment on the grounds that its arbitrary administration
violated the Eighth Amendment's prohibition of "cruel and unusual
punishments."[1] Although it later affirmed the death penalty's constitutionality, the Court over time added a number of restrictions governing both who could be subject to capital punishment and the
discretion juries should have to impose it. The Court said that its
determinations about whether imposition of capital (or other severe)

punishments is impermissibly "cruel and unusual" are governed by consideration of the "evolving standards of decency that mark the progress of a maturing society."[2]

Justice Scalia has been an ardent defender of the government's authority to use the death penalty as it sees fit. He has voted to uphold application of capital punishment to fifteen-year-old[3] and mentally retarded convicted criminals. His argument is, not surprisingly, a textual one; capital punishment is explicitly contemplated in the Constitution. Moreover, he contends that the Eighth Amendment's prohibition of cruel and unusual punishments represents no barrier to capital punishment since its use is rarely if ever "cruel" and cannot even remotely be considered "unusual," in light of its use throughout American history.

CALLINS v. COLLINS (1994)

Though content to defend the constitutionality of capital punishment on textual and historical grounds, Scalia has been persistent in making certain that policy arguments and emotional pleas made by the Court's more liberal justices do not go unanswered. In 1994, Justice Blackmun dissented from the Court's decision not to consider an appeal brought by a convicted murderer. Usually such routine decisions are not accompanied by opinions from the justices. However, Justice Blackmun used his dissent in this case to announce his conclusion that the death penalty, because of its imperfect application, was always "cruel and unusual" and, thus, unconstitutional. In a memorable phrase, he said he would no longer "tinker with the machinery of death."

Rather than letting Blackmun have the spotlight to make his new anti-death penalty declaration, Scalia filed a concurring opinion, in which he said that the

Court should follow the Constitution and enforce the death penalty. Pursuant to the Court's protocol for publishing opinions, Scalia's concurrence appeared before Blackmun's dissent and thus allowed him to pre-empt Blackmun.

Blackmun's statement began with a description of how the defendant, Bruce Callins, would be put to death. He said, "Intravenous tubes attached to his arms will carry the instrument of death, a toxic fluid designed specifically for the purpose of killing human beings. The witnesses, standing a few feet away, will behold Callins, no longer a defendant, an appellant, or a petitioner, but a man, strapped to a gurney, and seconds away from extinction." It is not clear if Blackmun included such specifics in an attempt to elicit sympathy for Callins. Whatever Blackmun's motivation, Justice Scalia noted that the lethal injection of Callins—a "convicted murderer"—seemed "enviable" compared with the brutal deaths suffered by Callins's and other killers' victims.

<hr />

JUSTICE SCALIA, CONCURRING.

Justice Blackmun dissents from the denial of certiorari in this case with a statement explaining why the death penalty "as currently administered" is contrary to the Constitution of the United States. That explanation often refers to "intellectual, moral and personal" perceptions, but never to the text and tradition of the Constitution. It is the latter, rather than the former that ought to control. The Fifth Amendment provides that "[n]o person shall be held to answer for a capital . . . crime, unless on a presentment or indictment of a Grand Jury, . . . nor be deprived of life, . . . without due process of law."

This clearly permits the death penalty to be imposed, and establishes beyond doubt that the death penalty is not one of the "cruel and unusual punishments" prohibited by the Eighth Amendment.

As Justice Blackmun describes, however, over the years since 1972, this Court has attached to the imposition of the death penalty two quite incompatible sets of commands: the sentencer's discretion to impose death must be closely confined, but the sentencer's discretion not to impose death (to extend mercy) must be unlimited. These commands were invented without benefit of any textual or historical support; they are the product of just such "intellectual, moral, and personal" perceptions as Justice Blackmun expresses today, some of which (viz., those that have been "perceived" simultaneously by five members of the Court) have been made part of what is called "the Court's Eighth Amendment jurisprudence."

Though Justice Blackmun joins those of us who have acknowledged the incompatibility of the Court's . . . jurisprudence, he unfortunately draws the wrong conclusion from the acknowledgment. He says:

> [T]he proper course when faced with irreconcilable constitutional commands is not to ignore one or the other, nor to pretend that the dilemma does not exist, but to admit the futility of the effort to harmonize them. This means accepting the fact that the death penalty cannot be administered in accord with our Constitution.

Surely a different conclusion commends itself—to wit, that at least one of these judicially announced irreconcilable commands which cause the Constitution to prohibit what its text explicitly permits must be wrong.

Convictions in opposition to the death penalty are often passionate and deeply held. That would be no excuse for reading them into a Constitution that does not contain them, even if they represented the convictions of a majority of Americans. Much less is there any excuse for using that course to thrust a minority's views upon the people. Justice Blackmun begins his statement by describing with poignancy the death of a convicted murderer by lethal injection. He chooses, as the case in which to make that statement, one of the less brutal of the murders that regularly come before us—the murder of a man ripped by a bullet suddenly and unexpectedly, with no opportunity to prepare himself and his affairs, and left to bleed to death on the floor of a tavern. The death-by-injection which Justice Blackmun describes looks pretty desirable next to that. It looks even better next to some of the other cases currently before us which Justice Blackmun did not select as the vehicle for his announcement that the death penalty is always unconstitutional—for example, the case of the 11-year-old girl raped by four men and then killed by stuffing her panties down her throat. How enviable a quiet death by lethal injection compared with that! If the people conclude that such more brutal deaths may be deterred by capital punishment; indeed, if they merely conclude that justice requires such brutal deaths to be avenged by capital punishment; the creation of false, untextual and unhistorical contradictions within "the Court's Eighth Amendment jurisprudence" should not prevent them.

ATKINS v. VIRGINIA (2002)

Daryl Atkins was arrested for abduction, armed robbery, and capital murder in the State of Virgina. Before the trial, a psychologist examined Atkins and found him to be "mildly mentally retarded." A jury, after finding aggravating circumstances, sentenced him to death.

The Supreme Court ruled that executions of mentally retarded criminals are "cruel and unusual punishments" prohibited by the Eighth Amendment to the Constitution. Though the Court had held the opposite thirteen years earlier, the majority in *Atkins* now found that a "national consensus" had developed as evidenced by the "dramatic shift in the state legislative landscape" toward abolishing the death penalty for mentally retarded individuals. The Court said it agreed with the states' move and did not believe that "the execution of the mentally retarded criminals will measurably advance the deterrent or the retributive purpose of the death penalty." The Court said the states' shift was part of "a much broader social and professional consensus" and pointed to the opposition of religious leaders and "the world community," including the European Union. In conclusion, the Court said the movement by some states and foreign counties toward abolition of capital punishment for the mentally retarded was a clear indicator that the practice was out of step with "evolving standards of decency."

Justice Scalia's frustration with the decision to limit the states' use of the death penalty comes through quite clearly from the start of his dissenting opinion. Charging the majority with drafting an opinion based on "nothing but the personal views of its members," Scalia said the Court once again ignored the text and history of the Eighth Amendment.

Scalia wrote that the Court "makes no pretense that execution of the mildly mentally retarded would have been considered 'cruel and unusual' in 1791." Thus, Scalia said, the Court needed to show that the practice has become inconsistent with modern standards of decency. Scalia contended the Court failed to support its claim that a "national consensus" had formed against the practice. He argued that the adoption of laws forbidding execution of the mentally retarded in eighteen states, representing less than half of the states that use the death penalty at all, fell far short of establishing a "national consensus" against the practice. Other arguments advanced by the Court were dismissed by Scalia as "feeble," "counter-indicative," and "irrelevant."

All of the majority's arguments are nothing more than "a game," Scalia charged, to distract from the Court's real rationale: the majority believed the Constitution confers on it the right to decide the acceptability of the death penalty based on the Justices' personal sense of decency and justice. Scalia scoffed at this interpretation and said the text of the Constitution authorizes no such "arrogant" assumption of authority. He then attempted to refute the majority's specific arguments supporting its view that capital punishment is "excessive" as applied to mentally retarded criminals. Scalia closed by bemoaning the addition of another restriction on states' use of the death penalty.

⚶

JUSTICE SCALIA, WITH WHOM THE CHIEF JUSTICE AND JUSTICE THOMAS JOIN, DISSENTING.

Today's decision is the pinnacle of our Eighth Amendment death-is-different jurisprudence. Not only does it, like all of that jurisprudence, find no support in the text or history of the Eighth Amendment; it does not even have support in current social attitudes regarding the conditions that render an otherwise just death penalty inappropriate. Seldom has an opinion of this Court rested so obviously upon nothing but the personal views of its members.

I

I begin with a brief restatement of facts that are abridged by the Court but important to understanding this case. After spending the day drinking alcohol and smoking marijuana, petitioner Daryl Renard Atkins and a partner in crime drove to a convenience store, intending to rob a customer. Their victim was Eric Nesbitt, an airman from Langley Air Force Base, whom they abducted, drove to a nearby automated teller machine, and forced to withdraw $200. They then drove him to a deserted area, ignoring his pleas to leave him unharmed. According to the co-conspirator, whose testimony the jury evidently credited, Atkins ordered Nesbitt out of the vehicle and, after he had taken only a few steps, shot him one, two, three, four, five, six, seven, eight times in the thorax, chest, abdomen, arms, and legs.

Seldom has an opinion of this Court rested so obviously upon nothing but the personal views of its Members.

The jury convicted Atkins of capital murder. At resentencing (the Virginia Supreme Court affirmed his conviction but remanded for resentencing because the trial court had used an improper verdict form), the jury heard extensive evidence of petitioner's alleged mental retardation. A psychologist testified that petitioner was mildly mentally retarded with an IQ of 59, that he was a "slow learne[r]," who showed a "lack of success in pretty much every domain of his life," and that he had an "impaired" capacity to appreciate the criminality of his conduct and to conform his conduct to the law. Petitioner's family members offered additional evidence in support of his mental retardation claim (e.g., that petitioner is a "follower"). The Commonwealth contested the evidence of retardation and presented testimony of a psychologist who found "absolutely no evidence other than the IQ score . . . indicating that [petitioner] was in the least bit mentally retarded" and concluded that petitioner was "of average intelligence, at least."

The jury also heard testimony about petitioner's 16 prior felony convictions for robbery, attempted robbery, abduction, use of a firearm, and maiming. The victims of these offenses provided graphic depictions of petitioner's violent tendencies: He hit one over the head with a beer bottle; he slapped a gun across another victim's face, clubbed her in the head with it, knocked her to the ground, and then helped her up, only to shoot her in the stomach. The jury sentenced petitioner to death. The Supreme Court of Virginia affirmed petitioner's sentence.

II

As the foregoing history demonstrates, petitioner's mental retardation was a *central issue* at sentencing. The jury concluded, however, that his alleged retardation was not a compelling reason to exempt him from the death penalty in light of the brutality of his crime and his long demonstrated propensity for violence. "In upsetting this particularized judgment on the basis of a constitutional absolute," the Court concludes that no one who is even slightly mentally retarded can have sufficient "moral responsibility to be subjected to capital punishment for any crime. As a sociological and moral conclusion that is implausible; and it is doubly implausible as an interpretation of the United States Constitution." *Thompson* v. *Oklahoma* (1988) (*Scalia*, J., dissenting).

Under our Eighth Amendment jurisprudence, a punishment is "cruel and unusual" if it falls within one of two categories: "those modes or acts of punishment that had been considered cruel and unusual at the time that the Bill of Rights was adopted," *Ford* v. *Wainwright* (1986), and modes of punishment that are inconsistent with modern "standards of decency," as evinced by objective indicia, the most important of which is "legislation enacted by the country's legislatures," *Penry* v. *Lynaugh* (1989).

The Court makes no pretense that execution of the mildly mentally retarded would have been considered "cruel and unusual" in 1791. Only the *severely* or *profoundly* mentally retarded, commonly known as "idiots," enjoyed any special status under the law at that time. They, like lunatics, suffered a "deficiency in will" rendering them unable to tell right from wrong. 4 W. Blackstone, Commentaries on the Laws of England 24 (1769) (hereinafter Blackstone); see also *Penry* ("[T]he term 'idiot' was generally used to describe persons who had a total lack of reason or understanding, or an inability to distinguish between good and evil") . . . Due to their incompetence, idiots were "excuse[d] from the guilt, and of course from the punishment, of any criminal action committed under such deprivation of the senses." 4 Blackstone 25. Instead, they were often committed to civil confinement or made wards of the State, thereby preventing them from "go[ing] loose, to the terror of the king's subjects." 4 Blackstone 25. Mentally retarded offenders with less severe impairments—those who were not "idiots"—suffered criminal prosecution and punishment, including capital punishment. . . .

The Court is left to argue, therefore, that execution of the mildly retarded is inconsistent with the "evolving standards of decency that mark the progress of a maturing society." *Trop* v. *Dulles* (1958). Before today, our opinions consistently emphasized that Eighth Amendment judgments regarding the existence of social "standards" "should be informed by objective factors to the maximum possible extent" and "should not be, or appear to be, merely the subjective views of individual Justices." *Coker* v. *Georgia* (1977). "First" among these objective factors are the "statutes passed by society's elected representatives," *Stanford* v. *Kentucky* (1989); because it "will rarely if ever be the case that the Members of this Court will have a better sense of the evolution in views of the American people than do their elected representatives," *Thompson* (*Scalia*, J., dissenting).

The Court pays lipservice to these precedents as it miraculously extracts a "national consensus" forbidding execution of the mentally retarded from the fact that 18 States—less than *half* (47%) of the 38 States that permit capital punishment (for whom the issue exists)—

have very recently enacted legislation barring execution of the mentally retarded. Even that 47% figure is a distorted one. If one is to say, as the Court does today, that *all* executions of the mentally retarded are so morally repugnant as to violate our national "standards of decency," surely the "consensus" it points to must be one that has set its righteous face against *all* such executions. Not 18 States, but only 7—18% of death penalty jurisdictions—have legislation of that scope. Eleven of those that the Court counts enacted statutes prohibiting execution of mentally retarded defendants *convicted after, or convicted of crimes committed after, the effective date* of the legislation; those already on death row, or consigned there before the statute's effective date, or even (in those States using the date of the crime as the criterion of retroactivity) tried in the future for murders committed many years ago, could be put to death. That is not a statement of absolute moral repugnance, but one of current preference between two tolerable approaches. Two of these States permit execution of the mentally retarded in other situations as well: Kansas apparently permits execution of all except the *severely* mentally retarded; New York permits execution of the mentally retarded who commit murder in a correctional facility.

But let us accept, for the sake of argument, the Court's faulty count. That bare number of States alone—*18*—should be enough to convince any reasonable person that no "national consensus" exists. How is it possible that agreement among 47% of the death penalty jurisdictions amounts to "consensus"? Our prior cases have generally required a much higher degree of agreement before finding a punishment cruel and unusual on "evolving standards" grounds. In *Coker*, we proscribed the death penalty for rape of an adult woman after finding that only one jurisdiction, Georgia, authorized such a punishment. In *Enmund*, we invalidated the death penalty for mere participation in a robbery in which an accomplice took a life, a punishment not permitted in 28 of the death penalty States (78%). In *Ford*, we supported the common-law prohibition of execution of the insane with the observation that "[t]his ancestral legacy has not outlived its time," since not a single State authorizes such punishment. In *Solem* v. *Helm* (1983), we invalidated a life sentence without parole under a recidivist statute by which the criminal "was treated more severely than he would have been in any other State." What the Court calls evidence of "consensus" in the present case (a fudged 47%) more closely resembles evidence that we found *inadequate* to establish consensus in earlier cases. *Tison* v. *Arizona* (1987) upheld a state law authorizing capital punishment for major participation in a felony with reckless indifference to life where only 11 of the 37 death penalty States (30%) prohibited such punishment. *Stanford* upheld a state law permitting execution of defendants who committed a capital crime at age 16 where only 15 of the 36 death penalty States (42%) prohibited death for such offenders.

Moreover, a major factor that the Court entirely disregards is that the legislation of all 18 States it relies on is still in its infancy. The oldest of the statutes is only 14 years old; five were enacted last year; over half were enacted within the past eight years. Few, if any, of the States have had sufficient experience with these laws to know whether they are sensible in the long term. It is "myopic to base sweeping constitutional principles upon the narrow experience of [a few] years." *Coker* (Burger, C. J., dissenting).

The Court attempts to bolster its embarrassingly feeble evidence of "consensus" with the following: "It is not so much the number of these States that is significant, but the *consistency* of the direction of change" (emphasis added). But in what *other* direction *could we possibly* see change? Given that 14 years ago *all* the death penalty statutes included the mentally retarded, *any* change (except precipitate undoing of what had just been done) was *bound to be* in the one direction the Court finds significant enough to overcome the lack of real consensus. That is to say, to be accurate the Court's "*consistency*-of-the-direction-of-change" point should be recast into the following unimpressive observation:"No State has yet undone its exemption of the mentally retarded, one for as long as 14 whole years." In any event, reliance upon "trends," even those of much longer duration than a mere 14 years, is a perilous basis for constitutional adjudication, as Justice O'Connor eloquently explained in *Thompson:*

In 1846, Michigan became the first State to abolish the death penalty.... In succeeding decades, other American States continued the trend towards abolition.... Later, and particularly after World War II, there ensued a steady and dramatic decline in executions.... In the 1950s and 1960s, more States abolished or radically restricted capital punishment, and executions ceased completely for several years beginning in 1968....

In 1972, when this Court heard arguments on the constitutionality of the death penalty, such statistics might have suggested that the practice had become a relic, implicitly rejected by a new societal consensus.... We now know that any inference of a societal consensus rejecting the death penalty would have been mistaken. But had this Court then declared the existence of such a consensus, and outlawed capital punishment, legislatures would very likely not have been able to revive it. The mistaken premise of the decision would have been frozen into constitutional law, making it difficult to refute and even more difficult to reject.

Her words demonstrate, of course, not merely the peril of riding a trend, but also the peril of discerning a consensus where there is none.

The Court's thrashing about for evidence of "consensus" includes reliance upon the *margins* by which state legislatures have enacted bans on execution of the retarded. Presumably, in applying our Eighth Amendment "evolving-standards-of-decency" jurisprudence, we will henceforth weigh not only how many States have agreed, but how many States have agreed *by how much*. Of course if the percentage of legislators voting for the bill is significant, surely the number of people *represented* by the legislators voting for the bill is also significant: the fact that 49% of the legislators in a State with a population of 60 million voted *against* the bill should be more impressive than the fact that 90% of the legislators in a state with a population of 2 million voted *for* it. (By the way, the population of the death penalty States that exclude the mentally retarded is only 44% of the population of all death penalty States.) This is quite absurd. What we have looked for in the past to "evolve" the Eighth Amendment is a consensus of the same sort as the consensus that *adopted* the Eighth Amendment: a consensus of the sovereign States that form the Union, not a nose count of Americans for and against.

> *What we have looked for in the past to "evolve" the Eighth Amendment is a consensus of the same sort as the consensus that adopted the Eighth Amendment: a consensus of the sovereign states that form the Union, not a nose count of Americans for and against.*

Even less compelling (if possible) is the Court's argument that evidence of "national consensus" is to be found in the infrequency with which retarded persons are executed in States that do not bar their execution. To begin with, what the Court takes as true is in fact quite doubtful. It is not at all clear that execution of the mentally retarded is "uncommon," as even the sources cited by the Court suggest. *If*, however, execution of the mentally retarded *is* "uncommon"; and if it is not a sufficient explanation of this that the retarded constitute a tiny fraction of society (1% to 3%); then surely the explanation is that mental retardation is a constitutionally mandated mitigating factor at sentencing. For that reason, even if there were uniform national sentiment in *favor* of executing the retarded in appropriate cases, one would still expect execution of the mentally retarded to be "uncommon." To adapt to the present case what the Court itself said in *Stanford*: "[I]t is not only possible, but overwhelmingly probable, that the very considerations which induce [today's majority] to believe that death should *never* be imposed on [mentally retarded] offenders ... cause prosecutors and juries to believe that it should *rarely* be imposed."

But the prize for the Court's Most Feeble Effort to fabricate "national consensus" must go to its appeal (deservedly relegated to a footnote) to the views of assorted professional and religious organizations, members of the so-called "world community," and respondents to opinion polls.

But the Prize for the Court's Most Feeble Effort to fabricate "national consensus" must go to its appeal (deservedly relegated to a footnote) to the views of assorted professional and religious organizations, members of the so-called "world community," and respondents to opinion polls. I agree with the Chief Justice that the views of professional and religious organizations and the results of opinion polls are irrelevant.

[Footnote] And in some cases positively counterindicative. The Court cites, for example, the views of the United States Catholic Conference, whose members are the active Catholic Bishops of the United States. The attitudes of that body regarding crime and punishment are so far from being representative, even of the views of Catholics, that they are currently the object of intense national (and entirely ecumenical) criticism.

Equally irrelevant are the practices of the "world community," whose notions of justice are (thankfully) not always those of our people. "We must never forget that it is a Constitution for the United States of America that we are expounding. . . . [W]here there is not first a settled consensus among our own people, the views of other nations, however enlightened the Justices of this Court may think them to be, cannot be imposed upon Americans through the Constitution." *Thompson* (*Scalia*, J., dissenting).

III

Beyond the empty talk of a "national consensus," the Court gives us a brief glimpse of what really underlies today's decision: pretension to a power confined *neither* by the moral sentiments originally enshrined in the Eighth Amendment (its original meaning) *nor even* by the current moral sentiments of the American people. "'[T]he Constitution,'" the Court says, "contemplates that in the end *our own judgment* will be brought to bear on the question of the acceptability of the death penalty under the Eighth Amendment'" (quoting *Coker*) (emphasis added). (The unexpressed reason for this unexpressed "contemplation" of the Constitution is presumably that really good lawyers have moral sentiments superior to those of the common herd, whether in 1791 or today.) The arrogance of this assumption of power takes one's breath away. And it explains, of course, why the Court can be so cavalier about the evidence of consensus. It is just a game, after all. "[I]n the end," it is the *feelings* and *intuition* of a majority of the Justices that count—"the perceptions of decency, or of penology, or of mercy, entertained . . . by a majority of the small and unrepresentative segment of our society that sits on this Court." *Thompson* (*Scalia*, J., dissenting).

The genuinely operative portion of the opinion, then, is the Court's statement of the reasons why it agrees with the contrived consensus it has found, that the "diminished capacities" of the mentally retarded render the death penalty excessive. The Court's analysis rests on two fundamental assumptions: (1) that the Eighth Amendment prohibits excessive punishments, and (2) that sentencing juries or judges are unable to account properly for the "diminished capacities" of the retarded. The first assumption is wrong, as I explained at length in *Harmelin* v. *Michigan* (1991). The Eighth Amendment is addressed to always-and-everywhere "cruel" punishments, such as the rack and the thumbscrew. But where the punishment is in itself permissible, "[t]he Eighth Amendment is not a ratchet, whereby a temporary consensus on leniency for a particular crime fixes a permanent constitutional maximum, disabling the States from giving effect to altered beliefs and responding to changed social conditions." The second assumption—inability of judges or juries to take proper account of mental retardation—is not only unsubstantiated, but contradicts the immemorial belief, here and in England, that they play an *indispensable* role in such matters:

[I]t is very difficult to define the indivisible line that divides perfect and partial insanity; but it must rest upon circumstances duly

to be weighed and considered both by the judge and jury, lest
on the one side there be a kind of inhumanity towards the
defects of human nature, or on the other side too great an indul-
gence given to great crimes.

1 HALE, PLEAS OF THE CROWN

Proceeding from these faulty assumptions, the Court gives two reasons why the death penalty is an excessive punishment for all mentally
retarded offenders. First, the "diminished capacities" of the mentally
retarded raise a "serious question" whether their execution contributes
to the "social purposes" of the death penalty, viz., retribution and
deterrence. (The Court conveniently ignores a third "social purpose"
of the death penalty—"incapacitation of dangerous criminals and the
consequent prevention of crimes that they may otherwise commit in
the future," *Gregg* v. *Georgia* (1976). But never mind; its discussion of
even the other two does not bear analysis.) Retribution is not
advanced, the argument goes, because the mentally retarded are *no
more culpable* than the average murderer, whom we have already held
lacks sufficient culpability to warrant the death penalty. Who says so?
Is there an established correlation between mental acuity and the ability to conform one's conduct to the law in such a rudimentary matter as murder? Are the mentally retarded really more disposed (and
hence more likely) to commit willfully cruel and serious crime than
others? In my experience, the opposite is true: being childlike generally suggests innocence rather than brutality.

Assuming, however, that there is a direct connection between
diminished intelligence and the inability to refrain from murder, what
scientific analysis can possibly show that a mildly retarded individual
who commits an exquisite torture-killing is "no more culpable" than

the "average" murderer in a holdup-gone-wrong or a domestic dispute? Or a moderately retarded individual who commits a series of 20 exquisite torture-killings? Surely culpability, and deservedness of the most severe retribution, depends not merely (if at all) upon the mental capacity of the criminal (above the level where he is able to distinguish right from wrong) but also upon the depravity of the crime—which is precisely why this sort of question has traditionally been thought answerable not by a categorical rule of the sort the Court today imposes upon all trials, but rather by the sentencer's weighing of the circumstances (both degree of retardation and depravity of crime) in the particular case. The fact that juries continue to sentence mentally retarded offenders to death for extreme crimes shows that society's moral outrage sometimes demands execution of retarded offenders. By what principle of law, science, or logic can the Court pronounce that this is wrong? There is none. Once the Court admits (as it does) that mental retardation does not render the offender morally *blameless*, there is no basis for saying that the death penalty is *never* appropriate retribution, no matter *how* heinous the crime. As long as a mentally retarded offender knows "the difference between right and wrong," only the sentencer can assess whether his retardation reduces his culpability enough to exempt him from the death penalty for the particular murder in question.

Are the mentally retarded really more disposed (and hence more likely) to commit willfully cruel and serious crime than others? In my experience, the opposite is true: being childlike generally suggests innocence rather than brutality.

As for the other social purpose of the death penalty that the Court discusses, deterrence: That is not advanced, the Court tells us, because

the mentally retarded are "less likely" than their nonretarded counterparts to "process the information of the possibility of execution as a
penalty and . . . control their conduct based upon that information."
Of course this leads to the same conclusion discussed earlier—that the
mentally retarded (because they are less deterred) are more likely to
kill—which neither I nor the society at large believes. In any event,
even the Court does not say that *all* mentally retarded individuals cannot "process the information of the possibility of execution as a
penalty and . . . control their conduct based upon that information"; it
merely asserts that they are "less likely" to be able to do so. But surely
the deterrent effect of a penalty is adequately vindicated if it successfully deters many, but not all, of the target class. Virginia's death
penalty, for example, does not fail of its deterrent effect simply because
some criminals are unaware that Virginia *has* the death penalty. In other
words, the supposed fact that *some* retarded criminals cannot fully
appreciate the death penalty has nothing to do with the deterrence
rationale, but is simply an echo of the arguments denying a retribution rationale, discussed and rejected above. I am not sure that a murderer is somehow less blameworthy if (though he knew his act was
wrong) he did not fully appreciate that he could die for it; but if so,
we should treat a mentally retarded murderer the way we treat an
offender who may be "less likely" to respond to the death penalty
because he was abused as a child. We do not hold him immune from
capital punishment, but require his background to be considered by
the sentencer as a mitigating factor.

The Court throws one last factor into its grab bag of reasons why
execution of the retarded is "excessive" in all cases: Mentally retarded
offenders "face a special risk of wrongful execution" because they are
less able "to make a persuasive showing of mitigation," "to give mean-

ingful assistance to their counsel," and to be effective witnesses. "Special risk" is pretty flabby language (even flabbier than "less likely")—and I suppose a similar "special risk" could be said to exist for just plain stupid people, inarticulate people, even ugly people. If this unsupported claim has any substance to it (which I doubt), it might support a due process claim in all criminal prosecutions of the mentally retarded; but it is hard to see how it has anything to do with an *Eighth Amendment* claim that execution of the mentally retarded is cruel and unusual. We have never before held it to be cruel and unusual punishment to impose a sentence in violation of some *other* constitutional imperative.

Today's opinion adds one more to the long list of substantive and procedural requirements impeding imposition of the death penalty imposed under this Court's assumed power to invent a death-is-different jurisprudence. None of those requirements existed when the Eighth Amendment was adopted, and some of them were not even supported by current moral consensus. They include prohibition of the death penalty for "ordinary" murder, *Godfrey*, for rape of an adult woman, *Coker*, and for felony murder absent a showing that the defendant possessed a sufficiently culpable state of mind, *Enmund*; prohibition of the death penalty for any person under the age of 16 at the time of the crime, *Thompson*; prohibition of the death penalty as the mandatory punishment for any crime, *Woodson* v. *North Carolina* (1976); a requirement that the sentencer not be given unguided discretion, *Furman* v. *Georgia* (1972); a requirement that the sentencer be empowered to take into account all mitigating circumstances, *Lockett* v. *Ohio* (1978); and a requirement that the accused receive a judicial evaluation of his claim of insanity before the sentence can be executed, *Ford*. There is something to be said for popular abolition of the death penalty; there is nothing to be said for its incremental abolition by this Court.

This newest invention promises to be more effective than any of the others in turning the process of capital trial into a game. One need only read the definitions of mental retardation adopted by the American Association of Mental Retardation and the American Psychiatric Association (set forth in the Court's opinion) to realize that the symptoms of this condition can readily be feigned. And whereas the capital defendant who feigns insanity risks commitment to a mental institution until he can be cured (and then tried and executed), the capital defendant who feigns mental retardation risks nothing at all. The mere pendency of the present case has brought us petitions by death row inmates claiming for the first time, after multiple habeas petitions, that they are retarded.

There is something to be said for popular abolition of the death penalty; there is nothing to be said for its incremental abolition by this Court.

Perhaps these practical difficulties will not be experienced by the minority of capital-punishment States that have very recently changed mental retardation from a mitigating factor (to be accepted or rejected by the sentencer) to an absolute immunity. Time will tell—and the brief time those States have had the new disposition in place (an average of 6.8 years) is surely not enough. But if the practical difficulties do not appear, and if the other States share the Court's perceived moral consensus that *all* mental retardation renders the death penalty inappropriate for *all* crimes, then that majority will presumably follow suit. But there is no justification for this Court's pushing them into the experiment—and turning the experiment into a permanent practice—on constitutional pretext. Nothing has changed the accuracy of Matthew

Hale's endorsement of the common law's traditional method for taking account of guilt-reducing factors, written over three centuries ago:

> [Determination of a person's incapacity] is a matter of great difficulty, partly from the easiness of counterfeiting this disability... and partly from the variety of the degrees of this infirmity, whereof some are sufficient, and some are insufficient to excuse persons in capital offenses....
>
> Yet the law of England hath afforded the best method of trial, that is possible, of this and all other matters of fact, namely, by a jury of twelve men all concurring in the same judgment, by the testimony of witnesses.... and by the inspection and direction of the judge.
>
> 1 Hale, Pleas of the Crown

I respectfully dissent.

CHAPTER SEVEN

RELIGIOUS FREEDOM

THE VERY FIRST WORDS in the Bill of Rights protect the freedom of Americans to practice their religion and guard them against the potential tyranny of government-sponsored religion. "Congress shall make no law respecting an establishment of religion, or prohibiting the free exercise thereof. . ." reads the First Amendment. The amendment's two clauses—known as the Establishment Clause and the Free Exercise Clause—have generated two separate issues for analysis by the courts.

The Establishment Clause of the First Amendment is the textual basis for what many consider the Constitution's requirement of a "wall of separation between church and state." Though the "wall of separation" phrase is nowhere to be found in the Constitution—it comes from a private letter written by Thomas Jefferson—the metaphor stuck and has been adopted by those who feel religion has no place in the public square. The Framers of the Constitution, of course, did not subscribe to such a separatist view. They were primarily concerned with preventing the establishment of a national church; indeed, the Establishment Clause did not even apply to state governments until 1947.[1] In that year, the Supreme Court, citing Jefferson's "wall," extended application of the clause not only with regard to who was covered (i.e. the states) but also concerning what government actions were covered. Laws that aid only one religion or that reveal a preference for one religion over another are unconstitutional, the Court said, but so, too, are laws that "aid all religions."[2]

As the Court constructed a higher wall between church and state, it was forced to consider the constitutionality of many government policies that arguably aided "all religions." For example, was it permissible for a state to provide any assistance to religious schools for textbooks or supplies? How would state laws fare that required students to observe a moment of silence that might be used for prayer? More fundamentally, what standards or guides should courts use to answer such questions?

Before Justice Scalia joined the Supreme Court, it had adopted in the case of *Lemon* v. *Kurtzman* (1971) a three-prong test for deciding legal challenges to government practices that purportedly "established" religion. The *Lemon* test, as it became known, requires the Court to strike down laws appearing to promote or aid religion unless it determines that (1) the government action had a secular purpose, (2) the government action's primary effect is not to advance religion, and (3) the action does not foster an "excessive entanglement" with religion. The *Lemon* test has been fiercely criticized by many legal scholars and even current Supreme Court justices for tipping the scales against religion.[3] These critics argue, among other things, that the Constitution does not forbid government from "advancing" religion generally, so long as it does not "play favorites" between various religions. Lately, the *Lemon* test is fallen into such disrepute that the Court sometimes ignores it altogether. This practice of ignoring but not overruling produced one of Scalia's most vivid and humorous opinions in *Lamb's Chapel*, which is included in this chapter.

Overall, Justice Scalia has been unsympathetic to claims that government action has unlawfully aided religion. Indeed, since joining the Court in 1986, Scalia has never written or joined an opinion that found a government authority had violated the Establishment Clause.[4]

The other religion clause of the First Amendment, the Free Exercise Clause, prohibits Congress and the states from interfering with an individual's ability to practice his or her religion. What constitutes interference is not always easy to determine. For example, the Court has held that the military's ban on wearing any hat (other than an official one) while on duty did not violate the Free Exercise right of an Orthodox Jewish soldier who wished to wear a yarmulke.[5] On the other hand, the Court has held that the Free Exercise rights of Seventh-Day Adventists were unconstitutionally abridged by a state law denying unemployment benefits to individuals who do not work on Saturdays, the Sabbath day for Adventists.[6]

The two religion commands are often raised in the same case. The Court examines whether a government action violates the Establishment Clause and if it does not, whether it overly burdens an individual's right to adhere to his or her religious customs.

Justice Scalia has been a very active participant in the religion clause cases. His most important opinion in the area is not one of his trademark colorful dissents. Rather, Scalia's opinion for the majority in *Employment Division of Oregon* v. *Smith* (1990) was noteworthy because it created a new rule for judging Free Exercise claims and because it disappointed many political conservatives. In *Smith*, Scalia and the Court ruled that Oregon could deny benefits to Native Americans who used peyote in violation of the state's drug laws. Though recognizing that the peyote was used in the Indians' religious ceremonies, Scalia wrote that the Free Exercise Clause does not protect activities that are made criminal by generally applicable and religion-neutral laws. To hold otherwise, Scalia argued, the Court would have to create special exemptions to all sorts of laws that various religious groups within the United States object to, for example, laws requiring payment of taxes and registration for military service, animal cruelty laws, and child labor laws.

Scalia appreciated the potential hardship that might arise from the Court's restraint. He wrote, "It may fairly be said that leaving accommodation to the political process will place at a disadvantage those religious practices that are not widely engaged in; but that unavoidable consequence of democratic government must be preferred to a system in which each conscience is a law unto itself or in which judges weigh the social importance of all laws against the centrality of all religious beliefs."[7] In Scalia's view, the Court is ill-suited to make determinations as to what religious practices are "central" to the exercise of an individual's faith. In order to avoid the Court wading into the realm of weighing such matters, he opts instead to leave the decision in the hands of the people acting through their elected officials.

In *Smith*, Scalia noted that Oregon could change its law to allow religious use of peyote, as other states had done. This acknowledgment is consistent with Scalia's strong belief that the Court should be deferential to legislative efforts to accommodate religious practices. "When a legislature acts to accommodate religion, particularly a minority sect, 'it follows the best of our traditions,'" Scalia wrote in one opinion.[8]

Besides *Smith*, Justice Scalia's most notable opinions have been dissents filed in cases where the majority used the Establishment Clause to invalidate legislative accommodations. Scalia has argued that religious practices that existed at the time the First Amendment was drafted cannot reasonably be considered unconstitutional when carried out today. His dissenting opinion in *Lee* v. *Weisman* (below) best represents his originalist argument.

LEE v. WEISMAN (1992)

This case arose from a challenge to a Rhode Island public school system's practice of inviting members of the clergy to offer prayers at the graduation ceremonies of its middle schools and high schools. In 1989, a middle school principal invited a rabbi to offer invocation and benediction prayers at the school's graduation. The principal provided the rabbi with a pamphlet entitled, "Guide for Civic Occasions," which was prepared by the National Conference of Christians and Jews. The principal instructed the rabbi to make the prayers nonsectarian. The rabbi's prayers included thanksgiving to God for the blessings found in America. One of the students and her father sued the school district, charging that the prayers amounted to government-required participation in religion.

A closely divided majority of the Supreme Court agreed that the school's practice violated the Establishment Clause of the First Amendment. The Court's decision did not rely on the *Lemon* test. Instead, it focused on the issue of coercion and the pressure that school sponsorship of the prayer would put on the non-believing student. The government has a duty, wrote Justice Anthony Kennedy for the Court, "to guard and respect that sphere of inviolable conscience and belief which is the mark of a free people."

Writing for the four dissenting justices, Scalia blasted the Court's decision for being completely out of touch with the history and traditions of religious freedom in the United States—specifically, the use of voluntary prayer at high school graduations and other public ceremonies. Scalia traced the long history of prayer in governmental ceremonies and proclamations. He argued that the potential harm of "coercion" that may be felt by the nonbeliever is outweighed by the benefit of having people of many different faiths be able to come together in the "unifying mechanism" of public prayer. Moreover, he belittled the Court for dabbling in psychology to support its finding of coercion.

Scalia began his dissent by pointing out the inconsistency in Justice Kennedy's religion clause interpretations. Scalia said he could not agree with Kennedy's majority opinion here because he already professed support for a history-and culture-searching analysis highlighted in a Court opinion from "three terms ago." That opinion was written by Justice Kennedy as well.

Scalia also referred to the *Durham* rule for insanity defense.[9] That rule, since abandoned, was widely criticized for allowing criminal defendants to escape punishment so long as a single psychiatrist testified that the crime was the product of "mental disease or defect." Scalia seemed to suggest that the Court's reliance on coercion in *Lee* v. *Weisman* might lead to a similarly absurd result whereby psychiatrists will have enormous influence in deciding which public displays of religion are permissible under the Constitution.

Last, Scalia's ability to see the logical consequences of the Court's reasoning is demonstrated here as he foresees the potential for a fight over the Pledge of Allegiance, in particular, its inclusion of the words "under God." Scalia said the Court's argument—that young adults need to be protected from even the slightest coercion—would likely lead it to find recitation of the Pledge at public ceremonies to violate the Establishment Clause. That issue reached the Supreme Court in 2003.

~~⊱⊰~~

JUSTICE SCALIA, WITH WHOM THE CHIEF JUSTICE, JUSTICE WHITE, AND JUSTICE THOMAS JOIN, DISSENTING.

Three Terms ago, I joined an opinion recognizing that the Establishment Clause must be construed in light of the "[g]overnment policies of accommodation, acknowledgment, and support for religion [that] are an accepted part of our political and cultural heritage." That opinion affirmed that "the meaning of the Clause is to be determined by reference to historical practices and understandings." It said that "[a] test for implementing the protections of the Establishment Clause that, if applied with consistency, would invalidate longstanding traditions cannot be a proper reading of the Clause." *County of Allegheny* v.

American Civil Liberties Union, Greater Pittsburgh Chapter (1989) (Kennedy, J., concurring in judgment in part and dissenting in part).

These views, of course, prevent me from joining today's opinion, which is conspicuously bereft of any reference to history. In holding that the Establishment Clause prohibits invocations and benedictions at public school graduation ceremonies, the Court—with nary a mention that it is doing so—lays waste a tradition that is as old as public school graduation ceremonies themselves, and that is a component of an even more longstanding American tradition of nonsectarian prayer to God at public celebrations generally. As its instrument of destruction, the bulldozer of its social engineering, the Court invents a boundless, and boundlessly manipulable, test of psychological coercion, which promises to do for the Establishment Clause what the *Durham* rule did for the insanity defense. Today's opinion shows more forcefully than volumes of argumentation why our Nation's protection, that fortress which is our Constitution, cannot possibly rest upon the changeable philosophical predilections of the Justices of this Court, but must have deep foundations in the historic practices of our people.

I

Justice Holmes' aphorism that "a page of history is worth a volume of logic" applies with particular force to our Establishment Clause jurisprudence. As we have recognized, our interpretation of the Establishment Clause should "compor[t] with what history reveals was the contemporaneous understanding of its guarantees." *Lynch* v. *Donnelly* (1984). "[T]he line we must draw between the permissible and the impermissible is one which accords with history and faithfully reflects the understanding of the Founding Fathers." *School Dist. of Abington* v.

Schempp (1963) (Brennan, J., concurring). "[H]istorical evidence sheds light not only on what the draftsmen intended the Establishment Clause to mean, but also on how they thought that Clause applied" to contemporaneous practices. *Marsh* v. *Chambers* (1983). Thus, "[t]he existence from the beginning of the Nation's life of a practice, [while] not conclusive of its constitutionality... is a fact of considerable import in the interpretation" of the Establishment Clause. *Walz* v. *Tax Comm'n of New York City* (1970) (Brennan, J., concurring).

The history and tradition of our Nation are replete with public ceremonies featuring prayers of thanksgiving and petition. Illustrations of this point have been amply provided in our prior opinions, but since the Court is so oblivious to our history as to suggest that the Constitution restricts "preservation and transmission of religious beliefs... to the private sphere," it appears necessary to provide another brief account.

From our Nation's origin, prayer has been a prominent part of governmental ceremonies and proclamations. The Declaration of Independence, the document marking our birth as a separate people, "appeal[ed] to the Supreme Judge of the world for the rectitude of our intentions" and avowed "a firm reliance on the protection of divine Providence." In his first inaugural address, after swearing his oath of office on a Bible, George Washington deliberately made a prayer a part of his first official act as President:

> [I]t would be peculiarly improper to omit in this first official act my fervent supplications to that Almighty Being who rules over the universe, who presides in the councils of nations, and whose providential aids can supply every human defect, that His benediction may consecrate to the liberties and happiness of the peo-

ple of the United States a Government instituted by themselves for these essential purposes.

Such supplications have been a characteristic feature of inaugural addresses ever since. Thomas Jefferson, for example, prayed in his first inaugural address: "[M]ay that Infinite Power which rules the destinies of the universe lead our councils to what is best, and give them a favorable issue for your peace and prosperity." In his second inaugural address, Jefferson acknowledged his need for divine guidance and invited his audience to join his prayer:

I shall need, too, the favor of that Being in whose hands we are, who led our fathers, as Israel of old, from their native land and planted them in a country flowing with all the necessaries and comforts of life; who has covered our infancy with His providence and our riper years with His wisdom and power, and to whose goodness I ask you to join in supplications with me that He will so enlighten the minds of your servants, guide their councils, and prosper their measures that whatsoever they do shall result in your good, and shall secure to you the peace, friendship, and approbation of all nations.

Similarly, James Madison, in his first inaugural address, placed his confidence:

[I]n the guardianship and guidance of that Almighty Being whose power regulates the destiny of nations, whose blessings have been so conspicuously dispensed to this rising Republic, and to whom we are bound to address our devout gratitude for the past, as well as our fervent supplications and best hopes for the future.

Most recently, President Bush, continuing the tradition established by President Washington, asked those attending his inauguration to bow their heads, and made a prayer his first official act as President.

Our national celebration of Thanksgiving likewise dates back to President Washington. As we recounted in *Lynch*:

> The day after the First Amendment was proposed, Congress urged President Washington to proclaim "a day of public thanksgiving and prayer, to be observed by acknowledging with grateful hearts the many and signal favours of Almighty God." President Washington proclaimed November 26, 1789, a day of thanksgiving to "offe[r] our prayers and supplications to the Great Lord and Ruler of Nations, and beseech Him to pardon our national and other transgressions. . . .

This tradition of Thanksgiving Proclamations—with their religious theme of prayerful gratitude to God—has been adhered to by almost every President.

The other two branches of the Federal Government also have a long-established practice of prayer at public events. As we detailed in *Marsh*, congressional sessions have opened with a chaplain's prayer ever since the First Congress. And this Court's own sessions have opened with the invocation "God save the United States and this Honorable Court" since the days of Chief Justice Marshall.

In addition to this general tradition of prayer at public ceremonies, there exists a more specific tradition of invocations and benedictions at public school graduation exercises. By one account, the first public high school graduation ceremony took place in Connecticut in July 1868—the very month, as it happens, that the Fourteenth Amendment (the vehicle by which the Establishment Clause has been applied against the States) was ratified—when "15 seniors from the Norwich Free Academy marched in their best Sunday suits and dresses into a church hall and waited through majestic music and long prayers." Brodinsky, Commencement Rites Obsolete? Not At All, A 10 Week Study Shows, 10 Updating School Board Policies, No. 4, p. 3 (Apr. 1979). As the Court obliquely acknowledges in describing the "customary features" of high school graduations, and as respondents do not contest, the invocation and benediction have long been recognized to be "as traditional as any other parts of the [school] graduation program and are widely established." H. McKown, Commencement Activities 56 (1931).

II

The Court presumably would separate graduation invocations and benedictions from other instances of public "preservation and transmission of religious beliefs" on the ground that they involve "psychological coercion." I find it a sufficient embarrassment that our Establishment Clause jurisprudence regarding holiday displays has come to "requir[e] scrutiny more commonly associated with interior decorators than with the judiciary." *American Jewish Congress* v. *Chicago* (CA 7 1987) (Easterbrook, J., dissenting). But interior decorating is a rock-hard science compared to psychology practiced by amateurs. A few citations of "[r]esearch in psychology" that have no particular bearing upon the precise issue here cannot disguise the fact that the Court has gone beyond the realm where judges know what they are doing. The Court's argument that state officials have "coerced" students to

I find it a sufficient embarrassment that our Establishment Clause jurisprudence regarding holiday displays has come to require scrutiny more commonly associated with interior decorators than with the judiciary. But interior decorating is a rock-hard science compared to psychology practiced by amateurs.

take part in the invocation and benediction at graduation ceremonies is, not to put too fine a point on it, incoherent.

The Court identifies two "dominant facts" that it says dictate its ruling that invocations and benedictions at public school graduation ceremonies violate the Establishment Clause. Neither of them is, in any relevant sense, true.

A

The Court declares that students' "attendance and participation in the [invocation and benediction] are, in a fair and real sense, obligatory." But what exactly is this "fair and real sense"? According to the Court, students at graduation who want "to avoid the fact or appearance of participation," in the invocation and benediction are *psychologically* obligated by "public pressure, as well as peer pressure, . . . to stand as a group or, at least, maintain respectful silence" during those prayers. This assertion—*the very linchpin of the Court's opinion*—is almost as intriguing for what it does not say as for what it says. It does not say, for example, that students are psychologically coerced to bow their heads, place their hands in a Durer-like prayer position, pay attention to the prayers, utter "Amen," or in fact pray. (Perhaps further intensive psychological research remains to be done on these matters.) It claims only that students are psychologically coerced "to stand . . . *or*, at least, maintain respectful silence." (emphasis added). Both halves of this disjunctive (both of which must amount to the fact or appearance of participation in prayer if the Court's analysis is to survive on its own terms) merit particular attention.

To begin with the latter: the Court's notion that a student who simply sits in "respectful silence" during the invocation and benediction (when all others are standing) has somehow joined—or would somehow be perceived as having joined—in the prayers is nothing short of ludicrous. We indeed live in a vulgar age. But surely "our social conventions" have not coarsened to the point that anyone who does not stand on his chair and shout obscenities can reasonably be deemed to have assented to everything said in his presence. Since the Court does not dispute that students exposed to prayer at graduation ceremonies retain (despite "subtle coercive pressures") the free will to sit, there is absolutely no basis for the Court's decision. It is fanciful enough to say that "a reasonable dissenter," standing head erect in a class of bowed heads, "could believe that the group exercise signified her own participation or approval of it." It is beyond the absurd to say that she could entertain such a belief while pointedly declining to rise.

But let us assume the very worst, that the nonparticipating graduate is "subtly coerced" ... to stand! Even that half of the disjunctive does not remotely establish a "participation" (or an "appearance of participation") in a religious exercise. The Court acknowledges that, "in our culture, standing ... can signify adherence to a view or simple respect for the views of others." (Much more often the latter than the former, I think, except perhaps in the proverbial town meeting, where one votes by standing.) But if it is a permissible inference that one who is standing is doing so simply out of respect for the prayers of others that are in progress, then how can it possibly be said that a "reasonable dissenter ... could believe that the group exercise signified her own participation or approval"? Quite obviously, it cannot.

I may add, moreover, that maintaining respect for the religious observances of others is a fundamental civic virtue that government (including the public schools) can and should cultivate—so that, even if it were the case that the displaying of such respect might be mistaken for taking part in the prayer, I would deny that the dissenter's interest in avoiding *even the false appearance of participation* constitutionally trumps the government's interest in fostering respect for religion generally.

The opinion manifests that the Court itself has not given careful consideration to its test of psychological coercion. For if it had, how could it observe, with no hint of concern or disapproval, that students stood for the Pledge of Allegiance, which immediately preceded Rabbi Gutterman's invocation? The government can, of course, no more coerce political orthodoxy than religious orthodoxy. Moreover, since the Pledge of Allegiance has been revised since *Barnette* to include the phrase "under God," recital of the Pledge would appear to raise the same Establishment Clause issue as the invocation and benediction. If students were psychologically coerced to remain standing during the invocation, they must also have been psychologically coerced, moments before, to stand for (and thereby, in the Court's view, take part in or appear to take part in) the Pledge. Must the Pledge therefore be barred from the public schools (both from graduation ceremonies and from the classroom)? In *Barnette*, we held that a public school student could not be

> *In Barnette, we held that a public school student could not be compelled to recite the Pledge; we did not even hint that she could not be compelled to observe respectful silence. . . . Logically, that ought to be the next project for the Court's bulldozer.*

compelled to recite the Pledge; we did not even hint that she could not be compelled to observe respectful silence—indeed, even to stand in respectful silence—when those who wished to recite it did so. Logically, that ought to be the next project for the Court's bulldozer.

I also find it odd that the Court concludes that high school graduates may not be subjected to this supposed psychological coercion, yet refrains from addressing whether "mature adults" may. I had thought that the reason graduation from high school is regarded as so significant an event is that it is generally associated with transition from adolescence to young adulthood. Many graduating seniors, of course, are old enough to vote. Why, then, does the Court treat them as though they were first-graders? Will we soon have a jurisprudence that distinguishes between mature and immature adults?

B

The other "dominant fac[t]" identified by the Court is that "[s]tate officials direct the performance of a formal religious exercise" at school graduation ceremonies. "Direct[ing] the performance of a formal religious exercise" has a sound of liturgy to it, summoning up images of the principal directing acolytes where to carry the cross, or showing the rabbi where to unroll the Torah. A Court professing to be engaged in a "delicate and fact-sensitive" line-drawing would better describe what it means as "prescribing the content of an invocation and benediction." But even that would be false. All the record shows is that principals of the Providence public schools, acting within their delegated authority, have invited clergy to deliver invocations and benedictions at graduations; and that Principal Lee invited Rabbi Gutterman, provided him a two-page pamphlet, prepared by the National Conference of Christians and Jews, giving general advice on inclusive prayer for civic occasions, and advised him that his prayers at graduation should be nonsectarian. How these facts can fairly be transformed into the charges that Principal Lee "directed and controlled the content of [Rabbi Gutterman's] prayer," that school officials "monitor prayer," and attempted to "'compose official prayers,'" and that the "government involvement with religious activity in this case is pervasive" is difficult to fathom. The Court identifies nothing in the record remotely suggesting that school officials have ever drafted, edited, screened, or censored graduation prayers, or that Rabbi Gutterman was a mouthpiece of the school officials.

These distortions of the record are, of course, not harmless error: without them, the Court's solemn assertion that the school officials could reasonably be perceived to be "enforc[ing] a religious orthodoxy," would ring as hollow, as it ought.

III

The deeper flaw in the Court's opinion does not lie in its wrong answer to the question whether there was state-induced "peer-pressure" coercion; it lies, rather, in the Court's making violation of the Establishment Clause hinge on such a precious question. The coercion that was a hallmark of historical establishments of religion was coercion of religious orthodoxy and of financial support by force of law and threat of penalty. Typically, attendance at the state church was required; only clergy of the official church could lawfully perform sacraments; and dissenters, if tolerated, faced an array of civil disabilities. Thus, for example, in the colony of Virginia, where the Church of England had been established, ministers were required by law to conform to the doctrine and rites of the Church of England; and all persons were required to attend church and observe the Sabbath, were tithed for the public support of Anglican ministers, and were taxed for the costs of building and repairing churches.

The Establishment Clause was adopted to prohibit such an establishment of religion at the federal level (and to protect state establishments of religion from federal interference). I will further acknowledge for the sake of argument that, as some scholars have argued, by 1790, the term "establishment" had acquired an additional meaning—"financial support of religion generally, by public taxation"—that reflected the development of "general or multiple" establishments, not limited to a single church. But that would still be an establishment coerced by *force of law*. And I will further concede that our constitutional tradition, from the Declaration of Independence and the first inaugural address of Washington, quoted earlier, down to the present day, has, with a few aberrations ruled out of order government-sponsored endorsement of religion—even when no legal coercion is present, and indeed even when no ersatz, "peer-pressure" psycho-coercion is present—where the endorsement is sectarian, in the sense of specifying details upon which men and women who believe in a benevolent, omnipotent Creator and Ruler of the world are known to differ (for example, the divinity of Christ). But there is simply no support for the proposition that the officially sponsored nondenominational invocation and benediction read by Rabbi Gutterman—with no one legally coerced to recite them—violated the Constitution of the United States. To the contrary, they are so characteristically American they could have come from the pen of George Washington or Abraham Lincoln himself.

Thus, while I have no quarrel with the Court's general proposition that the Establishment Clause "guarantees that government may not coerce anyone to support or participate in religion or its exercise," I see no warrant for expanding the concept of coercion beyond acts backed by threat of penalty—a brand of coercion that, happily, is readily discernible to those of us who have made a career of reading the disciples of Blackstone, rather than of Freud. The Framers were indeed opposed to coercion of religious worship by the National Government; but, as their own sponsorship of nonsectarian prayer in public events demonstrates, they understood that "[s]peech is not coercive; the listener may do as he likes." *American Jewish Congress* v. *Chicago*, 827 F.2d, at 132 (Easterbrook, J., dissenting).

> *I see no warrant for expanding the concept of coercion beyond acts backed by threat of penalty—a brand of coercion that, happily, is readily discernible to those of us who have made a career of reading the disciples of Blackstone, rather than of Freud.*

This historical discussion places in revealing perspective the Court's extravagant claim that the State has, "for all practical purposes," and "in every practical sense," compelled students to participate in prayers at graduation. Beyond the fact, stipulated to by the parties, that attendance at graduation is voluntary, there is nothing in the record to indicate that failure of attending students to take part in the invocation or benediction was subject to any penalty or discipline. Contrast this with, for example, the facts of *Barnette*: Schoolchildren were required by law to recite the Pledge of Allegiance; failure to do so resulted in expulsion, threatened the expelled child with the prospect of being sent to a reformatory for criminally inclined juveniles, and subjected his parents to prosecution (and incarceration) for causing delinquency. To characterize the "subtle coercive pressures" allegedly present here as the "practical" equivalent of the legal sanctions in *Barnette* is . . . well, let me just say it is not a "delicate and fact-sensitive" analysis.

The Court relies on our "school prayer" cases, *Engel* v. *Vitale* (1962) and School *Dist. of Abington* v. *Schempp* (1963). But whatever the merit of those cases, they do not support, much less compel, the Court's psychojourney. In the first place, *Engel* and *Schempp* do not constitute an exception to the rule, distilled from historical practice, that public ceremonies may include prayer; rather, they simply do not fall within the scope of the rule (for the obvious reason that school instruction is not a public ceremony). Second, we have made clear our understanding that school prayer occurs within a framework in which legal coercion to attend school (i.e., coercion under threat of penalty) provides the ultimate backdrop. In *Schempp*, for example, we emphasized that the prayers were "prescribed as part of the curricular activities of students who are *required by law* to attend school." (emphasis added). *Engel*'s suggestion that the school prayer program at issue there—which permitted students "to remain silent or be excused from the room"—involved "indirect coercive pressure" should be understood against this backdrop of legal coercion. The question whether the opt-out procedure in *Engel* sufficed to dispel the coercion resulting from the mandatory attendance requirement is quite different from the question whether forbidden coercion exists in an environment utterly devoid of legal compulsion. And finally, our school prayer cases turn in part on the fact that the classroom is inherently an instructional setting, and daily prayer there—where parents are not present to counter "the students' emulation of teachers as role models and the children's susceptibility to peer pressure," *Edwards* v. *Aguillard* (1987)—

> *The Court relies on our school prayer cases, Engel v. Vitale and School District of Abington v. Schempp. But whatever the merit of those cases, they do not support, much less compel, the Court's psychojourney.*

might be thought to raise special concerns regarding state interference
with the liberty of parents to direct the religious upbringing of their
children: "Families entrust public schools with the education of their
children, but condition their trust on the understanding that the classroom will not purposely be used to advance religious views that may
conflict with the private beliefs of the student and his or her family."
Voluntary prayer at graduation—a one-time ceremony at which parents, friends, and relatives are present—can hardly be thought to raise
the same concerns.

IV

Our Religion Clause jurisprudence has become bedeviled (so to speak)
by reliance on formulaic abstractions that are not derived from, but
positively conflict with, our long-accepted constitutional traditions.
Foremost among these has been the so-called *Lemon* test, which has
received well-earned criticism from many Members of this Court. The
Court today demonstrates the irrelevance of *Lemon* by essentially
ignoring it, and the interment of that case may be the one happy
byproduct of the Court's otherwise lamentable decision. Unfortunately,
however, the Court has replaced *Lemon* with its psycho-coercion test,
which suffers the double disability of having no roots whatever in our
people's historic practice and being as infinitely expandable as the reasons for psychotherapy itself.

Another happy aspect of the case is that it is only a jurisprudential
disaster, and not a practical one. Given the odd basis for the Court's
decision, invocations and benedictions will be able to be given at public school graduations next June, as they have for the past century and
a half, so long as school authorities make clear that anyone who
abstains from screaming in protest does not necessarily participate in

the prayers. All that is seemingly needed is an announcement, or perhaps a written insertion at the beginning of the graduation program, to the effect that, while all are asked to rise for the invocation and benediction, none is compelled to join in them, nor will be assumed, by rising, to have done so. That obvious fact recited, the graduates and their parents may proceed to thank God, as Americans have always done, for the blessings He has generously bestowed on them and on their country.

The reader has been told much in this case about the personal interest of Mr. Weisman and his daughter, and very little about the personal interests on the other side. They are not inconsequential. Church and state would not be such a difficult subject if religion were, as the Court apparently thinks it to be, some purely personal avocation that can be indulged entirely in secret, like pornography, in the privacy of one's room. For most believers, it is not that, and has never been. Religious men and women of almost all denominations have felt it necessary to acknowledge and beseech the blessing of God as a people, and not just as individuals, because they believe in the "protection of divine Providence," as the Declaration of Independence put it, not just for individuals but for societies; because they believe God to be, as Washington's first Thanksgiving Proclamation put it, the "Great Lord and Ruler of Nations." One can believe in the effectiveness of such public worship, or one can deprecate and deride it. But the long-standing American tradition of prayer at official ceremonies displays with unmistakable clarity that the Establishment Clause does not forbid the government to accommodate it.

The narrow context of the present case involves a community's celebration of one of the milestones in its young citizens' lives, and it is a bold step for this Court to seek to banish from that occasion, and from thousands of similar celebrations throughout this land, the expression of gratitude to God that a majority of the community wishes to make. The issue before us today is not the abstract philosophical question whether the alternative of frustrating this desire of a religious majority is to be preferred over the alternative of imposing "psychological coercion," or a feeling of exclusion, upon nonbelievers. Rather, the question is *whether a mandatory choice in favor of the former has been imposed by the United States Constitution.* As the age-old practices of our people show, the answer to that question is not at all in doubt.

I must add one final observation: the Founders of our Republic knew the fearsome potential of sectarian religious belief to generate civil dissension and civil strife. And they also knew that nothing, absolutely nothing, is so inclined to foster among religious believers of various faiths a toleration—no, an affection—for one another than voluntarily joining in prayer together, to the God whom they all worship and seek. Needless to say, no one should be compelled to do that, but it is a shame to deprive our public culture of the opportunity, and indeed the encouragement, for people to do it voluntarily. The Baptist or Catholic who heard and joined in the simple and inspiring prayers of Rabbi Gutterman on this official and patriotic occasion was inoculated from religious bigotry and prejudice in a manner that cannot be replicated. To deprive our society of that important unifying mechanism in order to spare the nonbeliever what seems to me the minimal inconvenience of standing, or even sitting in respectful nonparticipation, is as senseless in policy as it is unsupported in law.

For the foregoing reasons, I dissent.

LAMB'S CHAPEL v. CENTER MORICHES UNION FREE SCHOOL DISTRICT (1993)

The Center Moriches Union Free School District in New York enacted a policy of allowing civic and social uses of its schools, but prohibited use by any group for religious purposes. This policy was enforced to exclude the pastor of Lamb's Chapel, who sought to use the school facilities to show a film series by Dr. James Dobson on issues related to family values and child rearing. The pastor sued alleging violation of free speech under the First Amendment.

In ruling that the policy indeed violated the free speech rights of the pastor and his church, the Court majority also stated that use of the school by the church for its film presentation would not violate the Establishment Clause. The Court, after ignoring the *Lemon* test a year earlier in *Lee* v. *Weisman*, applied the test here and found the church's use of the school harmless.

Justice Scalia agreed with the Court's free speech conclusion, but wrote a separate opinion to point out the absurdity of the Court's use of *Lemon*. The image Scalia evokes to make his point qualifies this short opinion as one of his most memorable.

~≈◊◊≈~

JUSTICE SCALIA, WITH WHOM JUSTICE THOMAS JOINS, CONCURRING IN THE JUDGMENT.

I join the Court's conclusion that the District's refusal to allow use of school facilities for petitioners' film viewing, while generally opening the schools for community activities, violates petitioners' First Amendment free speech rights... I also agree with the Court that allowing Lamb's Chapel to use school facilities poses "no realistic danger" of a violation of the Establishment Clause, but I cannot accept most of its reasoning in this regard. The Court explains that the showing of petitioners' film on school property after school hours would not cause the community to "think that the District was endorsing religion or any particular creed," and further notes that access to school property would not violate the three-part test articulated in *Lemon* v. *Kurtzman* (1971).

Like some ghoul in a late-night horror movie that repeatedly sits up in its grave and shuffles abroad after being repeatedly killed and buried, Lemon stalks our Establishment Clause jurisprudence once again, frightening the little children and school attorneys of Center Moriches Union Free School District.

As to the Court's invocation of the *Lemon* test: Like some ghoul in a late-night horror movie that repeatedly sits up in its grave and shuffles abroad after being repeatedly killed and buried, *Lemon* stalks our Establishment Clause jurisprudence once again, frightening the little children and school attorneys of Center Moriches Union Free School District. Its most recent burial, only last Term, was, to be sure, not fully six feet under: Our decision in *Lee* v. *Weisman* conspicuously avoided using the supposed "test," but also declined the invitation to repudiate it. Over the years, however, no fewer than five of the currently sitting Justices have, in their own opinions, personally driven pencils through the creature's heart (the author of today's opinion repeatedly), and a sixth has joined an opinion doing so.

The secret of the *Lemon* test's survival, I think, is that it is so easy to kill. It is there to scare us (and our audience) when we wish it to do so, but we can command it to return to the tomb at will. When we wish to strike down a practice it forbids, we invoke it, see, e.g., *Aguilar*

v. *Fenton* (1985) (striking down state remedial education program administered in part in parochial schools); when we wish to uphold a practice it forbids, we ignore it entirely, see *Marsh* v. *Chambers* (1983) (upholding state legislative chaplains). Sometimes, we take a middle course, calling its three prongs "no more than helpful signposts," *Hunt* v. *McNair* (1973). Such a docile and useful monster is worth keeping around, at least in a somnolent state; one never knows when one might need him.

For my part, I agree with the long list of constitutional scholars who have criticized *Lemon* and bemoaned the strange Establishment Clause geometry of crooked lines and wavering shapes its intermittent use has produced. I will decline to apply *Lemon*—whether it validates or invalidates the government action in question—and therefore cannot join the opinion of the Court today.

I cannot join for yet another reason: the Court's statement that the proposed use of the school's facilities is constitutional because (among other things) it would not signal endorsement of religion in general. What a strange notion, that a Constitution which itself gives "religion in general" preferential treatment (I refer to the Free Exercise Clause) forbids endorsement of religion in general. The attorney general of New York not only agrees with that strange notion, he has an explanation for it: "Religious advocacy," he writes, "serves the community only in the eyes of its adherents, and yields a benefit only to those who already believe." Brief for Respondent Attorney General 24. That was *not* the view of those who adopted our Constitution, who believed that the public virtues inculcated by religion are a public good. It suffices to point out that, during the summer of 1789, when it was in the process of drafting the First Amendment, Congress enacted the Northwest Territory Ordinance that the Confederation Congress had adopted, in 1787—Article III of which provides, "Religion, morality, and knowledge, *being necessary to good government and the happiness of mankind*, schools and the means of education shall forever be encouraged." Unsurprisingly, then, indifference to "religion in general" is not what our cases, both old and recent, demand.

For the reasons given by the Court, I agree that the Free Speech Clause of the First Amendment forbids what respondents have done here. As for the asserted Establishment Clause justification, I would hold, simply and clearly, that giving Lamb's Chapel nondiscriminatory access to school facilities cannot violate that provision because it does not signify state or local embrace of a particular religious sect.

CHAPTER EIGHT

GENDER EQUALITY

~✦~

As with race, the Equal Protection Clause of the Fourteenth Amendment protects individuals from being unreasonably classified by gender. Before the 1970s, however, the Supreme Court gave wide latitude to the government to draw lines by sex. So long as the classification was considered "rationally related" to some "legitimate" government objective, it would be allowed.

Beginning in the 1970s, as attitudes about women's role in society changed, the Court began to take a harder look at gender classifications. From 1976 until its decision in *United States* v. *Virginia* in 1996, the Court upheld such classifications only if they served "important" (as opposed to merely "legitimate") government objectives and were "substantially related" (not just "rationally related") to achievement of those objectives.[1] This level of review, commonly referred to as "intermediate scrutiny," is easier to satisfy than the strict scrutiny standard used with race cases, but often results in classifications being struck down as unconstitutional. There have been exceptions. For example, the Supreme Court upheld the law requiring only men to register for the military draft[2] and also found constitutional a

California law holding adult men, but not women, criminally liable for statutory rape.[3]

Justice Scalia follows the Court's precedents and applies intermediate scrutiny to laws that distinguish between men and women. As the reader will observe in Scalia's dissent in *United States* v. *Virginia* below, he contends this level of review is more than sufficient given that women have a greater voice in our democratic system than racial and ethnic minorities. Women's greater political power, he believes, is a product of simple math; women make up the majority of eligible voters in the United States. Thus, they are less likely to be on the receiving end of discriminatory laws that violate the Equal Protection Clause.

UNITED STATES v. VIRGINIA (1996)

The Supreme Court was asked to decide the constitutionality of the Virginia Military Institute's (VMI) admissions policy. The State of Virginia had operated VMI as a men-only institution since 1839. The State defended its discriminatory policy on the grounds that its rigorous physical training requirements, deprivation of students' privacy, and boot camp-style method of training, including hazing, would be forced to change if women were admitted. The State also argued that the VMI's men-only military education furthered Virginia's efforts to provide diversity in educational approaches. Finally, the state proposed a separate military program at a pre-existing all-women private liberal arts college in Virginia.

In a 7–1 decision (Justice Thomas did not participate in the case because his son attended VMI at the time), the Supreme Court ruled that VMI's admissions policy violated the Equal Protection Clause of the Fourteenth Amendment. The majority said the admissions policy was based on overly broad generalizations about how women would fare in VMI's physically challenging program. Even if most women would be unable to keep up, some would be able, the Court said, and therefore should not be denied the opportunity to attend. The Court also dismissed the state's claim that the school fit in the state's policy of providing diversity, saying that Virginia did not have any all-women public universities. Lastly, the Court ruled that the proposed all-women military program did not fix the state's Equal Protection problems because the women's alternative did not include the same level of military training or have the same standard of academic excellence as existed at VMI.

In holding the VMI admissions policy unconstitutional, the Court ruled that gender distinctions will be invalidated unless a state demonstrates an "exceedingly persuasive justification" for the classification. In addition, the Court's majority said it will be more skeptical of the reasons put forth by States and other governments to justify gender line drawing, saying that a state's justification must describe actual state purposes, not rationalizations that hide discriminatory motivations.

Justice Scalia, the lone dissenter, wrote a long opinion that challenged the Court on nearly every facet of its decision. First, Scalia said the Court completely ignored the long-standing tradition of government support for men's military colleges. Using a line of reasoning he employs often in religious freedom cases, Scalia argued that the Constitution cannot possibly be read to outlaw a policy that has been in place for more than one hundred and fifty years.

Next, Scalia charged that the new burden on the state to show an "exceedingly persuasive justification" for denying women at VMI amounted to a "redefinition of intermediate scrutiny that makes it indistinguishable from strict scrutiny." He said this more searching scrutiny was unwarranted given that women are not a minority group that lacks recourse to change policy through the democratic process. Rejecting the new standard, Scalia went on to apply the traditional intermediate scrutiny analysis and concluded that Virginia had a legitimate, if not compelling, interest in providing "effective" education and that the factual record makes clear single-sex education at the college level is beneficial for both male and female students. Scalia criticized the Court for ignoring what was a clear factual record supporting the benefits of single-sex education.

Scalia's opinion also responded to a concurring opinion written by Chief Justice Rehnquist. Rehnquist agreed that VMI's admissions policy was unconstitutional but argued that the Court should not have used the new "exceedingly persuasive justification" test. Even under the standard "intermediate scrutiny" review, the Chief Justice wrote, the policy would fail because the state did not offer sufficient evidence to support its mission of providing educational diversity or of the benefits of the adversative method. Scalia argued that the evidence sought by the Chief Justice was either amply provided by the state or was considered a given in the litigation.

Scalia predicted the Court's rationale for invalidating VMI's admissions policy will someday be extended to close all single-sex schools in the United State, public and private. Finally, his opinion closed with a poignant reflection on the code of conduct all first-year students at VMI were required to keep with them. The code sets forth basic rules of gentlemanly behavior. Scalia said he is not aware whether the men of VMI followed the rules or not, but nevertheless found it "powerfully impressive that a public institution of higher education still in existence sought to have them do so."

—◦◦◦◦—

JUSTICE SCALIA, DISSENTING.

Today the Court shuts down an institution that has served the people of the Commonwealth of Virginia with pride and distinction for over a century and a half. To achieve that desired result, it rejects (contrary to our established practice) the factual findings of two courts below, sweeps aside the precedents of this Court, and ignores the history of our people. As to facts: it explicitly rejects the finding that there exist "gender-based developmental differences" supporting Virginia's restriction of the "adversative" method to only a men's institution, and the finding that the all-male composition of the Virginia Military Institute

(VMI) is essential to that institution's character. As to precedent: it drastically revises our established standards for reviewing sex-based classifications. And as to history: it counts for nothing the long tradition, enduring down to the present, of men's military colleges supported by both States and the Federal Government.

> *Today the Court shuts down an institution that has served the people of the Commonwealth of Virginia with pride and distinction for over a century and a half.*

Much of the Court's opinion is devoted to deprecating the closed-mindedness of our forebears with regard to women's education, and even with regard to the treatment of women in areas that have nothing to do with education. Closed-minded they were—as every age is, including our own, with regard to matters it cannot guess, because it simply does not consider them debatable. The virtue of a democratic system with a First Amendment is that it readily enables the people, over time, to be persuaded that what they took for granted is not so, and to change their laws accordingly. That system is destroyed if the smug assurances of each age are removed from the democratic process and written into the Constitution. So to counterbalance the Court's criticism of our ancestors, let me say a word in their praise: they left us free to change. The same cannot be said of this most illiberal Court, which has embarked on a course of inscribing one after another of the current preferences of the society (and in some cases only the counter-majoritarian preferences of the society's law-trained elite) into our Basic Law. Today it enshrines the notion that no substantial educational value is to be served by an all-men's military academy—so that the decision by the people of Virginia to maintain such an institution denies equal protection to women who cannot attend that institution but can attend others. Since it is entirely clear that the Constitution of the United States—the old one—takes no sides in this educational debate, I dissent.

I

I shall devote most of my analysis to evaluating the Court's opinion on the basis of our current equal protection jurisprudence, which regards this Court as free to evaluate everything under the sun by applying one of three tests: "rational basis" scrutiny, intermediate scrutiny, or strict scrutiny. These tests are no more scientific than their names suggest, and a further element of randomness is added by the fact that it is largely up to us which test will be applied in each case. Strict scrutiny, we have said, is reserved for state "classifications based on race or national origin and classifications affecting fundamental rights," *Clark* v. *Jeter* (1988). It is my position that the term "fundamental rights" should be limited to "interest[s] traditionally protected by our society," *Michael H.* v. *Gerald D.* (1989); but the Court has not accepted that view, so that strict scrutiny will be applied to the deprivation of whatever sort of right we consider "fundamental." We have no established criterion for "intermediate scrutiny" either, but essentially apply it when it seems like a good idea to load the dice. So far it has been applied to content-neutral restrictions that place an incidental burden on speech, to disabilities attendant to illegitimacy, and to discrimination on the basis of sex.

I have no problem with a system of abstract tests such as rational-basis, intermediate, and strict scrutiny (though I think we can do better than applying strict scrutiny and intermediate scrutiny whenever we feel like it). Such formulas are essential to evaluating whether the new restrictions that a changing society constantly imposes upon private conduct comport with that "equal protection" our society has always accorded in the past. But in my view the function of this Court is to *preserve* our society's values regarding (among other things) equal protection, not to *revise* them; to prevent backsliding from the degree of restriction the Constitution imposed upon democratic government, not to prescribe, on our own authority, progressively higher degrees. For that reason it is my view that, whatever abstract tests we may choose to devise, they cannot supersede—and indeed ought to be crafted *so as to reflect*—those constant and unbroken national traditions that embody the people's understanding of ambiguous constitutional texts. More specifically, it is my view that "when a practice not expressly prohibited by the text of the Bill of Rights bears the endorsement of a long tradition of open, widespread, and unchallenged use that dates back to the beginning of the Republic, we have no proper basis for striking it down." *Rutan* v. *Republican Party of Ill.* (1990) (Scalia, J., dissenting). The same applies, mutatis mutandis, to a practice asserted to be in violation of the post–Civil War Fourteenth Amendment.

The all-male constitution of VMI comes squarely within such a governing tradition. Founded by the Commonwealth of Virginia in 1839 and continuously maintained by it since, VMI has always admitted only men. And in that regard it has not been unusual. For almost all of VMI's more than a century and a half of existence, its single-sex status reflected the uniform practice for government-supported military colleges. Another famous Southern institution, The Citadel, has existed as a state-funded school of South Carolina since 1842. And all the federal military colleges—West Point, the Naval Academy at Annapolis, and even the Air Force Academy, which was not established until 1954—admitted only males for most of their history.

Their admission of women in 1976 (upon which the Court today relies) came not by court decree, but because the people, through their elected representatives, decreed a change. In other words, the tradition of having government-funded military schools for men is as well rooted in the traditions of this country as the tradition of sending only men into military combat. The people may decide to change the one tradition, like the other, through democratic processes; but the assertion that either tradition has been unconstitutional through the centuries is not law, but politics-smuggled-into-law.

> *The tradition of having government-funded military schools for men is as well rooted in the traditions of this country as the tradition of sending only men into military combat. The people may decide to change the one tradition, like the other, through democratic processes; but the assertion that either tradition has been unconstitutional through the centuries is not law, but politics-smuggled-into-law.*

And the same applies, more broadly, to single-sex education in general, which, as I shall discuss, is threatened by today's decision with the cut-off of all state and federal support. Government-run nonmilitary educational institutions for the two sexes have until very recently also been part of our national tradition. "[It is] [c]oeducation, historically, [that] is a novel educational theory. From grade school through high school, college, and graduate and professional training, much of the Nation's population during much of our history has been educated in sexually segregated classrooms." *Mississippi Univ. for Women* v. *Hogan* (1982) (Powell, J., dissenting). These traditions may of course be changed by the democratic decisions of the people, as they largely have been.

Today, however, change is forced upon Virginia, and reversion to single-sex education is prohibited nationwide, not by democratic processes but by order of this Court. Even while bemoaning the sorry, bygone days of "fixed notions" concerning women's education, the Court favors current notions so fixedly that it is willing to write them into the Constitution of the United States by application of custom-built "tests." This is not the interpretation of a Constitution, but the creation of one.

II

To reject the Court's disposition today, however, it is not necessary to accept my view that the Court's made-up tests cannot displace long-standing national traditions as the primary determinant of what the Constitution means. It is only necessary to apply honestly the test the Court has been applying to sex-based classifications for the past two decades. It is well settled, as Justice O'Connor stated some time ago for a unanimous Court, that we evaluate a statutory classification based on sex under a standard that lies "[b]etween th[e] extremes of rational basis review and strict scrutiny." *Clark* v. *Jeter.* We have denominated this standard "intermediate scrutiny" and under it have inquired whether the statutory classification is "substantially related to an important governmental objective." *Ibid.*

Before I proceed to apply this standard to VMI, I must comment upon the manner in which the Court avoids doing so. Notwithstanding our above-described precedents and their "'firmly established principles,'" *Heckler* v. *Mathews* (1984) (quoting *Hogan*), the United States urged us to hold in this case "that strict scrutiny is the correct constitutional standard for evaluating classifications that deny opportunities to individuals based on their sex." (This was in flat contradiction of the

Government's position below, which was, in its own words, to "stat[e] *unequivocally* that the appropriate standard in this case is 'intermediate scrutiny.'" The Court, while making no reference to the Government's argument, effectively accepts it.

Although the Court in two places recites the test as stated in *Hogan*, which asks whether the State has demonstrated "that the classification serves important governmental objectives and that the discriminatory means employed are substantially related to the achievement of those objectives," the Court never answers the question presented in anything resembling that form. When it engages in analysis, the Court instead prefers the phrase "exceedingly persuasive justification" from *Hogan*. The Court's nine invocations of that phrase and even its fanciful description of that imponderable as "the core instruction" of the Court's decisions in *J.E.B.* v. *Alabama ex rel. T. B.* and *Hogan* would be unobjectionable if the Court acknowledged that whether a "justification" is "exceedingly persuasive" must be assessed by asking "[whether] the classification serves important governmental objectives and [whether] the discriminatory means employed are substantially related to the achievement of those objectives." Instead, however, the Court proceeds to interpret "exceedingly persuasive justification" in a fashion that contradicts the reasoning of *Hogan* and our other precedents.

That is essential to the Court's result, which can only be achieved by establishing that intermediate scrutiny is not survived if there are *some* women interested in attending VMI, capable of undertaking its activities, and able to meet its physical demands. Thus, the Court summarizes its holding as follows:

In contrast to the generalizations about women on which Virginia rests, we note again these *dispositive* realities: VMI's implementing methodology is not *inherently* unsuitable to women; *some* women do well under the adversative model; *some* women, at least, would want to attend VMI if they had the opportunity; *some* women are capable of all of the individual activities required of VMI cadets and can meet the physical standards VMI now imposes on men. (internal quotation marks, citations, and punctuation omitted; emphasis added).

Similarly, the Court states that "[t]he Commonwealth's justification for excluding all women from 'citizen-soldier' training for which some are qualified . . . cannot rank as 'exceedingly persuasive'. . . ."

Only the amorphous "exceedingly persuasive justification" phrase, and not the standard elaboration of intermediate scrutiny, can be made to yield this conclusion that VMI's single-sex composition is unconstitutional because there exist several women (or, one would have to conclude under the Court's reasoning, a single woman) willing and able to undertake VMI's program. Intermediate scrutiny has never required a least-restrictive-means analysis, but only a "substantial relation" between the classification and the state interests that it serves. Thus, in *Califano* v. *Webster* (1977), we upheld a congressional statute that provided higher Social Security benefits for women than for men. We reasoned that "women . . . as such have been unfairly hindered from earning as much as men," but we did not require proof that each woman so benefited had suffered discrimination or that each disadvantaged man had not; it was sufficient that even under the former congressional scheme "women *on the average* received lower retirement benefits than men." (emphasis added). The reasoning in our other intermediate-scrutiny cases has similarly required only a substantial relation between end and means, not a perfect fit. In *Rostker*

v. *Goldberg* (1981), we held that selective-service registration could constitutionally exclude women, because even "assuming that a small number of women could be drafted for noncombat roles, Congress simply did not consider it worth the added burdens of including women in draft and registration plans." In *Metro Broadcasting, Inc.* v. *FCC* (1990), we held that a classification need not be accurate "in every case" to survive intermediate scrutiny so long as, "in the aggregate," it advances the underlying objective. There is simply no support in our cases for the notion that a sex-based classification is invalid unless it relates to characteristics that hold true in every instance.

Not content to execute a *de facto* abandonment of the intermediate scrutiny that has been our standard for sex-based classifications for some two decades, the Court purports to reserve the question whether, even in principle, a higher standard (*i.e.,* strict scrutiny) should apply. "The Court has," it says, "*thus far* reserved most stringent judicial scrutiny for classifications based on race or national origin . . ." (emphasis added); and it describes our earlier cases as having done no more than decline to "equat[e] gender classifications, *for all purposes,* to classifications based on race or national origin." (emphasis added). The wonderful thing about these statements is that they are not actually false—just as it would not be actually false to say that "our cases have thus far reserved the 'beyond a reasonable doubt' standard of proof for criminal cases," or that "we have not equated tort actions, for all purposes, to criminal prosecutions." But the statements are misleading, insofar as they suggest that we have not already categorically *held* strict scrutiny to be inapplicable to sex-based classifications. And the statements are irresponsible, insofar as they are calculated to destabilize current law. Our task is to clarify the law—not to muddy the waters, and not to exact overcompliance by intimidation. The States and the Federal Government are entitled to know *before they act* the standard to which they will be held, rather than be compelled to guess about the outcome of Supreme Court peek-a-boo.

The Court's intimations are particularly out of place because it is perfectly clear that, if the question of the applicable standard of review for sex-based classifications were to be regarded as an appropriate subject for reconsideration, the stronger argument would be not for elevating the standard to strict scrutiny, but for reducing it to rational-basis review. The latter certainly has a firmer foundation in our past jurisprudence: Whereas no majority of the Court has ever applied strict scrutiny in a case involving sex-based classifications, we routinely applied rational-basis review until the 1970s. And of course normal, rational-basis review of sex-based classifications would be much more in accord with the genesis of heightened standards of judicial review, the famous footnote in *United States v. Carolene Products Co.* (1938), which said (intimatingly) that we did not have to inquire in the case at hand:

> [W]hether prejudice against discrete and insular minorities may be a special condition, which tends seriously to curtail the operation of those political processes ordinarily to be relied upon to protect minorities, and which may call for a correspondingly more searching judicial inquiry.

The States and the Federal Government are entitled to know before they act the standard to which they will be held, rather than be compelled to guess about the outcome of Supreme Court peek-a-boo.

It is hard to consider women a "discrete and insular minority" unable to employ the "political processes ordinarily to be relied upon," when they constitute a majority of the electorate.

It is hard to consider women a "discrete and insular minorit[y]" unable to employ the "political processes ordinarily to be relied upon," when they constitute a majority of the electorate. And the suggestion that they are incapable of exerting that political power smacks of the same paternalism that the Court so roundly condemns. Moreover, a long list of legislation proves the proposition false. See, *e.g.,* Equal Pay Act of 1963; Title VII of the Civil Rights Act of 1964; Title IX of the Education Amendments of 1972; Women's Business Ownership Act of 1988; Violence Against Women Act of 1994.

III

With this explanation of how the Court has succeeded in making its analysis seem orthodox—and indeed, if intimations are to be believed, even overly generous to VMI—I now proceed to describe how the analysis should have been conducted. The question to be answered, I repeat, is whether the exclusion of women from VMI is "substantially related to an important governmental objective."

A

It is beyond question that Virginia has an important state interest in providing effective college education for its citizens. That single-sex instruction is an approach substantially related to that interest should be evident enough from the long and continuing history in this country of men's and women's colleges. But beyond that, as the Court of

Appeals here stated: "That single-gender education at the college level is beneficial to both sexes is a *fact established in this case*" (emphasis added).

The evidence establishing that fact was overwhelming—indeed, "virtually uncontradicted" in the words of the court that received the evidence. As an initial matter, Virginia demonstrated at trial that "[a] substantial body of contemporary scholarship and research supports the proposition that, although males and females have significant areas of developmental overlap, they also have differing developmental needs that are deep-seated." While no one questioned that for many students a coeducational environment was nonetheless not inappropriate, that could not obscure the demonstrated benefits of single-sex colleges. For example, the District Court stated as follows:

> One empirical study in evidence, not questioned by any expert, demonstrates that single-sex colleges provide better educational experiences than coeducational institutions. Students of both sexes become more academically involved, interact with faculty frequently, show larger increases in intellectual self-esteem and are more satisfied with practically all aspects of college experience (the sole exception is social life) compared with their counterparts in coeducational institutions. Attendance at an all-male college substantially increases the likelihood that a student will carry out career plans in law, business and college teaching, and also has a substantial positive effect on starting salaries in business. Women's colleges increase the chances that those who attend will obtain positions of leadership, complete the baccalaureate degree, and aspire to higher degrees.

"[I]n the light of this very substantial authority favoring single-sex education," the District Court concluded that "the VMI Board's decision to maintain an all-male institution is fully justified even without taking into consideration the other unique features of VMI's teaching and training." This finding alone, which even this Court cannot dispute, should be sufficient to demonstrate the constitutionality of VMI's all-male composition.

But besides its single-sex constitution, VMI is different from other colleges in another way. It employs a "distinctive educational method," sometimes referred to as the "adversative, or doubting, model of education." "Physical rigor, mental stress, absolute equality of treatment, absence of privacy, minute regulation of behavior, and indoctrination in desirable values are the salient attributes of the VMI educational experience." No one contends that this method is appropriate for all individuals; education is not a "one size fits all" business. Just as a State may wish to support junior colleges, vocational institutes, or a law school that emphasizes case practice instead of classroom study, so too a State's decision to maintain within its system one school that provides the adversative method is "substantially related" to its goal of good education. Moreover, it was uncontested that "if the state were to establish a women's VMI-type [*i.e.,* adversative] program, the program would attract an insufficient number of participants to make the program work" and it was found by the District Court that if Virginia were to include women in VMI, the school "would eventually find it necessary to drop the adversative system altogether." Thus, Virginia's options were an adversative method that excludes women or no adversative method at all.

There can be no serious dispute that, as the District Court found, single-sex education and a distinctive educational method "represent legitimate contributions to diversity in the Virginia higher education system." As a theoretical matter, Virginia's educational interest would have been *best* served (insofar as the two factors we have mentioned are concerned) by six different types of public colleges—an all-men's, an all-women's, and a coeducational college run in the "adversative method," and an all-men's, an all-women's, and a coeducational college run in the "traditional method." But as a practical matter, of course, Virginia's financial resources, like any State's, are not limitless, and the Commonwealth must select among the available options. Virginia thus has decided to fund, in addition to some 14 coeducational 4-year colleges, one college that is run as an all-male school on the adversative model: the Virginia Military Institute.

Virginia did not make this determination regarding the make-up of its public college system on the unrealistic assumption that no other colleges exist. Substantial evidence in the District Court demonstrated that the Commonwealth has long proceeded on the principle that " '[h]igher education resources should be viewed as a whole—public and private' "—because such an approach enhances diversity and because " 'it is academic and economic waste to permit unwarranted duplication.' " (quoting 1974 Report of the General Assembly Commission on Higher Education to the General Assembly of Virginia). It is thus significant that, whereas there are "four all-female private [colleges] in Virginia," there is only "one private all-male college," which "indicates that the private sector is providing for th[e] [former] form of education to a much greater extent that it provides for all-male education." In these circumstances, Virginia's election to fund one public all-male institution and one on the adversative model—and to concentrate its resources in a single entity that serves both these interests in diversity—is substantially related to the Commonwealth's important educational interests.

B

The Court today has no adequate response to this clear demonstration of the conclusion produced by application of intermediate scrutiny. Rather, it relies on a series of contentions that are irrelevant or erroneous as a matter of law, foreclosed by the record in this litigation, or both.

1. I have already pointed out the Court's most fundamental error, which is its reasoning that VMI's all-male composition is unconstitutional because "some women are capable of all of the individual activities required of VMI cadets" and would prefer military training on the adversative model. This unacknowledged adoption of what amounts to (at least) strict scrutiny is without antecedent in our sex-discrimination cases and by itself discredits the Court's decision.

2. The Court suggests that Virginia's claimed purpose in maintaining VMI as an all-male institution—its asserted interest in promoting diversity of educational options—is not "genuin[e]," but is a pretext for discriminating against women. To support this charge, the Court would have to impute that base motive to VMI's Mission Study Committee, which conducted a 3-year study from 1983 to 1986 and recommended to VMI's Board of Visitors that the school remain all male. The committee, a majority of whose members consisted of non-VMI graduates, "read materials on education and on women in the military," "made site visits to single-sex and newly coeducational institutions" including West Point and the Naval Academy, and "considered the reasons that other institutions had changed from single-sex to coeducational status"; its work was praised as "thorough" in the

accreditation review of VMI conducted by the Southern Association of Colleges and Schools. The Court states that "[w]hatever internal purpose the Mission Study Committee served—and however well meaning the framers of the report—we can hardly extract from that effort any Commonwealth policy evenhandedly to advance diverse educational options." But whether it is part of the evidence to prove that diversity *was* the Commonwealth's objective (its short report said nothing on that particular subject) is quite separate from whether it is part of the evidence to prove that anti-feminism *was not*. The relevance of the Mission Study Committee is that its very creation, its sober 3-year study, and the analysis it produced utterly refute the claim that VMI has elected to maintain its all-male student-body composition for some misogynistic reason.

The Court also supports its analysis of Virginia's "actual state purposes" in maintaining VMI's student body as all male by stating that there is no explicit statement in the record "'in which the Commonwealth has expressed itself'" concerning those purposes. That is wrong on numerous grounds. First and foremost, in its implication that such an explicit statement of "actual purposes" is needed. The Court adopts, in effect, the argument of the United States that since the exclusion of women from VMI in 1839 was based on the "assumptions" of the time "that men alone were fit for military and leadership roles," and since "[b]efore this litigation was initiated, Virginia never sought to supply a valid, contemporary rationale for VMI's exclusionary policy," "[t]hat failure itself renders the VMI policy invalid." This is an unheard-of doctrine. Each state decision to adopt or maintain a governmental policy need not be accompanied—in anticipation of litigation and on pain of being found to lack a relevant state interest—by a lawyer's contemporaneous recitation of the State's purposes. The

Constitution is not some giant Administrative Procedure Act, which imposes upon the States the obligation to set forth a "statement of basis and purpose" for their sovereign Acts. The situation would be different if what the Court assumes to have been the 1839 policy *had* been enshrined *and remained enshrined* in legislation—a VMI charter, perhaps, pronouncing that the institution's purpose is to keep women in their place. But since the 1839 policy was no more explicitly recorded than the Court contends the present one is, the mere fact that *today's* Commonwealth continues to fund VMI "is enough to answer [the United States'] contention that the [classification] was the 'accidental by-product of a traditional way of thinking about females.'" *Michael M.* (quoting *Califano*) (internal quotation marks omitted).

It is, moreover, not true that Virginia's contemporary reasons for maintaining VMI are not explicitly recorded. It is hard to imagine a more authoritative source on this subject than the 1990 Report of the Virginia Commission on the University of the 21st Century (1990 Report). As the parties stipulated, that report "notes that the hallmarks of Virginia's educational policy are 'diversity and autonomy.'" It said: "The formal system of higher education in Virginia includes a great array of institutions: state-supported and independent, two-year and senior, research and highly specialized, traditionally black *and single-sex.*" (emphasis added). The Court's only response to this is repeated reliance on the Court of Appeals' assertion that "'the only explicit [statement] that we have found in the record in which the Common-wealth has expressed itself with respect to gender distinctions'" (namely, the statement in the 1990 Report that the Commonwealth's institutions must "deal with faculty, staff, and students without regard to sex") had nothing to do with the purpose of diversity. This proves,

I suppose, that the Court of Appeals did not find a statement dealing with sex and diversity in the record; but the pertinent question (accepting the need for such a statement) is *whether it was there.* And the plain fact, which the Court does not deny, is that it *was.*

The Court contends that "[a] purpose genuinely to advance an array of educational options . . . is not served" by VMI. It relies on the fact that all of Virginia's *other* public colleges have become coeducational. The apparent theory of this argument is that unless Virginia pursues a great deal of diversity, its pursuit of some diversity must be a sham. This fails to take account of the fact that Virginia's resources cannot support all possible permutations of schools, and of the fact that Virginia coordinates its public educational offerings with the offerings of in-state private educational institutions that the Commonwealth provides money for its residents to attend and otherwise assists—which include four women's colleges.

The apparent theory of this argument is that unless Virginia pursues a great deal of diversity, its pursuit of some diversity must be a sham.

Finally, the Court unreasonably suggests that there is some pretext in Virginia's reliance upon decentralized decisionmaking to achieve diversity—its granting of substantial autonomy to each institution with regard to student-body composition and other matters. The Court adopts the suggestion of the Court of Appeals that it is not possible for "one institution with autonomy, but with no authority over any other state institution, [to] give effect to a state policy of diversity among institutions." (internal quotation marks omitted). If it were impossible for individual human beings (or groups of human beings) to act autonomously in effective pursuit of a common goal, the game of soccer would not exist. And where the goal is diversity in a free market for services, that tends to be achieved even by autonomous actors who act out of entirely selfish interests and make no effort to cooperate. Each Virginia institution, that is to say, has a natural incentive to make itself distinctive in order to attract a particular segment of student applicants. And of course none of the institutions is *entirely* autonomous; if and when the legislature decides that a particular school is not well serving the interest of diversity—if it decides, for example, that a men's school is not much needed—funding will cease.

If it were impossible for individual human beings (or groups of human beings) to act autonomously in effective pursuit of a common goal, the game of soccer would not exist.

[Footnote] The Court, unfamiliar with the Commonwealth's policy of diverse and independent institutions, and in any event careless of state and local traditions, must be forgiven by Virginians for quoting a reference to "'the Charlottesville campus'" of the University of Virginia. The University of Virginia, an institution even older than VMI, though not as old as another of the Commonwealth's universities, the College of William and Mary, occupies the portion of Charlottesville known, not as the "campus," but as "the grounds." More importantly, even if it were a "campus," there would be no need to specify "the Charlottesville campus," as one might refer to the Bloomington or Indianapolis campus of Indiana University. Unlike university systems with which the Court is perhaps more familiar, such as those in New York (*e.g.,* the State University of New York at Binghamton or Buffalo), Illinois (University of Illinois at Urbana-Champaign or at Chicago), and

California (University of California, Los Angeles, or University of California, Berkeley), there is only *one* University of Virginia. It happens (because Thomas Jefferson lived near there) to be located at Charlottesville. To many Virginians it is known, simply, as "the University," which suffices to distinguish it from the Commonwealth's other institutions offering 4-year college instruction. . . . .

3. In addition to disparaging Virginia's claim that VMI's single-sex status serves a state interest in diversity, the Court finds fault with Virginia's failure to offer education based on the adversative training method to women. It dismisses the District Court's "'findings' on 'gender-based developmental differences'" on the ground that "[t]hese 'findings' restate the opinions of Virginia's expert witnesses, opinions about typically male or typically female 'tendencies.'" How remarkable to criticize the District Court on the ground that its findings rest on the evidence (*i.e.,* the testimony of Virginia's witnesses)! That is what findings are supposed to do. It is indefensible to tell the Commonwealth that "[t]he burden of justification is demanding and it rests entirely on [you]," and then to ignore the District Court's findings *because* they rest on the evidence put forward by the Commonwealth—particularly when, as the District Court said, "[t]he evidence in the case . . . is *virtually uncontradicted,*" (emphasis added).

Ultimately, in fact, the Court does not deny the evidence supporting these findings. It instead makes evident that the parties to this litigation could have saved themselves a great deal of time, trouble, and expense by omitting a trial. The Court simply dispenses with the evidence submitted at trial—it never says that a single finding of the District Court is clearly erroneous—in favor of the Justices' own view of the world, which the Court proceeds to support with (1) references to observations of someone who is not a witness, nor even an educational expert, nor even a judge who reviewed the record or participated in the judgment below, but rather a judge who merely dissented from the Court of Appeals' decision not to rehear this litigation en banc, (2) citations of nonevidentiary materials such as *amicus curiae* briefs filed in this Court, and (3) various historical anecdotes designed to demonstrate that Virginia's support for VMI as currently constituted reminds the Justices of the "bad old days."

It is not too much to say that this approach to the litigation has rendered the trial a sham. But treating the evidence as irrelevant is absolutely necessary for the Court to reach its conclusion. Not a single witness contested, for example, Virginia's "substantial body of 'exceedingly persuasive' evidence . . . that some students, both male and female, benefit from attending a single-sex college" and "[that] [f]or those students, the opportunity to attend a single-sex college is a valuable one, likely to lead to better academic and professional achievement." Even the United States' expert witness "called himself a 'believer in single-sex education,'" although it was his "personal, philosophical preference," not one "born of educational-benefit considerations," "that single-sex education should be provided only by the private sector."

4. The Court contends that Virginia, and the District Court, erred, and "misperceived our precedent," by "train[ing] their argument on 'means' rather than 'end.'" The Court focuses on "VMI's mission," which is to produce individuals "imbued with love of learning, confident in the functions and attitudes of leadership, possessing a high sense of public service, advocates of the American democracy and free enterprise system, and ready . . . to defend their country in time of national peril." (quoting Mission Study Committee of the VMI Board

of Visitors, Report, May 16, 1986). "Surely," the Court says, "that goal is great enough to accommodate women."

This is lawmaking by indirection. What the Court describes as "VMI's mission" is no less the mission of *all* Virginia colleges. Which of them would the Old Dominion continue to fund if they did *not* aim to create individuals "imbued with love of learning, etc.," right down to being ready "to defend their country in time of national peril"? It can be summed up as "learning, leadership, and patriotism." To be sure, those general educational values are described in a particularly martial fashion in VMI's mission statement, in accordance with the military, adversative, and all-male character of the institution. But imparting those values *in that fashion*—i.e., in a military, adversative, all-male environment—is the *distinctive* mission of VMI. And as I have discussed (and both courts below found), *that* mission is *not* "great enough to accommodate women."

The Court's analysis at least has the benefit of producing foreseeable results. Applied generally, it means that whenever a State's ultimate objective is "great enough to accommodate women" (as it always will be), then the State will be held to have violated the Equal Protection Clause if it restricts to men even one means by which it pursues that objective—no matter how few women are interested in pursuing the objective by that means, no matter how much the single-sex program will have to be changed if both sexes are admitted, and no matter how beneficial that program has theretofore been to its participants.

5. The Court argues that VMI would not have to change very much if it were to admit women. The principal response to that argument is that it is irrelevant: If VMI's single-sex status is substantially related to the government's important educational objectives, as I have demonstrated above and as the Court refuses to discuss, that concludes

the inquiry. There should be no debate in the federal judiciary over "how much" VMI would be required to change if it admitted women and whether that would constitute "too much" change.

But if such a debate were relevant, the Court would certainly be on the losing side. The District Court found as follows: "[T]he evidence establishes that key elements of the adversative VMI educational system, with its focus on barracks life, would be fundamentally altered, and the distinctive ends of the system would be thwarted, if VMI were forced to admit females and to make changes necessary to accommodate their needs and interests." Changes that the District Court's detailed analysis found would be required include new allowances for personal privacy in the barracks, such as locked doors and coverings on windows, which would detract from VMI's approach of regulating minute details of student behavior, "contradict the principle that everyone is constantly subject to scrutiny by everyone else," and impair VMI's "total egalitarian approach" under which every student must be "treated alike";

The Court argues that VMI would not have to change very much if it were to admit women. The principal response to that argument is that it is irrelevant.

changes in the physical training program, which would reduce "[t]he intensity and aggressiveness of the current program"; and various modifications in other respects of the adversative training program that permeates student life. As the Court of Appeals summarized it, "the record supports the district court's findings that at least these three aspects of VMI's program—physical training, the absence of privacy, and the adversative approach—would be materially affected by coeducation, leading to a substantial change in the egalitarian ethos that is a critical aspect of VMI's training."

In the face of these findings by two courts below, amply supported by the evidence, and resulting in the conclusion that VMI would be fundamentally altered if it admitted women, this Court simply pronounces that "[t]he notion that admission of women would downgrade VMI's stature, destroy the adversative system and, with it, even the school, is a judgment hardly proved." The point about "downgrad[ing] VMI's stature" is a straw man; no one has made any such claim. The point about "destroy[ing] the adversative system" is simply false; the District Court not only stated that "[e]vidence supports this theory," but specifically concluded that while "[w]ithout a doubt" VMI could assimilate women, "it is equally without a doubt that VMI's present methods of training and education would have to be changed" by a "move away from its adversative new cadet system." And the point about "destroy[ing] the school," depending upon what that ambiguous phrase is intended to mean, is either false or else sets a standard much higher than VMI had to meet. It sufficed to establish, as the District Court stated, that VMI would be "significantly different" upon the admission of women and "would eventually find it necessary to drop the adversative system altogether."

6. Finally, the absence of a precise "all-women's analogue" to VMI is irrelevant. In *Mississippi Univ. for Women* v. *Hogan*, we attached no constitutional significance to the absence of an all-male nursing school. As Virginia notes, if a program restricted to one sex is necessarily unconstitutional unless there is a parallel program restricted to the other sex, "the opinion in *Hogan* could have ended with its first footnote, which observed that 'Mississippi maintains no other single-sex public university or college.'"

Although there is no precise female-only analogue to VMI, Virginia has created during this litigation the Virginia Women's Institute for Leadership (VWIL), a state-funded all-women's program run by Mary Baldwin College. I have thus far said nothing about VWIL because it is, under our established test, irrelevant, so long as *VMI's* all-male character is "substantially related" to an important state goal. But VWIL now exists, and the Court's treatment of it shows how far reaching today's decision is.

VWIL was carefully designed by professional educators who have long experience in educating young women. The program *rejects* the proposition that there is a "difference in the respective spheres and destinies of man and woman," *Bradwell* v. *State* (1873), and is designed to "provide an all-female program that will achieve substantially similar outcomes [to VMI's] in an all-female environment." After holding a trial where voluminous evidence was submitted and making detailed findings of fact, the District Court concluded that "there is a legitimate pedagogical basis for the different means employed [by VMI and VWIL] to achieve the substantially similar ends." The Court of Appeals undertook a detailed review of the record and affirmed. But it is Mary Baldwin College, which runs VWIL, that has made the point most succinctly:

> It would have been possible to develop the VWIL program to more closely resemble VMI, with adversative techniques associated with the rat line and barracks-like living quarters. Simply replicating an existing program would have required far less thought, research, and educational expertise. But such a facile approach would have produced a paper program with no real prospect of successful implementation.
>
> BRIEF FOR MARY BALDWIN COLLEGE

It is worth noting that none of the United States' own experts in the remedial phase of this litigation was willing to testify that VMI's adversative method was an appropriate methodology for educating women. This Court, however, does not care. Even though VWIL was carefully designed by professional educators who have tremendous experience in the area, and survived the test of adversarial litigation, the Court simply declares, with no basis in the evidence, that these professionals acted on " 'overbroad' generalizations."

C

A few words are appropriate in response to the concurrence, which finds VMI unconstitutional on a basis that is more moderate than the Court's but only at the expense of being even more implausible. The concurrence offers three reasons: First, that there is "scant evidence in the record" that diversity of educational offering was the real reason for Virginia's maintaining VMI. "Scant" has the advantage of being an imprecise term. I have cited the clearest statements of diversity as a goal for higher education in the 1990 Report, the 1989 Virginia Plan for Higher Education, the Budget Initiatives prepared in 1989 by the State Council of Higher Education for Virginia, the 1974 Report of the General Assembly Commission on Higher Education to the General Assembly of Virginia, and the 1969 Report of the Virginia Commission on Constitutional Revision. There is *no* evidence to the contrary, once one rejects (as the concurrence rightly does) the relevance of VMI's founding in days when attitude towards the education of women were different. Is this conceivably not enough to foreclose rejecting as clearly erroneous the District Court's determination regarding "the Commonwealth's objective of educational diversity"? Especially since it is absurd on its face even to *demand* "evidence" to prove that the Commonwealth's reason for maintaining a men's military academy is that a men's military academy provides a distinctive type of educational experience (*i.e.,* fosters diversity). What other purpose *would* the Commonwealth have? One may argue, as the Court does, that this *type* of diversity is designed only to indulge hostility toward women—but that is a separate point, explicitly rejected by the concurrence, and amply refuted by the evidence I have mentioned in discussing the Court's opinion. What is now under discussion—the concurrence's making central to the disposition of this litigation the supposedly "scant" evidence that Virginia maintained VMI in order to offer a diverse educational experience—is rather like making crucial to the lawfulness of the United States Army record "evidence" that its purpose is to do battle. A legal culture that has forgotten the concept of *res ipsa loquitur* ["the thing speaks for itself"] deserves the fate that it today decrees for VMI.

> *A legal culture that has forgotten the concept of res ipsa loquitur [the thing speaks for itself] deserves the fate that it today decrees for VMI.*

Second, the concurrence dismisses out of hand what it calls Virginia's "second justification for the single-sex admissions policy: maintenance of the adversative method." The concurrence reasons that "this justification does not serve an important governmental objective" because, whatever the record may show about the pedagogical benefits of *single-sex* education, "there is no similar evidence in the record that an adversative method is pedagogically beneficial or is any more likely to produce character traits than other methodologies." That is simply wrong. In reality, the pedagogical benefits of VMI's adversative approach were not only proved, but were a *given* in this litigation. The reason the woman applicant who prompted this suit wanted to enter VMI was assuredly not that she wanted to go to an all-male school; it would cease being all-male as soon as she entered. She wanted the distinctive adversative education that VMI provided, and the battle was joined (in the main) over whether VMI had a basis for excluding women from that approach. The Court's opinion recognizes this, and devotes much of its opinion to demonstrating that "'some women ... do well under [the] adversative model'" and that "[i]t is on behalf of these women that the United States has instituted this suit." Of course, in the last analysis it does not matter whether there are any benefits to the adversative method. The concurrence does not contest that there are benefits to *single-sex* education, and that alone suffices to make Virginia's case, since admission of a woman will even more surely put an end to VMI's single-sex education than it will to VMI's adversative methodology.

A third reason the concurrence offers in support of the judgment is that the Commonwealth and VMI were not quick enough to react to the "further developments" in this Court's evolving jurisprudence. Specifically, the concurrence believes it should have been clear after *Hogan* that "[t]he difficulty with [Virginia's] position is that the diversity benefited only one sex; there was single-sex public education available for men at VMI, but no corresponding single-sex public education available for women." If only, the concurrence asserts, Virginia had "made a genuine effort to devote comparable public resources to a facility for women, and followed through on such a plan, it might well have avoided an equal protection violation." That is to say, the concurrence believes that after our decision in *Hogan* (which held a program of the Mississippi University for Women to be unconstitutional—without any reliance on the fact that there was no corresponding Mississippi all-men's program), the Commonwealth should have known that what this Court expected of it was . . . yes!, the creation of a state all-women's program. Any lawyer who gave that advice to the Commonwealth ought to have been either disbarred or committed. (The proof of that pudding is today's 6-Justice majority opinion.) And any Virginia politician who proposed such a step when there were already four 4-year women's colleges in Virginia (assisted by state support that may well exceed, in the aggregate, what VMI costs) ought to have been recalled.

In any event, "diversity in the form of single-sex, as well as coeducational, institutions of higher learning" *is* "available to women as well as to men" in Virginia. The concurrence is able to assert the contrary only by disregarding the four all-women's private colleges in Virginia (generously assisted by public funds) and the Commonwealth's longstanding policy of coordinating public with private educational offerings. According to the concurrence, the *reason* Virginia's assistance to its four all-women's private colleges does not count is that "[t]he private women's colleges are treated by the State *exactly* as all other private schools are treated." But if Virginia cannot get *credit* for assisting women's education if it only treats women's private schools as it does all other private schools, then why should it get *blame* for assisting men's education if it only treats VMI as it does all other public schools? This is a great puzzlement.

IV

As is frequently true, the Court's decision today will have consequences that extend far beyond the parties to the litigation. What I

take to be the Court's unease with these consequences, and its resulting unwillingness to acknowledge them, cannot alter the reality.

A

Under the constitutional principles announced and applied today, single-sex public education is unconstitutional. By going through the
motions of applying a balancing test—asking whether the State has
adduced an "exceedingly persuasive justification" for its sex-based classification—the Court creates the illusion that government officials in
some future case will have a clear shot at justifying some sort of single-sex public education. Indeed, the Court seeks to create even a
greater illusion than that: It purports to have said nothing of relevance
to *other* public schools at all. "We address specifically and only an educational opportunity recognized...as 'unique'."

The Supreme Court of the United States does not sit to announce
"unique" dispositions. Its principal function is to establish *precedent*—
that is, to set forth principles of law that every court in America must
follow. As we said only this Term, we expect both ourselves and
lower courts to adhere to the "*rationale* upon which the Court based
the results of its earlier decisions." *Seminole Tribe of Fla* v. *Florida*
(1996) (emphasis added). That is the principal reason we publish our
opinions.

And the rationale of today's decision is sweeping: for sex-based
classifications, a redefinition of intermediate scrutiny that makes it
indistinguishable from strict scrutiny. Indeed, the Court indicates that
if any program restricted to one sex is "uniqu[e]," it must be opened
to members of the opposite sex "who have the will and capacity" to
participate in it. I suggest that the single-sex program that will not be

capable of being characterized as "unique" is not only unique but nonexistent.

[Footnote] In this regard, I note that the Court—which I concede is under no obligation to do so—provides no example of a program that *would* pass muster under its reasoning today: not even, for example, a football or wrestling program. On the Court's theory, any woman ready, willing, and physically able to participate in such a program would, *as a constitutional matter,* be entitled to do so.

In any event, regardless of whether the Court's rationale leaves some small amount of room for lawyers to argue, it ensures that single-sex public education is functionally dead. The costs of litigating the constitutionality of a single-sex education program, and the risks of ultimately losing that litigation, are simply too high to be embraced by public officials. Any person with standing to challenge any sex-based classification can haul the State into federal court and compel it to establish by evidence (presumably in the form of expert testimony) that there is an "exceedingly persuasive justification" for the classification. Should the courts happen to interpret that vacuous phrase as establishing a standard that is not utterly impossible of achievement, there is considerable risk that whether the standard has been met will not be determined on the basis of the record evidence—indeed, that will necessarily be the approach of any court that seeks to walk the path the Court has trod today. No state official in his right mind will buy such a high-cost, high-risk lawsuit by commencing a single-sex program. The enemies of single-sex education have won; by persuading only seven Justices (five would have been enough) that their view of the world is enshrined in the Constitution, they have effectively imposed that view on all 50 States.

This is especially regrettable because, as the District Court here determined, educational experts in recent years have increasingly come to "suppor[t] [the] view that substantial educational benefits flow from a single-gender environment, be it male or female, *that cannot be replicated in a coeducational setting.*" (emphasis added). "The evidence in th[is] case," for example, "is virtually uncontradicted" to that effect. Until quite recently, some public officials have attempted to institute new single-sex programs, at least as experiments. In 1991, for example, the Detroit Board of Education announced a program to establish three boys-only schools for inner-city youth; it was met with a lawsuit, a preliminary injunction was swiftly entered by a District Court that purported to rely on *Hogan* and the Detroit Board of Education voted to abandon the litigation and thus abandon the plan. Today's opinion assures that no such experiment will be tried again.

B

There are few extant single-sex public educational programs. The potential of today's decision for widespread disruption of existing institutions lies in its application to *private* single-sex education. Government support is immensely important to private educational institutions. Mary Baldwin College—which designed and runs VWIL—notes that private institutions of higher education in the 1990–1991 school year derived approximately 19 percent of their budgets from federal, state, and local government funds, *not including financial aid to students.* Charitable status under the tax laws is also highly significant for private educational institutions, and it is certainly not beyond the

Court that rendered today's decision to hold that a donation to a single-sex college should be deemed contrary to public policy and therefore not deductible if the college discriminates on the basis of sex.

The Court adverts to private single-sex education only briefly, and only to make the assertion (mentioned above) that "[w]e address specifically and only an educational opportunity recognized by the District Court and the Court of Appeals as 'unique.'" As I have already remarked, that assurance assures nothing, unless it is to be taken as a promise that in the future the Court will disclaim the reasoning it has used today to destroy VMI. The Government, in its briefs to this Court, at least purports to address the consequences of its attack on VMI for public support of private single-sex education. It contends that private colleges that are the direct or indirect beneficiaries of government funding are not thereby necessarily converted into state actors to which the Equal Protection Clause is then applicable. That is true. It is also virtually meaningless.

The issue will be not whether government assistance turns private colleges into state actors, but whether the government *itself* would be violating the Constitution by providing state support to single-sex colleges. For example, in *Norwood* v. *Harrison* (1973), we saw no room to distinguish between state operation of racially segregated schools and state support of privately run segregated schools. "Racial discrimination in state-operated schools is barred by the Constitution and '[i]t is also axiomatic that a state may not induce, encourage or promote private persons to accomplish what it is constitutionally forbidden to accomplish.'" *Id.* When the Government was pressed at oral argument concerning the implications of these cases for private single-sex education if government-provided single-sex education is unconstitutional, it stated that the implications will not be so disastrous, since

States *can* provide funding to *racially* segregated private schools, "depend[ing] on the circumstances." I cannot imagine what those "circumstances" might be, and it would be as foolish for private-school administrators to think that that assurance from the Justice Department will outlive the day it was made, as it was for VMI to think that the Justice Department's "unequivoca[l]" support for an intermediate-scrutiny standard in this litigation would survive the Government's loss in the courts below.

The only hope for state-assisted single-sex private schools is that the Court will not apply in the future the principles of law it has applied today. That is a substantial hope, I am happy and ashamed to say. After all, did not the Court today abandon the principles of law it has applied in our earlier sex-classification cases? And does not the Court positively invite private colleges to rely upon our ad-hocery by assuring them this litigation is "unique"? I would not advise the foundation of any new single-sex college (especially an all-male one) with the expectation of being allowed to receive any government support; but it is too soon to abandon in despair those single-sex colleges already in existence. It will certainly be possible for this Court to write a future opinion that ignores the broad principles of law set forth today, and that characterizes as utterly dispositive the opinion's perceptions that VMI was a uniquely prestigious all-male institution, conceived in chauvinism, etc., etc. I will not join that opinion.

Justice Brandeis said it is "one of the happy incidents of the federal system that a single courageous State may, if its citizens choose, serve as a laboratory; and try novel social and economic experiments without risk to the rest of the country." *New State Ice Co.* v. *Liebmann* (1932) (dissenting opinion). But it is one of the unhappy incidents of the federal system that a self-righteous Supreme Court, acting on its Members' personal view of what would make a "'more perfect Union,'" (a criterion only slightly more restrictive than a "more perfect world"), can impose its own favored social and economic dispositions nationwide. As today's disposition, and others this single Term, show, this places it beyond the power of a "single courageous State," not only to introduce novel dispositions that the Court frowns upon, but to reintroduce, or indeed even adhere to, disfavored dispositions that are centuries old. The sphere of self-government reserved to the people of the Republic is progressively narrowed.

It is one of the unhappy incidents of the federal system that a self-righteous Supreme Court, acting on its Members' personal view of what would make a "more perfect Union," (a criterion only slightly more restrictive than a "more perfect world"), can impose its own favored social and economic dispositions nationwide.

In the course of this dissent, I have referred approvingly to the opinion of my former colleague, Justice Powell, in *Mississippi Univ. for Women* v. *Hogan.* Many of the points made in his dissent apply with equal force here—in particular, the criticism of judicial opinions that purport to be "narro[w]" but whose "logic" is "sweepin[g]." But there is one statement with which I cannot agree. Justice Powell observed that the Court's decision in *Hogan,* which struck down a single-sex program offered by the Mississippi University for Women, had thereby "[l]eft without honor...an element of diversity that has characterized much of American education and enriched much of American life." Today's decision does not leave VMI without honor; no court opinion can do that.

In an odd sort of way, it is precisely VMI's attachment to such old-fashioned concepts as manly "honor" that has made it, and the system it represents, the target of those who today succeed in abolishing public single-sex education. The record contains a booklet that all first-year VMI students (the so-called "rats") were required to keep in their possession at all times. Near the end there appears the following period piece, entitled "The Code of a Gentleman": "Without a strict observance of the fundamental Code of Honor, no man, no matter how 'polished,' can be considered a gentleman. The honor of a gentleman demands the inviolability of his word, and the incorruptibility of his principles. He is the descendant of the knight, the crusader; he is the defender of the defenseless and the champion of justice . . . or he is not a Gentleman. "A Gentleman . . . Does not discuss his family affairs in public or with acquaintances . . . Does not speak more than casually about his girl friend."

"Does not go to a lady's house if he is affected by alcohol. He is temperate in the use of alcohol. Does not lose his temper; nor exhibit anger, fear, hate, embarrassment, ardor or hilarity in public. Does not hail a lady from a club window. A gentleman never discusses the merits or demerits of a lady. Does not mention names exactly as he avoids the mention of what things cost. Does not borrow money from a friend, except in dire need. Money borrowed is a debt of honor, and must be repaid as promptly as possible. Debts incurred by a deceased parent, brother, sister or grown child are assumed by honorable men as a debt of honor. Does not display his wealth, money or possessions. Does not put his manners on and off, whether in the club or in a ball-room. He treats people with courtesy, no matter what their social position may be. Does not slap strangers on the back nor so much as lay a finger on a lady. Does not 'lick the boots of those above' nor 'kick the face of those below him on the social ladder.' Does not take advantage of another's helplessness or ignorance and assumes that no gentleman will take advantage of him."

"A Gentleman respects the reserves of others, but demands that others respect those which are his. A Gentleman can become what he wills to be. . . ." I do not know whether the men of VMI lived by this code; perhaps not. But it is powerfully impressive that a public institution of higher education still in existence sought to have them do so. I do not think any of us, women included, will be better off for its destruction.

CHAPTER NINE

FREE SPEECH

"CONGRESS SHALL MAKE NO LAW abridging the freedom of speech." Many Americans cherish the First Amendment's protection of freedom of speech more than any other liberty in the Bill of Rights. It was written into the Constitution by a generation of Americans that did not always permit or enjoy the full exercise of that freedom. Yet the Framers believed that truth—so necessary for enlightened self-government—would best be served by competition in a "marketplace of ideas."[1]

That marketplace has grown over the years. The First Amendment has been extended by federal courts to cover nude dancing, shouting obscenities, flag burning, pornography, and even refusing to wear a necktie.[2] Although some doubt whether the First Amendment was meant to cover such "speech," no one doubts that a fundamental purpose of the First Amendment was the protection of political speech. Indeed, political speech is said to lie at the heart of the First Amendment.

Justice Scalia has supported efforts to protect traditional speech. He has also supported protection of expressive activity when government laws sought to limit that activity solely because of its communicative aspect. The clearest example of this was his vote to strike down a federal law criminalizing the destruction of the American flag. Scalia joined the Court's opinion in *U.S.* v. *Eichman* (1990), which held the law was aimed directly and unconstitutionally at suppressing a manner of communicating opposition to the U.S. government and its policies.

Although Scalia has not been as willing as his colleagues to protect some categories of speech—pornography, to name one—he has forcefully defended two clear (but unpopular) exercises of First Amendment rights: election-related speech and anti-abortion protest. Scalia has said the Court uses an "ad hoc nullification machine" to eliminate its normal constitutional analyses whenever the issue before it involves abortion.

In *Hill* v. *Colorado* (2000), the Court upheld a Colorado law that prohibited any person from approaching within eight feet of another person near a health care facility without that person's consent.[3] Although the Court is normally hostile to prior restraints on speech, the Court said the restriction was valid because it was narrowly tailored, as required by its precedents, to advance the State's interest in protecting its citizens' rights to be let alone from unwanted speech.

Though the Court said the statute did not regulate content of speech, Scalia noted that statute specifically targeted "oral protest," "counseling," and "education" outside medical clinics, making clear that silencing anti-abortion protest was the objective of the law. Scalia said, "I have no doubt this regulation would be deemed content based in an instant if the case before us involved antiwar protesters, or union members seeking to 'educate' the public about the reasons for their strike."[4] In addition to challenging the law's purpose, Scalia attacked the Court's finding that the law was narrowly tailored to serve the state's interest. He wrote, "[I]f protecting people from unwelcome communications . . . is a compelling state interest, the First Amendment is a dead letter. And if . . . forbidding peaceful, nonthreatening, but uninvited speech from a distance closer than eight feet is a 'narrowly tailored' means of preventing the obstruction of entrance to medical facilities, . . . the narrow tailoring must refer not to the standards of Versace, but to those of Omar the tentmaker."[5]

The Court decided *Hill* on the same day it issued its opinion in *Stenberg* v. *Carhart*. In *Stenberg*, the Court invalidated Nebraska's law banning partial-birth abortions (see chapter five). Scalia said that since abortion—"even abortion of a live-and-kicking child"—was removed from the democratic process by the Court, the only way anti-abortion advocates can have a voice is to persuade individuals of the rightness of their views. The *Hill* decision, he said, made even that effort more difficult. Scalia concluded:

Does the deck seem stacked? You bet. . . . [T]oday's decision is not an isolated distortion of our traditional constitutional principles, but is one of many aggressively proabortion novelties announced by the Court in recent years. Today's distortions, however, are particularly blatant. Restrictive views of the First Amendment that have been in dissent since the 1930s suddenly find themselves in the majority. "Uninhibited, robust, and wide open" debate is replaced by the power of the State to protect an unheard-of "right to be left alone" on the public streets.[6]

Scalia has also fought to protect the freedom of individuals, groups, and corporations to participate in political campaigns. Specifically, he has argued that campaign contributions and expenditures are too closely associated with protected political speech to be regulated by the government without a showing of compelling interest in limiting them. And trying to create a "level playing field," Scalia has argued, is not compelling. In a 1990 case involving Michigan's ban on corporate contributions, Scalia wrote:

> Perhaps the Michigan law before us here has an unqualifiedly noble objective—to equalize the political debate by preventing disproportionate expression of corporations' point of view. But governmental abridgement of liberty is always undertaken with the very best of announced objectives (dictators promise to bring order, not tyranny), and often with the very best of genuinely intended objectives (zealous policemen conduct unlawful searches in order to put dangerous felons behind bars). The premise of our Bill of Rights, however, is that there are some things—even some seemingly desirable things—that government cannot be trusted to do. The very first of these is establishing restrictions upon speech that will assure "fair" political debate.[7]

Because Scalia believes political speech is at the core of the First Amendment, he is very skeptical of any legislative effort to limit election-related speech. Of course, there are some who do not think limiting the amount of money an individual or corporate entity can contribute to a campaign, or prohibiting some sources from contributing at all, is a significant limitation on speech protected by the First Amendment. In addition, some think that the large amounts of money spent on campaigns alone creates at least an "appearance of corruption" that must be fixed in order to preserve the integrity of our democratic government. These forces were behind the law that was challenged in *McConnell* v. *Federal Election Commission* (2003).

MCCONNELL v. FEDERAL
ELECTION COMMISSION (2003)

In response to the widely condemned abuses of the 1972 presidential election, Congress in 1974 passed an amendment to strengthen the Federal Election Campaign Act of 1971. Both the 1971 law and 1974 amendment were designed to provide greater regulation of the system of financing federal campaigns. The new laws had numerous features, including creation of the Federal Election Commission, new limits on the amounts that could be contributed to and spent by candidates, and a voluntary system of public financing for presidential campaigns.

After a challenge to the laws' constitutionality, the Supreme Court in its landmark *Buckley* v. *Valeo* (1976) decision upheld parts of the regulatory regime, including limits on contributions to candidates, and invalidated others. The Court said that campaign fundraising and spending involved First Amendment freedoms and therefore could only be limited if the government had a compelling purpose and the regulation was narrowly tailored to serve that purpose. The Court ruled that limiting the amount of money that could be given directly to a candidate was justified as a way of reducing corruption or the appearance of corruption that might arise from making a large donation of money.

Congress and the Court left donations from individuals and corporations to national political parties unregulated because the fear of corruption was not as great; the parties were barred from using unregulated money to directly benefit candidates. The contributions were used for party-building activities, get-out-the vote efforts, and issue advocacy. With limits on direct giving upheld, the unregulated contributions to the parties—known commonly as "soft money"—began to grow in size and number. Some Members of Congress and so-called good government groups began to complain that these large contributions were corrupting the legislative process. They pointed to the fact that soft money was sometimes solicited by the parties with lures of access to Members of Congress. If the system was not corrupt, it sure looked like it, they argued.

In 2002, Congress passed the Bipartisan Campaign Finance Reform Act (BCRA).[8] The law was very complex, but had two major features. The first was a ban on soft money. The second was regulation of "issue advocacy." Issue advocacy, as its name suggests, refers to advertising designed to call attention to one or more public policy issues. Sponsors of issue ads were not required by law to disclose the names of their donors or the amount they spent on such ads. Only advertisements that specifically urged listeners or viewers to support or oppose a candidate were regulated.

Because issue ads began to closely resemble candidate ads—the ads might say, "Pollution is killing children. Senator Jones supports pollution. Call Senator Jones and tell him to save our children by opposing pollution"—Congress thought the ads should be more tightly regulated. In order to address the ads most likely intended to influence an election, Congress decided to ban issue ads that mention a candidate's name during the sixty days before any general election. This provision was very controversial because it would serve to muffle groups that truly wished to educate voters about a politician's record at the most effective time, the days preceding the election. A diverse group of politically active associations ranging from the AFL-CIO to the National Rifle Association argued that BCRA abridged their First Amendment rights.

The Supreme Court in 2003 narrowly voted to uphold both main provisions of the Act. The Court said new evidence helped to establish that enormous soft-money contributions, especially from corporations, had a corrosive effect on the legislative process and citizens' confidence in the integrity of their government. Combating that corrosion represented a compelling government interest, and prohibiting these donations was deemed a legitimate means, the Court said.

Scalia joined three dissenting opinions that largely argued that the Court's opinion was not faithful to the text and spirit of the First Amendment, nor to the Court's own precedents. In his separate dissent, Scalia did not go deep into the weeds about the Court's constitutional analyses of each provision of BCRA. Instead, he expressed confusion that the Court, which in recent years had wrapped a constitutional blanket around "virtual child pornography" and other "inconsequential forms of expression," did not in *McConnell* protect speech "the First Amendment is meant to protect: the right to criticize the government."

He then attacked three "fallacious propositions" upon which BCRA was premised and which, he said, were accepted by the Court. Scalia's opinion—especially his argument concerning the amount of money spent on elections—is a good example of his willingness to challenge the Court's majority when it advances a policy argument to limit a freedom that is explicitly protected by the Constitution. Disputing the claim that there is too much money spent on politics, Scalia wrote, "If our democracy is drowning from this much spending, it cannot swim."

Scalia said the motivation behind BCRA and the resulting litigation is suppression of speech that criticizes the government. He argued that some members of Congress might be motivated by a noble purpose, but since others might merely wish to avoid criticism, the course most faithful to the First Amendment is "to assume the worst, and to rule the regulation of political speech 'for fairness' sake' simply out of bounds." Scalia concluded by predicting that Congress would enact additional measures to limit spending and speech in the future, and that the Court's decision in *McConnell* would make it difficult, if not impossible, to rescue the First Amendment by striking down those future measures.

~≈◎❀◎≈~

JUSTICE SCALIA, CONCURRING WITH RESPECT TO BCRA TITLES III AND IV, DISSENTING WITH RESPECT TO BCRA TITLES I AND V, AND CONCURRING IN THE JUDGMENT IN PART AND DISSENTING IN PART WITH RESPECT TO BCRA TITLE II.

. . . This is a sad day for the freedom of speech. Who could have imagined that the same Court which, within the past four years, has sternly disapproved of restrictions upon such inconsequential forms of expression as virtual child pornography, tobacco advertising, dissemination of illegally intercepted communications, and sexually explicit cable programming, would smile with favor upon a law that cuts to the heart of what the First Amendment is meant to protect: the right to criticize the government. For that is what the most offensive provisions of this legislation are all about. We are governed by Congress, and this legislation prohibits the criticism of Members of Congress by those entities most capable of giving such criticism loud voice: national political parties and corporations, both of the commercial and the not-for-profit sort. It forbids pre-election criticism of incumbents by corporations, even not-for-profit corporations, by use of their general funds; and forbids national-party use of "soft" money to fund "issue ads" that incumbents find so offensive.

To be sure, the legislation is evenhanded: It similarly prohibits criticism of the candidates who oppose Members of Congress in their reelection bids. But as everyone knows, this is an area in which evenhandedness is not fairness. If *all* electioneering were evenhandedly prohibited, incumbents would have an enormous advantage. Likewise, if incumbents and challengers are limited to the same quantity of electioneering, incumbents are favored. In other words, *any* restriction upon a type of campaign speech that is equally available to challengers and incumbents tends to favor incumbents.

Beyond that, however, the present legislation *targets* for prohibition certain categories of campaign speech that are particularly harmful to incumbents. Is it accidental, do you think, that incumbents raise about three times as much "hard money"—the sort of funding generally *not* restricted by this legislation—as do their challengers? Or that lobbyists (who seek the favor of incumbents) give 92 percent of their money in "hard" contributions? Is it an oversight, do you sup-

pose, that the so-called "millionaire provisions" raise the contribution
limit for a candidate running against an individual who devotes to the
campaign (as challengers often do) great personal wealth, but do not
raise the limit for a candidate running against
an individual who devotes to the campaign (as
incumbents often do) a massive election "war
chest"? And is it mere happenstance, do you
estimate, that national-party funding, which is
severely limited by the Act, is more likely to
assist cash-strapped challengers than flush-
with-hard-money incumbents? Was it unin-
tended, by any chance, that incumbents are free
personally to receive some soft money and
even to solicit it for other organizations, while
national parties are not?

*Is it mere happenstance,
do you estimate, that
national-party funding,
which is severely limited
by the Act, is more likely
to assist cash-strapped
challengers than flush-
with-hard-money
incumbents?*

  I wish to address three fallacious propositions
that might be thought to justify some or all of
the provisions of this legislation—only the last of which is explicitly
embraced by the principal opinion for the Court, but all of which
underlie, I think, its approach to these cases.

(A) Money is Not Speech

It was said by congressional proponents of this legislation, with support from the law reviews, that since this legislation regulates nothing
but the expenditure of money for speech, as opposed to speech itself,
the burden it imposes is not subject to full First Amendment scrutiny;
the government may regulate the raising and spending of campaign
funds just as it regulates other forms of conduct, such as burning draft
cards or camping out on the National Mall. That proposition has been

endorsed by one of the two authors of today's principal opinion:"The right to use one's own money to hire gladiators, [and] to fund 'speech by proxy,'... [are] property rights ... not entitled to the same protection as the right to say what one pleases." *Nixon* v. *Shrink Missouri Government PAC* (2000) (Stevens, J., concurring). Until today, however, that view has been categorically rejected by our jurisprudence. As we said in *Buckley* v. *Valeo* (1976), "this Court has never suggested that the dependence of a communication on the expenditure of money operates itself to introduce a nonspeech element or to reduce the exacting scrutiny required by the First Amendment."

Our traditional view was correct, and today's cavalier attitude toward regulating the financing of speech (the "exacting scrutiny" test of *Buckley* is not uttered in any majority opinion, and is not observed in the ones from which I dissent) frustrates the fundamental purpose of the First Amendment. In any economy operated on even the most rudimentary principles of division of labor, effective public communication requires the speaker to make use of the services of others. An author may write a novel, but he will seldom publish and distribute it himself. A freelance reporter may write a story, but he will rarely edit, print, and deliver it to subscribers. To a government bent on suppressing speech, this mode of organization presents opportunities: Control any cog in the machine, and you can halt the whole apparatus. License printers, and it matters little whether authors are still free to write. Restrict the sale of books, and it matters little who prints them. Predictably, repressive regimes have exploited these principles by attacking all levels of the production and dissemination of ideas. See, *e.g.*, Printing Act of 1662 (punishing printers, importers, and booksellers); Printing Act of 1649 (punishing authors, printers, booksellers, importers, and buyers). In response to this threat, we have interpreted the First Amendment broadly. See, *e.g.*, *Bantam Books, Inc.* v. *Sullivan* (1963) ("The constitutional guarantee of freedom of the press embraces the circulation of books as well as their publication . . .").

Division of labor requires a means of mediating exchange, and in a commercial society, that means is supplied by money. The publisher pays the author for the right to sell his book; it pays its staff who print and assemble the book; it demands payments from booksellers who bring the book to market. This, too, presents opportunities for repression: Instead of regulating the various parties to the enterprise individually, the government can suppress their ability to coordinate by regulating their use of money. What good is the right to print books without a right to buy works from authors? Or the right to publish newspapers without the right to pay deliverymen? The right to speak would be largely ineffective if it did not include the right to engage in financial transactions that are the incidents of its exercise.

This is not to say that *any* regulation of money is a regulation of speech. The government may apply general commercial regulations to those who use money for speech if it applies them evenhandedly to those who use money for other purposes. But where the government singles out money used to fund speech as its legislative object, it is acting against speech as such, no less than if it had targeted the paper on which a book was printed or the trucks that deliver it to the bookstore.

History and jurisprudence bear this out. The best early examples derive from the British efforts to tax the press after the lapse of licensing statutes by which the press was first regulated. The Stamp Act of 1712 imposed levies on all newspapers, including an additional tax for each advertisement. It was a response to unfavorable war coverage, "obvious[ly] . . . designed to check the publication of those newspapers and pamphlets which depended for their sale on their cheapness and sensationalism." F. Siebert, Freedom of the Press in England, 1476–1776 (1952). It succeeded in killing off approximately half the newspapers in England in its first year. *Id*. In 1765, Parliament applied a similar Act to the Colonies. The colonial Act likewise placed exactions on sales and advertising revenue, the latter at 2s. per advertisement, which was "by any standard . . . excessive, since the publisher himself received only from 3 to 5s. and still less for repeated insertions." A. Schlesinger, Prelude to Independence: The Newspaper War on Britain, 1764–1776 (1958). The founding generation saw these taxes as grievous incursions on the freedom of the press.

We have kept faith with the Founders' tradition by prohibiting the selective taxation of the press. And we have done so whether the tax was the product of illicit motive or not. These press-taxation cases belie the claim that regulation of money used to fund speech is not regulation of speech itself. A tax on a newspaper's advertising revenue does not prohibit anyone from saying anything; it merely appropriates part of the revenue that a speaker would otherwise obtain. That is even a step short of totally prohibiting advertising revenue—which would be analogous to the total prohibition of certain campaign-speech contributions in the present cases. Yet it is unquestionably a violation of the First Amendment.

Many other cases exemplify the same principle that an attack upon the funding of speech is an attack upon speech itself. In *Schaumburg* v. *Citizens for a Better Environment* (1980), we struck down an ordinance limiting the amount charities could pay their solicitors. In *Simon & Schuster, Inc.* v. *Members of N.Y. State Crime Victims Bd.* (1991), we held unconstitutional a state statute that appropriated the proceeds of criminals' biographies for payment to the victims. And in *Rosenberger* v. *Rector and Visitors of Univ. of Va.* (1995), we held unconstitutional a university's discrimination in the disbursement of funds to speakers on the basis of viewpoint. Most notable, perhaps, is our famous opinion in *New York Times Co.* v. *Sullivan* (1964), holding that paid advertisements in a newspaper were entitled to full First Amendment protection:

> Any other conclusion would discourage newspapers from carrying "editorial advertisements" of this type, and so might shut off an important outlet for the promulgation of information and ideas by persons who do not themselves have access to publishing facilities—who wish to exercise their freedom of speech even though they are not members of the press. The effect would be to shackle the First Amendment in its attempt to secure "the widest possible dissemination of information from diverse and antagonistic sources." *Id*. (citations omitted).

This passage was relied on in *Buckley* for the point that restrictions on the expenditure of money for speech are equivalent to restrictions on speech itself. That reliance was appropriate. If denying protection to paid-for speech would "shackle the First Amendment," so also does forbidding or limiting the right to pay for speech.

It should be obvious, then, that a law limiting the amount a person can spend to broadcast his political views is a direct restriction on speech. That is no different from a law limiting the amount a newspaper can pay its editorial staff or the amount a charity can pay its leafletters. It is equally clear that a limit on the amount a candidate can *raise* from any one individual for the purpose of speaking is also a direct limitation on speech. That is no different from a law limiting the amount a publisher can accept from any one shareholder or lender, or the amount a newspaper can charge any one advertiser or customer.

(B) POOLING MONEY IS NOT SPEECH

Another proposition which could explain at least some of the results of today's opinion is that the First Amendment right to spend money for speech does not include the right to combine with others in spending money for speech. Such a proposition fits uncomfortably with the concluding words of our Declaration of Independence:"And for the support of this Declaration, . . . we mutually pledge to each other our Lives, *our Fortunes* and our sacred Honor." (Emphasis added.) The freedom to associate with others for the dissemination of ideas— not just by singing or speaking in unison, but by pooling financial resources for expressive purposes—is part of the freedom of speech.

> Our form of government is built on the premise that every cit-
> izen shall have the right to engage in political expression and
> association. This right was enshrined in the First Amendment of
> the Bill of Rights. Exercise of these basic freedoms in America
> has traditionally been through the media of political associations.
> Any interference with the freedom of a party is simultaneously
> an interference with the freedom of its adherents.
>
> NAACP v. BUTTON (1963) (INTERNAL QUOTATION MARKS OMITTED)

The First Amendment protects political association as well as political expression. The constitutional right of association expli-cated in *NAACP v. Alabama* (1958) stemmed from the Court's recognition that "[e]ffective advocacy of both public and private points of view, particularly controversial ones, is undeniably enhanced by group association." Subsequent decisions have made clear that the First and Fourteenth Amendments guarantee "freedom to associate with others for the common advancement of political beliefs and ideas, . . .

BUCKLEY

We have said that "implicit in the right to engage in activities protected by the First Amendment" is "a corresponding right to associate with others in pursuit of a wide variety of political, social, economic, educational, religious, and cultural ends." *Roberts* v. *United States Jaycees* (1984). That "right to associate . . . in pursuit" includes the right to pool financial resources.

If it were otherwise, Congress would be empowered to enact legislation requiring newspapers to be sole proprietorships, banning their use of partnership or corporate form. That sort of restriction would be an obvious violation of the First Amendment, and it is incomprehensible why the conclusion should change when what is at issue is the pooling of funds for the most important (and most perennially threatened) category of speech: electoral speech. The principle that such financial association does not enjoy full First Amendment protection threatens the existence of all political parties.

(c) Speech by Corporations Can Be Abridged

The last proposition that might explain at least some of today's casual abridgment of free-speech rights is this: that the particular form of association known as a corporation does not enjoy full First Amendment protection. Of course the text of the First Amendment does not limit its application in this fashion, even though "[b]y the end of the eighteenth century the corporation was a familiar figure in American economic life." C. Cooke, Corporation, Trust and Company 92 (1951). Nor is there any basis in reason why First Amendment rights should not attach to corporate associations—and we have said so. In *First Nat. Bank of Boston* v. *Bellotti* (1978), we held unconstitutional a state prohibition of corporate speech designed to influence the vote on referendum proposals. We said:

> [T]here is practically universal agreement that a major purpose of [the First] Amendment was to protect the free discussion of governmental affairs. If the speakers here were not corporations, no one would suggest that the State could silence their proposed speech. It is the type of speech indispensable to decisionmaking in a democracy, and this is no less true because the speech comes from a corporation rather than an individual. The inherent worth of the speech in terms of its capacity for informing the public does not depend upon the identity of its source, whether corporation, association, union, or individual. *Id.* (internal quotation marks, footnotes, and citations omitted).

In *NAACP* v. *Button,* we held that the NAACP could assert First Amendment rights "on its own behalf, . . . though a corporation," and that the activities of the corporation were "modes of expression and association protected by the First and Fourteenth Amendments." In *Pacific Gas & Elec. Co.* v. *Public Util. Comm'n of Cal.* (1986), we held unconstitutional a state effort to compel corporate speech. "The identity of the speaker," we said, "is not decisive in determining whether speech is protected. Corporations and other associations, like individuals, contribute to the 'discussion, debate, and the dissemination of information and ideas' that the First Amendment seeks to foster." And in *Buckley*, we held unconstitutional FECA's limitation upon independent corporate expenditures.

The Court changed course in *Austin* v. *Michigan Chamber of Commerce* (1990), upholding a state prohibition of an independent corporate expenditure in support of a candidate for state office. I dissented in that case and remain of the view that it was error. In the modern world, giving the government power to exclude corporations from the political debate enables it effectively to muffle the voices that best represent the most significant segments of the economy and the most passionately held social and political views. People who associate—who pool their financial resources—for purposes of economic enterprise overwhelmingly do so in the corporate form; and with increasing frequency, incorporation is chosen by those who associate to defend and promote particular ideas—such as the American Civil Liberties Union and the National Rifle Association, parties to these cases. Imagine, then, a government that wished to suppress nuclear power—or oil and gas exploration, or automobile manufacturing, or gun ownership, or civil liberties—and that had the power to prohibit corporate advertising against its proposals. To be sure, the individuals involved in, or benefited by, those industries, or interested in those causes, could (given enough time) form political action committees or other associations to make their case. But the organizational form in which those enterprises already *exist*, and in which they can most quickly and most effectively get their message across, is the corporate form. The First Amendment does not in my view permit the restriction of that political speech. And the same holds true for corporate electoral speech: A candidate should not be insulated from the most effective speech that the major participants in the economy and major incorporated interest groups can generate.

But what about the danger to the political system posed by "amassed wealth"? The most direct threat from that source comes in the form of undisclosed favors and payoffs to elected officials—which have already been criminalized, and will be rendered no more discoverable by the legislation at issue here. The use of corporate wealth (like individual wealth) to speak to the electorate is unlikely to "distort" elections—*especially* if disclosure requirements *tell* the people where the speech is coming from. The premise of the First Amendment is that the American people are neither sheep nor fools, and hence fully capable of considering both the substance of the speech presented to them and its proximate and ultimate source. If that premise is wrong, our democracy has a much greater problem to overcome than merely the influence of amassed wealth. Given the premises of democracy, there is no such thing as *too much* speech.

> *The premise of the First Amendment is that the American people are neither sheep nor fools.*

But, it is argued, quite apart from its effect upon the electorate, corporate speech in the form of contributions to the candidate's campaign, or even in the form of independent expenditures supporting the candidate, engenders an obligation which is later paid in the form of greater access to the officeholder, or indeed in the form of votes on particular bills. Any *quid-pro-quo* agreement for votes would of course violate criminal law, and actual payoff *votes* have not even been claimed by those favoring the restrictions on corporate speech. It cannot be denied, however, that corporate (like noncorporate) allies will have greater access to the officeholder, and that he will tend to favor the same causes as those who support him (which is usually *why* they supported him). That is the nature of politics—if not indeed human nature—and how this can properly be considered "corruption" (or "the appearance of corruption") with regard to corporate allies and not with regard to other allies is beyond me. If the Bill of Rights had intended an exception to the freedom of speech in order to combat this malign proclivity of the office-holder to agree with those who agree with him, and to speak more with his supporters than his opponents, it would surely have said so. It did not do so, I think, because the juice is not worth the squeeze. Evil corporate (and private affluent) influences are well enough checked (so long as adequate campaign-expenditure disclosure rules exist) by the politician's fear of being portrayed as "in the pocket" of so-called moneyed interests. The incremental benefit obtained by muzzling corporate speech is more than offset by loss of the information and persuasion that corporate speech can contain. That, at least, is the assumption of a constitutional guarantee which prescribes that Congress shall make no law abridging the freedom of speech.

But let us not be deceived. While the Government's briefs and arguments before this Court focused on the horrible "appearance of corruption," the most passionate floor statements during the debates on this legislation pertained to so-called attack ads, which the Constitution surely protects, but which Members of Congress analogized to "crack cocaine," "drive-by shooting[s]," and "air pollution."

But let us not be deceived. While the Government's briefs and arguments before this Court focused on the horrible "appearance of corruption," the most passionate floor statements during the debates on this legislation pertained to so-called attack ads, which the Constitution surely protects, but which Members of Congress analogized to "crack cocaine," "drive-by shootings," and "air pollution."

There is good reason to believe that the ending of negative campaign ads was the principal attraction of the legislation. A Senate sponsor said, "I hope that we will not allow our attention to be distracted from the real issues at hand—how to raise the tenor of the debate in our elections and give people real choices. No one benefits from negative ads. They don't aid our Nation's political dialog." Cong. Rec. (remarks of Sen. McCain). He assured the body that "[y]ou cut off the soft money, you are going to see a lot less of that [attack ads]. Prohibit unions and corporations, and you will see a lot less of that. If you demand full disclosure for those who pay for those ads, you are going to see a lot less of that. . . ." Cong. Rec. (remarks of Sen. McCain).

Another theme prominent in the legislative debates was the notion that there is too much money spent on elections. The first principle of "reform" was that "there should be less money in politics." (remarks of Sen. Murray). "The enormous amounts of special interest money that flood our political system have become a cancer in our democracy" (remarks of Sen. Kennedy). "[L]arge sums of money drown out the voice of the average voter" (remarks of Rep. Langevin). The system of campaign finance is "drowning in money." (remarks of Rep. Menendez). And most expansively:

> Despite the ever-increasing sums spent on campaigns, we have not seen an improvement in campaign discourse, issue discussion or voter education. More money does not mean more ideas, more substance or more depth. Instead, it means more of what voters complain about most. More 30-second spots, more negativity and an increasingly longer campaign period.
>
> REMARKS OF SENATOR KERRY

Perhaps voters do detest these 30-second spots—though I suspect they detest even more hour-long campaign-debate interruptions of their favorite entertainment programming. Evidently, however, these ads *do persuade* voters, or else they would not be so routinely used by sophisticated politicians of all parties. The point, in any event, is that it is not the proper role of those who govern us to judge which campaign speech has "substance" and "depth" (do you think it might be that which is least damaging to incumbents?) and to abridge the rest.

And what exactly are these outrageous sums frittered away in determining who will govern us? A report prepared for Congress concluded that the total amount, in hard and soft money, spent on the 2000 federal elections was between $2.4 and $2.5 billion. *All* campaign spending in the United States, including state elections, ballot initiatives, and judicial elections, has been estimated at $3.9 billion for 2000, which was a year that "shattered spending and contribution records." Even taking this last, larger figure as the benchmark, it means that Americans spent about half as much electing all their Nation's officials, state and federal, as they spent on movie tickets ($7.8 billion); about a fifth as much as they spent on cosmetics and perfume ($18.8 billion); and about a sixth as much as

Americans spent about half as much electing all their Nation's officials, state and federal, as they spent on movie tickets ($7.8 billion); about a fifth as much as they spent on cosmetics and perfume ($18.8 billion); and about a sixth as much as they spent on pork (the nongovernmental sort) ($22.8 billion). If our democracy is drowning from this much spending, it cannot swim.

they spent on pork (the nongovernmental sort) ($22.8 billion). If our democracy is drowning from this much spending, it cannot swim.

Which brings me back to where I began: This litigation is about preventing criticism of the government. I cannot say for certain that many, or some, or even any, of the Members of Congress who voted for this legislation did so not to produce "fairer" campaigns, but to mute criticism of their records and facilitate reelection. Indeed, I will stipulate that all those who voted for the Act believed they were acting for the good of the country. There remains the problem of the Charlie Wilson Phenomenon, named after Charles Wilson, former president of General Motors, who is supposed to have said during the Senate hearing on his nomination as Secretary of Defense that "what's good for General Motors is good for the country." Those in power, even giving them the benefit of the greatest good will, are inclined to believe that what is good for them is good for the country. Whether in prescient recognition of the Charlie Wilson Phenomenon, or out of fear of good old-fashioned, malicious, self-interested manipulation, "[t]he fundamental approach of the First Amendment . . . was to assume the worst, and to rule the regulation of political speech 'for fairness' sake' simply out of bounds." *Austin* (Scalia, J., dissenting). Having abandoned that approach to a limited extent in *Buckley*, we abandon it much further today.

We will unquestionably be called upon to abandon it further still in the future. The most frightening passage in the lengthy floor debates on this legislation is the following assurance given by one of the cosponsoring Senators to his colleagues:

> *Those in power, even giving them the benefit of the greatest good will, are inclined to believe that what is good for them is good for the country.*

This is a modest step, it is a first step, it is an essential step, but it does not even begin to address, in some ways, the fundamental problems that exist with the hard money aspect of the system.

CONGRESSIONAL RECORD (STATEMENT OF SENATOR FEINGOLD)

The system indeed. The first instinct of power is the retention of power, and, under a Constitution that requires periodic elections, that is best achieved by the suppression of election-time speech. We have witnessed merely the second scene of Act I of what promises to be a lengthy tragedy. In scene 3 the Court, having abandoned most of the First Amendment weaponry that *Buckley* left intact, will be even less equipped to resist the incumbents' writing of the rules of political debate. The federal election campaign laws, which are already (as today's opinions show) so voluminous, so detailed, so complex, that no ordinary citizen dare run for office, or even contribute a significant sum, without hiring an expert advisor in the field, can be expected to grow more voluminous, more detailed, and more complex in the years to come—and always, always, with the objective of reducing the excessive amount of speech.

CHAPTER TEN

NON-SPEECH AND
UN-FREE SPEECH

❦

A S ILLUSTRATED IN THE PREVIOUS CHAPTER, Justice Scalia views with suspicion laws that regulate political speech because he views protection of such speech to be the main purpose of the First Amendment. He is not sympathetic to free speech claims brought by individuals involved in pornography and indecency. Scalia's lack of sympathy does not reflect a belief that certain speech or expressive conduct is merely less important, but that the conduct involved is not speech at all. For example, the issue of nude dancing has come before the Supreme Court at least twice during Scalia's tenure.[1] In both cases, Scalia has voted to uphold local indecency laws from challenge by nude dancers. Scalia argued that public nudity is the object of the law's prohibition, not dancing, and said nudity is not speech. Unlike with flag burning—where the conduct itself was banned because of its communicative purpose—the expressive component of dancing is not what is being targeted by the laws and any limit on expression is incidental.

Scalia also has voted to deny First Amendment protection to artists seeking federal subsidies for their work. Saying the issue is one of government discretion in the exercise of its spending power, Scalia said artists are free to create indecent works, but are not entitled to make taxpayers foot the bill. Thus, if an artist wishes to accept federal money for his work, he must accept the rules that go with the money—even if they limit his artistic expression.

BARNES v. GLEN THEATER, INC. (1991)

The State of Indiana enacted a law to combat public indecency, which, among other things, prohibited appearing nude in public. Two strip bars in South Bend and their dancers challenged the law, arguing that the First Amendment's right of free expression prevents enforcement of the public indecency law against nude dancing.

The Supreme Court, in a 5–4 decision, upheld the Indiana law. The majority conceded that nude dancing constitutes expressive conduct, but said the established test for reviewing expression-limiting laws was satisfied. Specifically, the law furthered the state's interest in protecting order and morality. The interest in protecting morality was unrelated to suppressing free expression, since banning public nudity, not expressive dancing, was the object of the law. Finally, the incidental restriction on the dancers' rights— they were forced to wear pasties and G-strings—was no greater than was essential to furthering Indiana's interest.

Justice Scalia concurred with the Court's opinion but wrote separately to state his view that the majority's First Amendment analysis was not appropriate. He wrote that the indecency measure was a general law regulating conduct and was not specifically directed at expression. Thus, the Court need not inquire as to whether the slight limitation on expression was justified by an important government interest. The First Amendment did not apply.

~∞◦∞~

JUSTICE SCALIA, CONCURRING IN THE JUDGMENT.

I agree that the judgment of the Court of Appeals must be reversed. In my view, however, the challenged regulation must be upheld, not because it survives some lower level of First-Amendment scrutiny, but because, as a general law regulating conduct and not specifically directed at expression, it is not subject to First Amendment scrutiny at all.

I

Indiana's public indecency statute provides:

(a) A person who knowingly or intentionally, in a public place:
  (1) engages in sexual intercourse;
  (2) engages in deviate sexual conduct;
  (3) appears in a state of nudity; or
  (4) fondles the genitals of himself or another person; commits public indecency, a Class A misdemeanor.
(b) "Nudity" means the showing of the human male or female genitals, pubic area, or buttocks with less than a fully opaque covering, the showing of the female breast with less than a fully opaque covering of any part of the nipple, or the showing of covered male genitals in a discernibly turgid state.

INDIANA CODE 35-45-4-I (1988)

On its face, this law is not directed at expression in particular. As Judge Easterbrook put it in his dissent below: "Indiana does not regulate dancing. It regulates public nudity.... Almost the entire domain of Indiana's statute is unrelated to expression, unless we view nude beaches and topless hot dog vendors as speech." *Miller* v. *Civil City of South Bend* (CA7 1990). The intent to convey a "message of eroticism" (or any other message) is not a necessary element of the statutory offense of public indecency; nor does one commit that statutory offense by conveying the most explicit "message of eroticism," so long as he does not commit any of the four specified acts in the process.

Indiana's statute is in the line of a long tradition of laws against public nudity, which have never been thought to run afoul of traditional understanding of "the freedom of speech." Public indecency—including public nudity—has long been an offense at common law. Indiana's first public nudity statute predated by many years the appearance of nude barroom dancing. It was general in scope, directed at all public nudity, and not just at public nude expression; and all succeeding statutes, down to the present one, have been the same. Were it the case that Indiana in practice targeted only expressive nudity, while turning a blind eye to nude beaches and unclothed purveyors of hot dogs and machine tools, it might be said that what posed as a regulation of conduct in general was in reality a regulation of only communicative conduct. Respondents have adduced no evidence of that. Indiana officials have brought many public indecency prosecutions for activities having no communicative element.

The dissent confidently asserts that the purpose of restricting nudity in public places in general is to protect nonconsenting parties from offense; and argues that, since only consenting, admission-paying patrons see respondents dance, that purpose cannot apply, and the only remaining purpose must relate to the communicative elements of the performance. Perhaps the dissenters believe that "offense to others" ought to be the only reason for restricting nudity in public places generally, but there is no basis for thinking that our society has ever shared that Thoreauvian "you-may-do-what-you-like-so-long-as-it-does-not-injure-someone-else" beau ideal—much less for thinking that it was written into the Constitution. The purpose of Indiana's nudity law would be violated, I think, if 60,000 fully consenting adults crowded into the Hoosierdome to display their genitals to one another, even if there were not an offended innocent in the crowd. Our society prohibits, and all human societies have prohibited, certain activities not because they harm others but because they are considered, in the traditional phrase, "contra bonos mores," i.e., immoral. In American society, such prohibitions have included, for example, sadomasochism, cockfighting, bestiality, suicide, drug use, prostitution, and sodomy. While there may be great diversity of view on whether various of these prohibitions should exist (though I have found few ready to abandon, in principle, all of them) there is no doubt that, absent specific constitutional protection for the conduct involved, the Constitution does not prohibit them simply because they regulate "morality." The purpose of the Indiana statute, as both its text and the manner of its enforcement demonstrate, is to enforce the traditional moral belief that people should not expose their private parts indiscriminately, regardless of whether those who see them are disedified. Since that is so, the dissent has no basis for positing that, where only thoroughly edified adults are present, the purpose must be repression of communication.

The purpose of Indiana's nudity law would be violated, I think, if 60,000 fully consenting adults crowded into the Hoosierdome to display their genitals to one another, even if there were not an offended innocent in the crowd.

II

Since the Indiana regulation is a general law not specifically targeted at expressive conduct, its application to such conduct does not, in my view, implicate the First Amendment.

The First Amendment explicitly protects "the freedom of speech [and] of the press"—oral and written speech—not "expressive conduct." When any law restricts speech, even for a purpose that has nothing to do with the suppression of communication (for instance, to reduce noise, see *Saia* v. *New York* (1948), to regulate election campaigns, see *Buckley* v. *Valeo* (1976), or to prevent littering, see *Schneider* v. *State* (1939)), we insist that it meet the high First Amendment standard of justification. But virtually every law restricts conduct, and virtually any prohibited conduct can be performed for an expressive purpose—if only expressive of the fact that the actor disagrees with the prohibition. See, e.g., *Florida Free Beaches, Inc.* v. *Miami*, 734 F.2d 608 (1984) (nude sunbathers challenging public indecency law claimed their "message" was that nudity is not indecent). It cannot reasonably be demanded, therefore, that every restriction of expression incidentally produced by a general law regulating conduct pass normal First Amendment scrutiny, or even—as some of our cases have suggested—that it be justified by an "important or substantial" government interest. Nor do our holdings require such justification: we have never invalidated the application of a general law simply because the conduct that it reached was being engaged in for expressive purposes and the government could not demonstrate a sufficiently important state interest.

This is not to say that the First Amendment affords no protection to expressive conduct. Where the government prohibits conduct precisely because of its communicative attributes, we hold the regulation unconstitutional. See, e.g., *United States* v. *Eichman* (1990) (burning flag); *Texas* v. *Johnson* (1989) (same); *Spence* v. *Washington* (1974) (defacing flag); *Tinker* v. *Des Moines Independent Community School District* (1969) (wearing black arm bands); *Brown* v. *Louisiana* (1966) (participating in silent sit-in); *Stromberg* v. *California* (1931) (flying a red flag). In each of the foregoing cases, we explicitly found that suppressing communication was the object of the regulation of conduct. Where that has not been the case, however—where suppression of communicative use of the conduct was merely the incidental effect of forbidding the conduct for other reasons—we have allowed the regulation to stand. As we clearly expressed the point in *Johnson*:

> The government generally has a freer hand in restricting expressive conduct than it has in restricting the written or spoken word. It may not, however, proscribe particular conduct *because* it has expressive elements. What might be termed the more generalized guarantee of freedom of expression makes the communicative nature of conduct an inadequate *basis* for singling out that conduct for proscription (internal quotations and citations omitted; emphasis in original).

All our holdings (though admittedly not some of our discussion) support the conclusion that "the only First Amendment analysis applicable to laws that do not directly or indirectly impede speech is the threshold inquiry of whether the purpose of the law is to suppress communication. If not, that is the end of the matter so far as First Amendment guarantees are concerned; if so, the court then proceeds to determine whether there is substantial justification for the proscription." *Community for Creative Non-Violence* v. *Watt*, 703 F.2d 586 (1983) (Scalia, J., dissenting) (footnote omitted; emphasis omitted), rev'd, *Clark* v. *Community for Creative Non-Violence* (1984). Such a regime ensures that the government does not act to suppress communication, without requiring that all conduct-restricting regulation (which means in effect all regulation) survive an enhanced level of scrutiny.

We have explicitly adopted such a regime in another First Amendment context: that of Free Exercise. In *Employment Division, Oregon Dept. of Human Resources* v. *Smith* (1990), we held that general laws not specifically targeted at religious practices did not require heightened First Amendment scrutiny even though they diminished some people's ability to practice their religion. "The government's ability to enforce generally applicable prohibitions of socially harmful conduct, like its ability to carry out other aspects of public policy, 'cannot depend on measuring the effects of a governmental action on a religious objector's spiritual development.'" *Id.*, quoting *Lyng* v. *Northwest Indian Cemetery Protective Assn.* (1988). There is even greater reason to apply this approach to the regulation of expressive conduct. Relatively few can plausibly assert that their illegal conduct is being engaged in for religious reasons; but almost anyone can violate almost any law as a means of expression. In the one case, as in the other, if the law is not directed against the protected value (religion or expression) the law must be obeyed.

III

While I do not think the plurality's conclusions differ greatly from my own, I cannot entirely endorse its reasoning. The plurality purports to apply to this general law, insofar as it regulates this allegedly expressive conduct, an intermediate level of First Amendment scrutiny: the government interest in the regulation must be "'imortant or substantial,'" quoting *O'Brien*. As I have indicated, I do not believe such a heightened standard exists. I think we should avoid wherever possible, moreover, a method of analysis that requires judicial assessment of the "importance" of government interests—and especially of government interests in various aspects of morality.

Neither of the cases that the plurality cites to support the "importance" of the State's interest here is in point. *Paris Adult Theatre I* v. *Slaton* and *Bowers* v. *Hardwick* did uphold laws prohibiting private conduct based on concerns of decency and morality; but neither opinion held that those concerns were particularly "important" or "substantial," or amounted to anything more than a rational basis for regulation. *Sla-*

ton involved an exhibition which, since it was obscene and at least to some extent public, was unprotected by the First Amendment; the State's prohibition could therefore be invalidated only if it had no rational basis. We found that the State's "right . . . to maintain a decent society" provided a "legitimate" basis for regulation—even as to obscene material viewed by consenting adults. In *Bowers*, we held that, since homosexual behavior is not a fundamental right, a Georgia law prohibiting private homosexual intercourse needed only a rational basis in order to comply with the Due Process Clause. Moral opposition to homosexuality, we said, provided that rational basis. I would uphold the Indiana statute on precisely the same ground: moral opposition to nudity supplies a rational basis for its prohibition, and since the First Amendment has no application to this case, no more than that is needed.

Indiana may constitutionally enforce its prohibition of public nudity even against those who choose to use public nudity as a means of communication. The State is regulating conduct, not expression, and those who choose to employ conduct as a means of expression must make sure that the conduct they select is not generally forbidden. For these reasons, I agree that the judgment should be reversed.

NATIONAL ENDOWMENT FOR THE ARTS
v. FINLEY (1998)

For a small agency of the federal government, the National Endowment for the Arts (NEA) created an enormous controversy in the 1980s and early 1990s. Some of the agency's grants were used to create "art" that many Americans found objectionable. Perhaps the most infamous award went to Andres Serrano, who created Piss Christ, which was a photograph of Jesus Christ submerged in urine.

While liberals in Congress defended the NEA on First Amendment grounds, conservatives thought the agency was insulting taxpayers by funding patently offensive art with their money. In addition to trying to eliminate the agency's budget, conservatives sought to ensure that no more grants would go to offensive projects or artists.

In 1990, a bipartisan compromise was reached via enactment of a law directing the chairperson of the NEA to establish procedures for judging grant applications. According to the law, "artistic excellence and artistic merit are the criteria by which applications are judged, taking into consideration general standards of decency and respect for the diverse beliefs and values of the American public..." Four performing artists challenged the law, arguing that it violated their First Amendment rights by rejecting their application on political grounds. They also argued that the law was too vague in that it did not give applicants sufficient guidance as to what types of art would be disfavored under the NEA's guidelines.

The Supreme Court, in an opinion written by Justice O'Connor, held that the law did not violate artists' First Amendment rights. O'Connor wrote that while government grants cannot discriminate based on the viewpoint of the recipient, the NEA provision is not viewpoint-based. She said it merely required the NEA to consider "decency and respect" standards when judging applications. In addition, O'Connor and the majority ruled that the law was not impermissibly vague; it simply added some imprecise considerations to an already subjective process for awarding federal grants.

Justice Scalia concurred with the Court's decision to uphold the law, but strongly rejected its reasoning. He conceded that the law discriminates against artists who create works that are indecent or not respectful of the beliefs and values of the American public. However, Scalia said this discrimination is not unconstitutional because it does not abridge the grant applicant's freedom to make indecent art; it merely removes taxpayer funding as the source. The artists could fund their works with private support. "The NEA is far from the sole source of funding for art—even indecent, disrespectful, or just plain bad art," wrote Scalia. Finally, with regard to vagueness, Scalia said that that concern should not apply to funding decisions. He pointed out that the NEA's pre-existing standard already was vague, as evidenced by fact that previous grants had been given for "everything from the playing of Beethoven to a depiction of crucifix immersed in urine."

~∞⊕⊕∞~

Justice Scalia, with whom Justice Thomas joins, concurring in the judgment.

"The operation was a success, but the patient died." What such a procedure is to medicine, the Court's opinion in this case is to law. It sustains the constitutionality of 20 U.S.C. § 954(d)(1) by gutting it. The most avid congressional opponents of the provision could not have asked for more. I write separately because, unlike the Court, I think that § 954(d)(1) must be evaluated as written, rather than as distorted by the agency it was meant to control. By its terms, it establishes content and viewpoint-based criteria upon which grant applications are to be evaluated. And that is perfectly constitutional.

> *The operation was a success, but the patient died. What such a procedure is to medicine, the Court's opinion in this case is to law.*

I
The Statute Means What It Says

Section 954(d)(1) provides:

No payment shall be made under this section except upon application therefore which is submitted to the National Endowment for the Arts in accordance with regulations issued and procedures established by the Chairperson. In establishing such regulations and procedures, the Chairperson shall ensure that "(1) artistic excellence and artistic merit are the criteria by which applications are judged, taking into consideration general standards of decency and respect for the diverse beliefs and values of the American public."

The phrase "taking into consideration general standards of decency and respect for the diverse beliefs and values of the American public" is what my grammar-school teacher would have condemned as a dangling modifier: There is no noun to which the participle is attached (unless one jumps out of paragraph (1) to press "Chairperson" into service). Even so, it is clear enough that the phrase is meant to apply to those who do the judging. The application reviewers must take into account "general standards of decency" and "respect for the diverse beliefs and values of the American public" when evaluating artistic excellence and merit. One can regard this as either suggesting that decency and respect are elements of what Congress regards as artistic excellence and merit, or as suggesting that decency and respect are factors to be taken into account in *addition* to artistic excellence and merit. But either way, it is entirely, 100% clear that decency and respect are to be taken into account in evaluating applications.

This is so apparent that I am at a loss to understand what the Court has in mind (other than the gutting of the statute) when it speculates that the statute is merely "advisory." General standards of decency and respect for Americans' beliefs and values *must* (for the statute says that the Chairperson "shall ensure" this result) be taken into account (see, *e.g.*, American Heritage Dictionary (3d ed. 1992):"consider... [t]o take into account; bear in mind") in evaluating all applications. This does not mean that those factors must always be dispositive, but it *does* mean that they must always be considered. The method of compliance proposed by the National Endowment for the Arts (NEA)—selecting diverse review panels of artists and nonartists that reflect a wide range of geographic and cultural perspective—is so obviously inadequate that it insults the intelligence. A diverse panel membership increases the odds that, *if and when* the panel takes the factors into account, it *will* reach an accurate assessment of what they demand. But it in no way increases the odds that the panel will take the factors into consideration—much less *ensures* that the panel will do so, which is the Chairperson's duty under the statute. Moreover, the NEA's fanciful reading of § 954(d)(1) would make it wholly superfluous. Section 959(c) already requires the Chairperson to "issue regulations and establish procedures ... to ensure that all panels are composed, to the extent practicable, of individuals reflecting ... diverse artistic and cultural points of view."

The statute requires the decency and respect factors to be considered in evaluating *all* applications—not, for example, just those applications relating to educational programs, or intended for a particular audience. Just as it would violate the statute to apply the artistic excellence and merit requirements to only select categories of applications, it would violate the statute to apply the decency and respect factors less than universally. A reviewer may, of course, give varying weight to the factors depending on the context, and in some categories of cases (such as the Court's example of funding for symphony orchestras) the factors may rarely if ever affect the outcome; but § 954(d)(1) requires the factors to be considered in every case.

I agree with the Court that § 954(d)(1) "imposes no categorical requirement," in the sense that it does not require the denial of all applications that violate general standards of decency or exhibit disrespect for the diverse beliefs and values of Americans. ... But the factors need not be conclusive to be discriminatory. To the extent a particular applicant exhibits disrespect for the diverse beliefs and values of the American public or fails to comport with general standards of decency, the likelihood that he will receive a grant diminishes. In other words, the presence of the "tak[e] into consideration" clause "cannot be regarded as mere surplusage; it means something," *Potter* v. *United States* (1894). And the "something" is that the decisionmaker, all else being equal, will favor applications that display decency and respect, and disfavor applications that do not.

This unquestionably constitutes viewpoint discrimination. That conclusion is not altered by the fact that the statute does not "compe[l]" the denial of funding any more than a provision imposing a five-point handicap on all black applicants for civil service jobs is saved from being race discrimination by the fact that it does not compel the rejection of black applicants. If viewpoint discrimination in this context is unconstitutional (a point I shall address anon), the law is invalid unless there are some situations in which the decency and respect factors *do not constitute viewpoint discrimination*. And there is none. The applicant who displays "decency," that is, "[c]onformity to prevailing standards of propriety or modesty," American Heritage Dictionary 483 (3d ed. 1992) (def. 2), and the applicant who displays "respect," that is, "deferential regard," for the diverse beliefs and values of the American people, *id.*, at 1536 (def. 1), will *always* have an edge over an applicant who displays the opposite. And finally, the conclusion of viewpoint discrimination is not affected by the fact that what constitutes "decency" or "the diverse beliefs and values of the American people" is difficult to pin down—any more than a civil-service preference in favor of those who display "Republican-Party values" would be rendered nondiscriminatory by the fact that there is plenty of room for argument as to what Republican-Party values might be.

The "political context surrounding the adoption of the 'decency and respect' clause," which the Court discusses at some length does not change its meaning or affect its constitutionality. All that is proved by the various statements that the Court quotes from the Report of the Independent Commission and the floor debates is (1) that the provision was not meant categorically to exclude any particular viewpoint (which I have conceded, and which is plain from the text), and (2) that the language was not meant to do anything that is unconstitutional. That in no way propels the Court's leap to the countertextual conclusion that the provision was merely "aimed at reforming procedures," and cannot be "utilized as a tool for invidious viewpoint discrimination." It is evident in the legislative history that § 954(d)(1) was prompted by, and directed at, the public funding of such offensive productions as Serrano's "Piss Christ," the portrayal of a crucifix immersed in urine, and Mapplethorpe's show of lurid homoerotic photographs. Thus, even if one strays beyond the plain text it is perfectly clear that the statute was meant to disfavor—that is, to discriminate against—such productions. Not to ban their funding absolutely, to be sure (though as I shall discuss, that also would not have been unconstitutional); but to make their funding more difficult.

More fundamentally, of course, all this legislative history has no valid claim upon our attention at all. It is a virtual certainty that very few of the Members of Congress who voted for this language both (1) knew of, and (2) agreed with, the various statements that the Court has culled from the Report of the Independent Commission and the floor debate (probably conducted on an almost empty floor). And it is wholly irrelevant that the statute was a "bipartisan proposal introduced as a counterweight" to an alternative proposal that would directly restrict funding on the basis of viewpoint. We do not judge statutes as if we are surveying the scene of an accident; each one is reviewed, not on the basis of how much worse it could have been, but on the basis of what it says. It matters not whether this enactment was the product of the most partisan alignment in history or whether, upon its passage, the Members all linked arms and sang, "The more we get together, the happier we'll be." It is "not consonant with our scheme of government for a court to inquire into the motives of legislators." *Tenney* v. *Brandhove* (1951). The law at issue in this case is to be found in the text of § 954(d)(1), which passed both Houses and was signed by the President, U. S. Const., Art. I, §7. And that law unquestionably disfavors—discriminates against—indecency and disrespect for the diverse beliefs and values of the American people. I turn, then, to whether such viewpoint discrimination violates the Constitution.

> *It matters not whether this enactment was the product of the most partisan alignment in history or whether, upon its passage, the Members all linked arms and sang, "The more we get together, the happier we'll be."*

II

What The Statute Says Is Constitutional

The Court devotes so much of its opinion to explaining why this statute means something other than what it says that it neglects to cite the constitutional text governing our analysis. The First Amendment reads: "Congress shall make no law. . . *abridging* the freedom of speech." U. S. Const., Amdt. 1 (emphasis added). To abridge is "to contract, to diminish; to deprive of." T. Sheridan, A Complete Dictionary of the

English Language (6th ed. 1796). With the enactment of § 954(d)(1), Congress did not *abridge* the speech of those who disdain the beliefs and values of the American public, nor did it abridge indecent speech. Those who wish to create indecent and disrespectful art are as unconstrained now as they were before the enactment of this statute. Avant-garde artistes such as respondents remain entirely free to epater les bourgeois; they are merely deprived of the additional satisfaction of having the bourgeoisie taxed to pay for it. It is preposterous to equate the denial of taxpayer subsidy with measures "'aimed at the *suppression* of dangerous ideas.'" *Regan* v. *Taxation with Representation of Wash.* (1983) (emphasis added) (quoting *Cammarano* v. *United States* (1959), in turn quoting *Speiser v . Randall* (1958)). "The reason that denial of participation in a tax exemption or other subsidy scheme does not necessarily 'infringe' a fundamental right is that—unlike direct restriction or prohibition—such a denial does not, as a general rule, have any significant coercive effect." *Arkansas Writers' Project, Inc.* v. *Ragland* (1987) (Scalia, J., dissenting).

One might contend, I suppose, that a threat of rejection by the only available source of free money would constitute coercion and hence "abridgment" within the meaning of the First Amendment. I would not agree with such a contention, which would make the NEA the mandatory patron of all art too indecent, too disrespectful, or even too *kitsch* to attract private support. But even if one accepts the contention, it would have no application here. The NEA is far from the sole source of funding for

> *Avant-garde artistes such as respondents remain entirely free to epater les bourgeois [to shock the middle classes]; they are merely deprived of the additional satisfaction of having the bourgeoisie taxed to pay for it.*

art—even indecent, disrespectful, or just plain bad art. Accordingly, the Government may earmark NEA funds for projects it deems to be in the public interest without thereby abridging speech.

Section 954(d)(1) is no more discriminatory, and no less constitutional, than virtually every other piece of funding legislation enacted by Congress. "The Government can, without violating the Constitution, selectively fund a program to encourage certain activities it believes to be in the public interest, without at the same time funding an alternative program. . . ." *Rust* v. *Sullivan* (1991). As we noted in *Rust*, when Congress chose to establish the National Endowment for Democracy it was not constitutionally required to fund programs encouraging competing philosophies of government—an example of funding discrimination that cuts much closer than this one to the core of *political* speech which is the primary concern of the First Amendment. It takes a particularly high degree of chutzpah for the NEA to contradict this proposition, since the agency itself discriminates—and is required by law to discriminate—in favor of artistic (as opposed to scientific, or political, or theological) expression. Not all the common folk, or even all great minds, for that matter, think that is a good idea. In 1800, when John Marshall told John Adams that a recent immigration of Frenchmen would include talented artists, "Adams denounced all Frenchmen, but most especially 'schoolmasters, painters, poets, &C.' He warned Marshall that the fine arts were like germs that infected healthy constitutions." J. Ellis, After the Revolution: Profiles of Early American Culture 36 (1979). Surely the NEA itself is nothing less than an institutionalized discrimination against that point of view. Nonetheless, it is constitutional, as is the congressional determination to favor decency and respect for beliefs and values over the opposite because such favoritism does not "abridge" anyone's freedom of speech.

Respondents, relying on *Rosenberger* v. *Rector and Visitors of Univ. of Va.* (1995), argue that viewpoint-based discrimination is impermissible unless the government is the speaker or the government is "disburs[ing] public funds to private entities to convey a governmental message." It is impossible to imagine why that should be so; one would think that directly involving the government itself in the viewpoint discrimination (if it is unconstitutional) would make the situation even worse. Respondents are mistaken. It is the very business of government to favor and disfavor points of view on (in modern times, at least) innumerable subjects—which is the main reason we have decided to elect those who run the government, rather than save money by making their posts hereditary. And it makes not a bit of difference, insofar as either common sense or the Constitution is concerned, whether these officials further their (and, in a democracy, our) favored point of view by achieving it directly (having government-employed artists paint pictures, for example, or government-employed doctors perform abortions); or by advocating it officially (establishing an Office of Art Appreciation, for example, or an Office of Voluntary Population Control); or by giving money to others who achieve or advocate it (funding private art classes, for example, or Planned Parenthood). None of this has anything to do with abridging anyone's speech. *Rosenberger*, as the Court explains, found the viewpoint discrimination unconstitutional, not because funding of "private" speech was involved, but because the government had established a limited public forum—to which the NEA's granting of highly selective (if not highly discriminating) awards bears no resemblance.

The nub of the difference between me and the Court is that I regard the distinction between "abridging" speech and funding it as a fundamental divide, on this side of which the First Amendment is inapplicable. The Court, by contrast, seems to believe that the First Amendment, despite its words, has some ineffable effect upon funding, imposing constraints of an indeterminate nature which it announces (without troubling to enunciate any particular test) are not violated by the statute here—or, more accurately, are not violated by the quite different, emasculated statute that it imagines. "[T]he Government," it says, "may allocate competitive funding according to criteria that would be impermissible were direct regulation of speech or a criminal penalty at stake." The Government, *I* think, may allocate both competitive and noncompetitive funding *ad libitum*, insofar as the First Amendment is concerned.

Finally, what is true of the First Amendment is also true of the constitutional rule against vague legislation: it has no application to funding. Insofar as it bears upon First Amendment concerns, the vagueness doctrine addresses the problems that arise from government *regulation* of expressive conduct, not government grant programs. In the former context, vagueness produces an abridgment of lawful speech; in the latter it produces, at worst, a waste of money. I cannot refrain from observing, however, that if the vagueness doctrine were applicable, the agency charged with making grants under a statutory standard of "artistic excellence"—and which has itself thought that standard met by everything from the playing of Beethoven to a depiction of a crucifix immersed in urine—would be of more dubious constitutional validity than the "decency" and "respect" limitations that respondents (who demand to be judged on the same strict standard of "artistic excellence") have the humorlessness to call too vague.

In its laudatory description of the accomplishments of the NEA, the Court notes with satisfaction that "only a handful of the agency's roughly 100,000 awards have generated formal complaints." The Congress that felt it necessary to enact § 954(d)(1) evidently thought it much more noteworthy that any money exacted from American taxpayers had been used to produce a crucifix immersed in urine, or a display of homoerotic photographs. It is no secret that the provision was prompted by, and directed at, the funding of such offensive productions. Instead of banning the funding of such productions absolutely, which I think would have been entirely constitutional, Congress took the lesser step of requiring them to be disfavored in the evaluation of grant applications. The Court's opinion today renders even that lesser step a nullity. For that reason, I concur only in the judgment.

CHAPTER ELEVEN

HOMOSEXUALITY

❦

JUST AS THE GOVERNMENT sometimes classifies people by race and gender, it also enacts policies providing for different treatment based on sexuality. Prohibitions of adoption by homosexual couples is one example. All classifications other than those based on race, national origin, gender, or illegitimacy have traditionally been given the broadest deference by the courts. Courts will uphold distinctions based on sexuality if they find that there was a rational basis for the classification. This is a very low threshold to meet, since state legislatures usually have some reason for passing the laws they do.

In its 1986 decision in *Bowers* v. *Hardwick*, the Supreme Court upheld a Georgia law that criminalized sodomy. Though the law did not single out homosexual sodomy, the challenge to the law was brought by a homosexual man who was caught in the act and arrested. The Court specifically refused to extend to sodomy the privacy right it had created and used previously to protect contraceptive use by married individuals in *Griswold* v. *Connecticut* (1965) and abortion in *Roe* v. *Wade* (1973). Writing for the majority, Justice White said not all "private sexual conduct between consenting adults" deserves constitutional protection.[1] Because sodomy had been outlawed by all fifty states as late as 1961 and remained illegal in half the states when *Bowers* was decided, the Court found it could not properly be considered a "fundamental right" that was "deeply rooted in this Nation's history or tradition." Finding no support for a right to sodomy in the text of the Constitution or in the country's history, the Court said that consensual sodomy could be regulated by the state.

Justice Scalia's opinions make clear that he believes a state's desire to protect traditional sexual mores constitutes a rational basis for regulating private sexual conduct. Indeed, Scalia argued, if Bowers prevented consensual sodomy from escaping criminal prosecution and prison, certainly a state could take more modest steps to disfavor homosexual conduct or, at least, to avoid giving preferential treatment to homosexuals.

This latter issue came to the Supreme Court in 1996 via a challenge to an amendment to the Colorado State Constitution. The amendment, adopted by the voters of Colorado in a referendum, prohibited the state government or any counties or cities within the state from giving homosexuals, as a class, special protection. In *Romer* v. *Evans* (1996), the Supreme Court struck down the Colorado amendment, ruling that the law did not have a rational justification and therefore violated the Equal Protection Clause of the Fourteenth Amendment.[2]

Justice Scalia vigorously disagreed. In his view, the Court's holding in *Bowers* protected the right of states to pass laws that disfavor homosexuality. The amendment at issue in *Romer* did not even go that far, but merely denied them from receiving special treatment under Colorado law. Scalia wrote that the Court's opinion contradicted *Bowers* and "places the prestige of this institution behind the proposition that opposition to homosexuality is as reprehensible as racial or religious bias."[3]

Particularly galling to Scalia, it seems, was the Court's assertion that the constitutional amendment was fueled by simple bigotry. Scalia wrote, "The Court has mistaken a Kulturkampf for a fit of spite." In that Kulturkampf (or culture war), Scalia says, many Americans view homosexuality as morally repugnant, not out of hatred, but rather in the same way they view other harmful conduct—"murder, for example, polygamy, or cruelty to animals"—as immoral. Far from being "un-American," Scalia argued, this moral disapproval is what "produced the centuries-old criminal laws that we held constitutional in *Bowers*."

In *Romer*, the Court, without addressing *Bowers* head-on, specifically took the reason and hence the life out of it. It would be seven years until *Bowers*' death was officially pronounced in *Lawrence* v. *Texas*.

LAWRENCE v. TEXAS (2003)

In 2003, a challenge against a Texas law prohibiting certain intimate sexual conduct between individuals of the same sex was brought by two homosexual men who were arrested and convicted for engaging in sodomy in their home. A majority of the Supreme Court, while not declaring homosexual sodomy a "fundamental right," struck down the law saying it was protected by the same "right to privacy" created in by the Court in *Griswold* and extended thereafter. In striking down the law, the Court expressly overruled *Bowers* v. *Hardwick*. The majority did not explicitly apply "strict scrutiny" review (appropriate when "fundamental rights" are abridged) or "rational basis" review (which the Court applied in *Bowers* to homosexual conduct). Instead, it said simply that moral opposition by a majority of voters is not a sufficient reason for outlawing consensual sex between same-sex individuals. The Texas law furthered "no legitimate state interest which can justify its intrusion into the personal and private life of the individual," the majority held.

In a concurring opinion, Justice Sandra Day O'Connor agreed the law should be invalidated, but disagreed with the Court's analysis and overturning of *Bowers*. Instead of relying on "substantive due process" and the right to privacy in the Fourteenth Amendment, O'Connor, said the Court should have used Equal Protection analysis as it did in *Romer* to strike down the law. Because the law discriminated against homosexuals—only sex acts between same-sex individuals were punishable—it could be upheld only if there was a rational basis for the law. O'Connor found the state's justification, promotion of morality, lacking. She wrote, "Moral disapproval of a group, like a bare desire to harm the group, is an interest that is insufficient to satisfy rational basis review under the Equal Protection Clause."

The biting opening of Justice Scalia's dissenting opinion can only be appreciated if one is familiar with the *Casey* joint opinion's refusal a decade earlier to overturn *Roe* because of *stare decisis* considerations (see chapter five). Scalia ridiculed the joint opinion authors' chest-beating adherence to the nineteen-year-old *Roe* with the *Lawrence* majority's breezy reversal of the seventeen-year-old *Bowers*. Further, he noted that the majority's argument for overturning *Bowers*—it had been undermined by a torrent of heavy criticism—also applied with equal force to *Roe*. In *Casey*, however, the joint opinion said that the criticism of *Roe* was a reason to uphold it—"to overrule under fire . . . would subvert the Court's legitimacy," the joint opinion read.

In addition to pointing out the Court's hypocrisy, Scalia chastised the majority for criticizing *Bowers'* conclusion that sodomy is not a fundamental right, but not having the temerity to expressly reverse that determination. Scalia said the country's long tradition of criminalizing homosexual sodomy makes clear that it is not a fundamental right. He argued that the state's interest in protecting morality—the same reason it outlaws bigamy, adult incest, and obscenity—provided a rational basis for maintaining the law against sodomy. Conversely, he argued, if the majority of the Court does not believe promoting morality is even a legitimate state interest, none of these prohibitions could be defended from challenge.

Scalia then turned his attention to Justice O'Connor's concurring opinion. He refuted her equal protection argument by noting that Texas's sodomy law on its face applies equally to men and women, homosexuals and heterosexuals. Further, he said even that if there were unequal treatment, the state's interest in protecting morality provides a rational basis to uphold the distinction.

Finally, Scalia took aim at both the Court and O'Connor for undercutting the rationale for prohibiting same-sex marriages. "If moral disapprobation of homosexual conduct is 'no legitimate state interest' for purposes of proscribing that conduct . . . what justification could there possibly be for denying the benefits of marriage to homosexuals exercising '[t]he liberty protected by the Constitution'?" Scalia asked rhetorically. Eight months after *Lawrence* was decided, the Massachusetts Supreme Court struck down the state's gay marriage ban. It appears the United States Supreme Court will have to answer Scalia's question sooner than even he probably expected.

~∽∞⚬∞∾~

JUSTICE SCALIA, WITH WHOM THE CHIEF JUSTICE AND JUSTICE THOMAS JOIN, DISSENTING.

"Liberty finds no refuge in a jurisprudence of doubt." *Planned Parenthood of Southeastern Pa.* v. *Casey* (1992). That was the Court's sententious response, barely more than a decade ago, to those seeking to overrule *Roe* v. *Wade*. The Court's response today, to those who have engaged in a 17-year crusade to overrule *Bowers* v. *Hardwick* (1986) is very different. The need for stability and certainty presents no barrier.

Most of the rest of today's opinion has no relevance to its actual holding—that the Texas statute "furthers no legitimate state interest which can justify" its application to petitioners under rational-basis review. Though there is discussion of "fundamental proposition[s]" and "fundamental decisions" nowhere does the Court's opinion declare that homosexual sodomy is a "fundamental right" under the Due Process Clause; nor does it subject the Texas law to the standard of review that would be appropriate (strict scrutiny) if homosexual sodomy *were* a "fundamental right." Thus, while overruling the *outcome* of *Bowers*, the Court leaves strangely untouched its central legal conclusion: "[R]espondent would have us announce . . . a fundamental right to engage in homosexual sodomy. This we are quite unwilling to do." Instead the Court simply describes petitioners' conduct as "an exercise of their liberty"—which it undoubtedly is—and proceeds to apply an unheard-of form of rational-basis review that will have far-reaching implications beyond this case.

I

I begin with the Court's surprising readiness to reconsider a decision rendered a mere 17 years ago in *Bowers* v. *Hardwick*. I do not myself believe in rigid adherence to *stare decisis* in constitutional cases; but I do believe that we should be consistent rather than manipulative in invoking the doctrine. Today's opinions in support of reversal do not bother to distinguish—or indeed, even bother to mention—the paean to *stare decisis* coauthored by three Members of today's majority in *Planned Parenthood* v. *Casey*. There, when *stare decisis* meant preservation of judicially invented abortion rights, the widespread criticism of *Roe* was strong reason to *reaffirm* it:

> Where, in the performance of its judicial duties, the Court decides a case in such a way as to resolve the sort of intensely divisive controversy reflected in *Roe*[,] . . . its decision has a dimension that the resolution of the normal case does not carry. . . . [T]o overrule under fire in the absence of the most compelling reason . . . would subvert the Court's legitimacy beyond any serious question.

Today, however, the widespread opposition to *Bowers*, a decision resolving an issue as "intensely divisive" as the issue in *Roe*, is offered as a reason in favor of *overruling* it. Gone, too, is any "enquiry" (of the sort conducted in *Casey*) into whether the decision sought to be overruled has "proven 'unworkable,' " *Casey*.

Today's approach to *stare decisis* invites us to overrule an erroneously decided precedent (including an "intensely divisive" decision) *if:* (1) its foundations have been "eroded" by subsequent decisions; (2) it has been subject to "substantial and continuing" criticism; and (3) it has not induced "individual or societal reliance" that counsels against overturning. The problem is that *Roe* itself—which today's majority surely has no disposition to overrule—satisfies these conditions to at least the same degree as *Bowers*.

(1) A preliminary digressive observation with regard to the first factor: The Court's claim that *Planned Parenthood* v. *Casey* "casts some doubt" upon the holding in *Bowers* (or any other case, for that matter) does not withstand analysis. As far as its holding is concerned, *Casey* provided a *less* expansive right to abortion than did *Roe*, *which was already on the books when Bowers was decided*. And if the Court is referring not to the holding of *Casey*, but to the dictum of its famed sweet-mystery-of-life passage ("'At the heart of liberty is the right to define one's own concept of existence, of meaning, of the universe, and of the mystery of human life'"): That "casts some doubt" upon either the totality of our jurisprudence or else (presumably the right answer) nothing at all. I have never heard of a law that attempted to restrict one's "right to define" certain concepts; and if the passage calls into question the government's power to regulate *actions based on* one's self-defined "concept of existence, etc.," it is the passage that ate the rule of law.

I do not quarrel with the Court's claim that *Romer* v. *Evans* "eroded" the "foundations" of *Bowers*' rational-basis holding. But *Roe* and *Casey* have been equally "eroded" by *Washington* v. *Glucksberg* (1997) which held that *only* fundamental rights which are " 'deeply rooted in this Nation's history and tradition' " qualify for anything other than rational basis scrutiny under the doctrine of "substantive due process." *Roe* and *Casey*, of course, subjected the restriction of abortion to heightened scrutiny without even attempting to establish that the freedom to abort *was* rooted in this Nation's tradition.

I have never heard of a law that attempted to restrict one's "right to define" certain concepts; and if the passage calls into question the government's power to regulate actions based on one's self-defined "concept of existence, etc.," it is the passage that ate the rule of law.

(2) *Bowers*, the Court says, has been subject to "substantial and continuing [criticism], disapproving of its reasoning in all respects, not just as to its historical assumptions." Exactly what those nonhistorical criticisms are, and whether the Court even agrees with them, are left unsaid, although the Court does cite two books. Of course, *Roe* too (and by extension *Casey*) had been (and still is) subject to unrelenting criticism, including criticism from the two commentators cited by the Court today.

(3) That leaves, to distinguish the rock-solid, unamendable disposition of *Roe* from the readily overrulable *Bowers*, only the third factor. "[T]here has been," the Court says, "no individual or societal reliance on *Bowers* of the sort that could counsel against overturning its holding..." It seems to me that the "societal reliance" on the principles confirmed in *Bowers* and discarded today has been overwhelming.

Countless judicial decisions and legislative enactments have relied on the ancient proposition that a governing majority's belief that certain sexual behavior is "immoral and unacceptable" constitutes a rational basis for regulation. We ourselves relied extensively on *Bowers* when we concluded, in *Barnes* v. *Glen Theatre, Inc.* (1991), that Indiana's public indecency statute furthered "a substantial government interest in protecting order and morality." State laws against bigamy, same-sex marriage, adult incest, prostitution, masturbation, adultery, fornication, bestiality, and obscenity are likewise sustainable only in light of *Bowers'* validation of laws based on moral choices. Every single one of these laws is called into question by today's decision; the Court makes no effort to cabin the scope of its decision to exclude them from its holding. The impossibility of distinguishing homosexuality from other traditional "morals" offenses is precisely why *Bowers* rejected the rational-basis challenge. "The law," it said, "is constantly based on notions of morality, and if all laws representing essentially moral choices are to be invalidated under the Due Process Clause, the courts will be very busy indeed."

What a massive disruption of the current social order, therefore, the overruling of *Bowers* entails. Not so the overruling of *Roe*, which would simply have restored the regime that existed for centuries before 1973, in which the permissibility of and restrictions upon abortion were determined legislatively State-by-State. *Casey*, however, chose to base its *stare decisis* determination on a different "sort" of reliance. "[P]eople," it said, "have organized intimate relationships and made choices that define their views of themselves and their places in society, in reliance on the availability of abortion in the event that contraception should fail." This falsely assumes that the consequence of overruling *Roe* would have been to make abortion unlawful. It would not; it would merely have *permitted* the States to do so. Many States would unquestionably have declined to prohibit abortion, and others would not have prohibited it within six months (after which the most significant reliance interests would have expired). Even for persons in States other than these, the choice would not have been between abortion and childbirth, but between abortion nearby and abortion in a neighboring State.

To tell the truth, it does not surprise me, and should surprise no one, that the Court has chosen today to revise the standards of *stare decisis* set forth in *Casey*. It has thereby exposed *Casey's* extraordinary deference to precedent for the result-oriented expedient that it is.

II

Having decided that it need not adhere to *stare decisis*, the Court still must establish that *Bowers* was wrongly decided and that the Texas statute, as applied to petitioners, is unconstitutional.

[The Texas anti-sodomy statute] undoubtedly imposes constraints on liberty. So do laws prohibiting prostitution, recreational use of heroin, and, for that matter, working more than 60 hours per week in a bakery. But there is no right to "liberty" under the Due Process Clause, though today's opinion repeatedly makes that claim. ("The liberty protected by the Constitution allows homosexual persons the right to make this choice"); ("'These matters . . . are central to the liberty protected by the Fourteenth Amendment'"); ("Their right to liberty under the Due Process Clause gives them the full right to engage in their conduct without intervention of the government"). The Fourteenth Amendment *expressly allows* States to deprive their citizens of "liberty," so long as "due process of law" is provided:

No state shall . . . deprive any person of life, liberty, or property,
without due process of law.

AMDT. 14 (EMPHASIS ADDED)

Our opinions applying the doctrine known as "substantive due
process" hold that the Due Process Clause prohibits States from
infringing *fundamental* liberty interests, unless the infringement is narrowly tailored to serve a compelling state interest. *Washington* v.
Glucksberg. We have held repeatedly, in cases the Court today does not
overrule, that *only* fundamental rights qualify for this so-called "heightened scrutiny" protection—that is, rights which are "'deeply rooted
in this Nation's history and tradition,'" *ibid.* All other liberty interests
may be abridged or abrogated pursuant to a validly enacted state law
if that law is rationally related to a legitimate state interest.

Bowers held, first, that criminal prohibitions of homosexual sodomy
are not subject to heightened scrutiny because they do not implicate
a "fundamental right" under the Due Process Clause. Noting that
"[p]roscriptions against that conduct have ancient roots," that "[s]od-
omy was a criminal offense at common law and was forbidden by the
laws of the original 13 States when they ratified the Bill of Rights,"
and that many States had retained their bans on sodomy, *Bowers* concluded that a right to engage in homosexual sodomy was not "'deeply
rooted in this Nation's history and tradition.'"

The Court today does not overrule this holding. Not once does it
describe homosexual sodomy as a "fundamental right" or a "fundamental liberty interest," nor does it subject the Texas statute to strict
scrutiny. Instead, having failed to establish that the right to homosexual
sodomy is "'deeply rooted in this Nation's history and tradition,'" the
Court concludes that the application of Texas's statute to petitioners'

conduct fails the rational-basis test, and overrules *Bowers'* holding to the contrary. "The Texas statute furthers no legitimate state interest which can justify its intrusion into the personal and private life of the individual."

I shall address that rational-basis holding presently. First, however, I address some aspersions that the Court casts upon *Bowers'* conclusion that homosexual sodomy is not a "fundamental right"—even though, as I have said, the Court does not have the boldness to reverse that conclusion.

III

The Court's description of "the state of the law" at the time of *Bowers* only confirms that *Bowers* was right. The Court points to *Griswold* v. *Connecticut* (1965). But that case *expressly disclaimed* any reliance on the doctrine of "substantive due process," and grounded the so-called "right to privacy" in penumbras of constitutional provisions *other than* the Due Process Clause. *Eisenstadt* v. *Baird* (1972), likewise had nothing to do with "substantive due process"; it invalidated a Massachusetts law prohibiting the distribution of contraceptives to unmarried persons solely on the basis of the Equal Protection Clause. Of course *Eisenstadt* contains well known dictum relating to the "right to privacy," but this referred to the right recognized in *Griswold*—a right penumbral to the *specific* guarantees in the Bill of Rights, and not a "substantive due process" right.

Roe v. *Wade* recognized that the right to abort an unborn child was a "fundamental right" protected by the Due Process Clause. The *Roe* Court, however, made no attempt to establish that this right was "'deeply rooted in this Nation's history and tradition'"; instead, it based its conclusion that "the Fourteenth Amendment's concept of personal liberty... is broad enough to encompass a woman's decision whether or not to terminate her pregnancy" on its own normative judgment that anti-abortion laws were undesirable. We have since rejected *Roe's* holding that regulations of abortion must be narrowly tailored to serve a compelling state interest, see *Planned Parenthood* v. *Casey*... and thus, by logical implication, *Roe's* holding that the right to abort an unborn child is a "fundamental right."

After discussing the history of antisodomy laws, the Court proclaims that, "it should be noted that there is no longstanding history in this country of laws directed at homosexual conduct as a distinct matter." This observation in no way casts into doubt the "definitive [historical] conclusion" on which *Bowers* relied: that our Nation has a longstanding history of laws prohibiting *sodomy in general*—regardless of whether it was performed by same-sex or opposite-sex couples:

> It is obvious to us that neither of these formulations would extend a fundamental right to homosexuals to engage in acts of consensual sodomy. Proscriptions against that conduct have ancient roots. *Sodomy* was a criminal offense at common law and was forbidden by the laws of the original 13 States when they ratified the Bill of Rights. In 1868, when the Fourteenth Amendment was ratified, all but 5 of the 37 States in the Union had *criminal sodomy laws*. In fact, until 1961, all 50 States outlawed *sodomy*, and today, 24 States and the District of Columbia continue to provide criminal penalties for *sodomy* performed in private and between consenting adults. Against this background, to claim that a right to engage in such conduct is "deeply rooted in this Nation's history and tradition" or "implicit in the concept of ordered liberty" is, at best, facetious.

It is (as *Bowers* recognized) entirely irrelevant whether the laws in our long national tradition criminalizing homosexual sodomy were "directed at homosexual conduct as a distinct matter." Whether homosexual sodomy was prohibited by a law targeted at same-sex sexual relations or by a more general law prohibiting both homosexual and heterosexual sodomy, the only relevant point is that it *was* criminalized—which suffices to establish that homosexual sodomy is not a right "deeply rooted in our Nation's history and tradition." The Court today agrees that homosexual sodomy was criminalized and thus does not dispute the facts on which *Bowers actually* relied.

Next the Court makes the claim, again unsupported by any citations, that "[l]aws prohibiting sodomy do not seem to have been enforced against consenting adults acting in private." The key qualifier here is "acting in private"—since the Court admits that sodomy laws *were* enforced against consenting adults (although the Court contends that prosecutions were "infrequent"). I do not know what "acting in private" means; surely consensual sodomy, like heterosexual intercourse, is rarely performed on stage. If all the Court means by "acting in private" is "on private premises, with the doors closed and windows covered," it is entirely unsurprising that evidence of enforcement would be hard to come by. (Imagine the circumstances that would enable a search warrant to be obtained for a residence on the ground that there was probable cause to believe that consensual sodomy was then and there occurring.) Surely that lack of evidence would not sustain the propo-

> *I do not know what "acting in private" means; surely consensual sodomy, like heterosexual intercourse, is rarely performed on stage.*

sition that consensual sodomy on private premises with the doors closed and windows covered was regarded as a "fundamental right," even though all other consensual sodomy was criminalized. There are 203 prosecutions for consensual, adult homosexual sodomy reported in the West Reporting system and official state reporters from the years 1880–1995. See W. Eskridge, Gaylaw: Challenging the Apartheid of the Closet (1999) (hereinafter Gaylaw). There are also records of 20 sodomy prosecutions and 4 executions during the colonial period. J. Katz, Gay/Lesbian Almanac (1983). Bowers' conclusion that homosexual sodomy is not a fundamental right "deeply rooted in this Nation's history and tradition" is utterly unassailable.

Realizing that fact, the Court instead says: "[W]e think that our laws and traditions in the past half century are of most relevance here. These references show *an emerging awareness* that liberty gives substantial protection to adult persons in deciding how to conduct their private lives *in matters pertaining to sex*." (emphasis added). Apart from the fact that such an "emerging awareness" does not establish a "fundamental right," the statement is factually false. States continue to prosecute all sorts of crimes by adults "in matters pertaining to sex": prostitution, adult incest, adultery, obscenity, and child pornography. Sodomy laws, too, have been enforced "in the past half century," in which there have been 134 reported cases involving prosecutions for consensual, adult, homosexual sodomy. In relying, for evidence of an "emerging recognition," upon the American Law Institute's 1955 recommendation not to criminalize "'consensual sexual relations conducted in private,'" the Court ignores the fact that this recommendation was "a point of resistance in most of the states that considered adopting the Model Penal Code" Gaylaw 159.

In any event, an "emerging awareness" is by definition not "deeply rooted in this Nation's history and tradition[s]," as we have said "fundamental right" status requires. Constitutional entitlements do not spring into existence because some States choose to lessen or eliminate criminal sanctions on certain behavior. Much less do they spring into existence, as the Court seems to believe, because *foreign nations* decriminalize conduct. The *Bowers* majority opinion *never* relied on "values we share with a wider civilization," but rather rejected the claimed right to sodomy on the ground that such a right was not "'deeply rooted in *this Nation's* history and tradition,'" (emphasis added). *Bowers'* rational-basis holding is likewise devoid of any reliance on the views of a "wider civilization." The Court's discussion of these foreign views (ignoring, of course, the many countries that have retained criminal prohibitions on sodomy) is therefore meaningless dicta. Dangerous dicta, however, since "this Court...should not impose foreign moods, fads, or fashions on Americans." *Foster* v. *Florida* (2002) (Thomas, J., concurring in denial of certiorari).

IV

I turn now to the ground on which the Court squarely rests its holding: the contention that there is no rational basis for the law here under attack. This proposition is so out of accord with our jurisprudence—indeed, with the jurisprudence of *any* society we know—that it requires little discussion.

The Texas statute undeniably seeks to further the belief of its citizens that certain forms of sexual behavior are "immoral and unacceptable"—the same interest furthered by criminal laws against fornication, bigamy, adultery, adult incest, bestiality, and obscenity. *Bowers* held that this *was* a legitimate state interest. The Court today reaches the opposite conclusion. The Texas statute, it says, "furthers *no legitimate state interest* which can justify its intrusion into the personal and private life of the individual" (emphasis addded). The Court embraces instead Justice Stevens' declaration in his *Bowers* dissent, that "the fact that the governing majority in a State has traditionally viewed a particular practice as immoral is not a sufficient reason for upholding a law prohibiting the practice." This effectively decrees the end of all morals legislation. If, as the Court asserts, the promotion of majoritarian sexual morality is not even a *legitimate* state interest, none of the above-mentioned laws can survive rational-basis review.

V

Finally, I turn to petitioners' equal-protection challenge, which no Member of the Court save Justice O'Connor embraces: On its face [the Texas law] applies equally to all persons. Men and women, heterosexuals and homosexuals, are all subject to its prohibition of deviate sexual intercourse with someone of the same sex. To be sure, §21.06 does distinguish between the sexes insofar as concerns the partner with whom the sexual acts are performed: men can violate the law only with other men, and women only with other women. But this cannot itself be a denial of equal protection, since it is precisely the same distinction regarding partner that is drawn in state laws prohibiting marriage with someone of the same sex while permitting marriage with someone of the opposite sex.

The objection is made, however, that the antimiscegenation laws invalidated in *Loving* v. *Virginia* (1967), similarly were applicable to whites and blacks alike, and only distinguished between the races insofar as the *partner* was concerned. In *Loving*, however, we correctly applied heightened scrutiny, rather than the usual rational-basis review, because the Virginia statute was "designed to maintain White Supremacy." A racially discriminatory purpose is always sufficient to subject a law to strict scrutiny, even a facially neutral law that makes no mention of race. No purpose to discriminate against men or women as a class can be gleaned from the Texas law, so rational-basis review applies. That review is readily satisfied here by the same rational basis that satisfied it in *Bowers*—society's belief that certain forms of sexual behavior are "immoral and unacceptable." This is the same justification that supports many other laws regulating sexual behavior that make a distinction based upon the identity of the partner—for example, laws against adultery, fornication, and adult incest, and laws refusing to recognize homosexual marriage.

Justice O'Connor argues that the discrimination in this law which must be justified is not its discrimination with regard to the sex of the partner but its discrimination with regard to the sexual proclivity of the principal actor.

> While it is true that the law applies only to conduct, the conduct targeted by this law is conduct that is closely correlated with being homosexual. Under such circumstances, Texas' sodomy law is targeted at more than conduct. It is instead directed toward gay persons as a class.

Of course the same could be said of any law. A law against public nudity targets "the conduct that is closely correlated with being a nudist," and hence "is targeted at more than conduct"; it is "directed toward nudists as a class." But be that as it may. Even if the Texas law *does* deny equal protection to "homosexuals as a class," that denial *still* does not need to be justified by anything more than a rational basis, which our cases show is satisfied by the enforcement of traditional notions of sexual morality.

Justice O'Connor simply decrees application of "a more searching form of rational basis review" to the Texas statute. The cases she cites do not recognize such a standard, and reach their conclusions only after finding, as required by conventional rational-basis analysis, that no conceivable legitimate state interest supports the classification at issue. Nor does Justice O'Connor explain precisely what her "more searching form" of rational-basis review consists of. It must at least mean, however, that laws exhibiting "'a . . . desire to harm a politically unpopular group,'" are invalid *even though* there may be a conceivable rational basis to support them.

This reasoning leaves on pretty shaky grounds state laws limiting marriage to opposite-sex couples. Justice O'Connor seeks to preserve them by the conclusory statement that "preserving the traditional institution of marriage" is a legitimate state interest. But "preserving the traditional institution of marriage" is just a kinder way of describing the State's *moral disapproval* of same-sex couples. Texas's interest in § 21.06 could be recast in similarly euphemistic terms: "preserving the traditional sexual mores of our society." In the jurisprudence Justice O'Connor has seemingly created, judges can validate laws by characterizing them as "preserving the traditions of society" (good); or invalidate them by characterizing them as "expressing moral disapproval" (bad).

Today's opinion is the product of a Court, which is the product of a law-profession culture, that has largely signed on to the so-called homosexual agenda, by which I mean the agenda promoted by some homosexual activists directed at eliminating the moral opprobrium that has traditionally attached to homosexual conduct. I noted in an earlier opinion the fact that the American Association of Law Schools (to which any reputable law school *must* seek to belong) excludes from membership any school that refuses to ban from its job-interview facilities a law firm (no matter how small) that does not wish to hire as a prospective partner a person who openly engages in homosexual conduct.

One of the most revealing statements in today's opinion is the Court's grim warning that the criminalization of homosexual conduct is "an invitation to subject homosexual persons to discrimination both in the public and in the private spheres." It is clear from this that the Court has taken sides in the culture war, departing from its role of assuring, as neutral observer, that the democratic rules of engagement are observed. Many Americans do not want persons who openly engage in homosexual conduct as partners in their business, as scout-masters for their children, as teachers in their children's schools, or as boarders in their home. They view this as protecting themselves and their families from a lifestyle that they believe to be immoral and destructive. The Court views it as "discrimination" which it is the function of our judgments to deter. So imbued is the Court with the law profession's anti-anti-homosexual culture, that it is seemingly unaware that the attitudes of that culture are not obviously "mainstream"; that in most States what the Court calls "discrimination" against those who engage in homosexual acts is perfectly legal; that proposals to ban such "discrimination" under Title VII have repeatedly been rejected by Congress; that in some cases such "discrimina-

> *So imbued is the Court with the law profession's anti-anti-homosexual culture, that it is seemingly unaware that the attitudes of that culture are not obviously "mainstream."*

tion" is *mandated* by federal statute, see 10 U.S.C. § 654(b)(1) (mandating discharge from the armed forces of any service member who engages in or intends to engage in homosexual acts); and that in some cases such "discrimination" is a constitutional right, see *Boy Scouts of America* v. *Dale* (2000).

Let me be clear that I have nothing against homosexuals, or any other group, promoting their agenda through normal democratic means. Social perceptions of sexual and other morality change over time, and every group has the right to persuade its fellow citizens that its view of such matters is the best. That homosexuals have achieved some success in that enterprise is attested to by the fact that Texas is one of the few remaining States that criminalize private, consensual homosexual acts. But persuading one's fellow citizens is one thing, and imposing one's views in absence of democratic majority will is something else. I would no more *require* a State to criminalize homosexual acts—or, for that matter, display *any* moral disapprobation of them—than I would *forbid* it to do so. What Texas has chosen to do is well within the range of traditional democratic action, and its hand should not be stayed through the invention of a brand-new "constitutional right" by a Court that is impatient of democratic change. It is indeed true that "later generations can see that laws once thought necessary and proper in fact serve only to oppress"; and when that happens, later generations can repeal those laws. But it is the premise of our system that those judgments are to be made by the people, and not imposed by a governing caste that knows best.

One of the benefits of leaving regulation of this matter to the people rather than to the courts is that the people, unlike judges, need not carry things to their logical conclusion. The people may feel that their disapprobation of homosexual conduct is strong enough to disallow homosexual marriage, but not strong enough to criminalize private homosexual acts—and may legislate accordingly. The Court today pretends that it possesses a similar freedom of action, so that that we need not fear judicial imposition of homosexual marriage, as has recently occurred in Canada (in a decision that the Canadian Government has chosen not to appeal). At the end of its opinion—after having laid waste the foundations of our rational-basis jurisprudence—the Court says that the present case "does not involve whether the government must give formal recognition to any relationship that homosexual persons seek to enter." Do not believe it. More illuminating than this bald, unreasoned disclaimer is the progression of thought displayed by an earlier passage in the Court's opinion, which notes the constitutional protections afforded to "personal decisions relating to *marriage*, procreation, contraception, family relationships, child rearing, and education," and then declares that "[p]ersons in a homosexual relationship may seek autonomy for these purposes, just as heterosexual persons do." (emphasis added). Today's opinion dismantles the structure of constitutional law that has permitted a distinction to be made between heterosexual and homosexual unions, insofar as formal recognition in marriage is concerned. If moral disapproval of homosexual conduct is "no legitimate state interest" for purposes of proscribing that conduct; and if, as the Court coos (casting aside all pretense of neutrality), "[w]hen sexuality finds overt expression in intimate conduct with another person, the conduct can be but one element in a personal bond that is more enduring," what justification

One of the benefits of leaving regulation of this matter to the people rather than to the courts is that the people, unlike judges, need not carry things to their logical conclusion.

could there possibly be for denying the benefits of marriage to homosexual couples exercising "[t]he liberty protected by the Constitution." Surely not the encouragement of procreation, since the sterile and the elderly are allowed to marry. This case "does not involve" the issue of homosexual marriage only if one entertains the belief that principle and logic have nothing to do with the decisions of this Court. Many will hope that, as the Court comfortingly assures us, this is so.

The matters appropriate for this Court's resolution are only three: Texas's prohibition of sodomy neither infringes a "fundamental right" (which the Court does not dispute), nor is unsupported by a rational relation to what the Constitution considers a legitimate state interest, nor denies the equal protection of the laws. I dissent.

CHAPTER TWELVE

OTHER "RIGHTS"

THE SUPREME COURT has occasionally extended constitutional protection to individual freedoms other than those enumerated in the Bill of Rights. Under the theory of "substantive due process," it is believed that the word "liberty" in the Due Process Clause of the Fourteenth Amendment includes substantive (and not merely procedural) limitations on a state's power to regulate personal conduct. Courts most commonly use substantive due process to declare certain activities—abortion, child-rearing, marriage, sodomy, among others—to be "fundamental" rights, even though they are not mentioned specifically or even generally in the Constitution.

When determining whether an asserted right is "fundamental" and therefore constitutionally protected, the Supreme Court will usually look at both the nature of the interest and its historical treatment under the law. If the right being asserted involves a highly personal interest including family or sexual relations, then the Court is likely to deem it a fundamental right. An asserted right is also aided by a showing that society has historically accorded strong protection for the activity. If a right is deemed "fundamental" by the Court, almost any regulation of the activity protected by that right will be invalidated.

Many conservative constitutional scholars, including Justice Scalia, have been very critical of substantive due process theory. They argue that the lack of textual basis for creating new rights gives unelected judges too much discretion to advance their sense of right and wrong, thereby undermining the rule of law. Scalia wrote succinctly in one case, "The entire practice of using the Due Process Clause to add judicially favored rights to the limitations upon democracy set forth in the Bill of Rights (usually under the rubric of so-called "substantive due process") is in my view judicial usurpation."[1]

Scalia and other critics note that the Constitution contains procedures for amending it. If additional protections are thought necessary to ward off government interference with personal freedoms, a concerned majority should work to amend the Constitution, as one did in 1920 to add the Nineteenth Amendment and grant women the right to vote.

Although some critics accuse Scalia of opposing judicial creation of new rights simply because he does not favor the rights being created, the charge does not withstand scrutiny. Scalia has opposed creation of new rights even when he is sympathetic to the claimant. Indeed, he has voted against constitutional protection for many freedoms championed by political conservatives, including, among others, the "right" of parents to direct the upbringing of their children and the "right" of companies to avoid having to pay "excessive" punitive damage awards. In another case, a taxpayer asked the Court to strike down on substantive due process grounds a law that increased his taxes retroactively. The Supreme Court rejected that claim. In his concurring opinion, Scalia wrote, "I welcome this recognition that the Due Process Clause does not prevent retroactive taxes, since I believe that the Due Process Clause guarantees no substantive rights, but only (as it says) process."[2]

Scalia went on to note that the Court seemed much more sympathetic to personal rights, such as abortion, than economic rights as this case involved. He concluded, "The picking and choosing among various rights to be accorded 'substantive due process' protection is alone enough to arouse suspicion; but the categorical and inexplicable exclusion of so-called economic rights (even though the Due Process Clause explicitly applies to property) unquestionably involves policy-making rather than neutral legal analysis. I would follow the text of the Constitution, which sets forth certain substantive rights that cannot be taken away, and adds, beyond that, a right to due process when life, liberty, or property is to be taken away."[3]

The opinions below—involving assertions of a new right to refuse medical treatment and a right of parents to determine who may visit their children—give substance to the view that Scalia is consistent in his opposition to judicially created rights. The Court accepts both into the Constitution; Scalia, neither.

CRUZAN v. MISSOURI DEPARTMENT OF HEALTH (1990)

Nancy Cruzan was involved in an automobile accident and suffered severe brain damage. In a "persistent vegetative state," she had some motor reflexes but was oblivious to her surroundings. She received nutrition through a feeding-and-hydration tube. After it became apparent Cruzan would not regain her mental faculties, her parents sought a court order directing the removal of her feeding-and-hydration tube. It was known to all involved that removal of the tube would result in Cruzan's death. The Supreme Court of Missouri refused to approve the order because it did not find "clear and convincing evidence" that Cruzan would have wanted to withdraw lifesaving equipment under such circumstances.

The Supreme Court, in a closely divided 5–4 decision, held that Cruzan had a "liberty" interest protected by the Fourteenth Amendment to refuse unwanted medical procedures. The majority, however, ruled that the State of Missouri also had an important interest in preserving life. This interest justified a requirement that there is "clear and convincing evidence" of an incompetent patient's wish to decline life-sustaining treatment. Because this level of evidence was not present, the Court agreed with the Missouri Supreme Court's ruling against the Cruzans.

Justice Scalia wrote an opinion agreeing with the Court's decision but disagreeing with its approach. Specifically, Scalia objected to the majority's determination that refusal of medical treatment was constitutionally protected. He argued that the "right" to refuse treatment was equivalent to a right to commit suicide, which had never been recognized by the Court and which was in plain opposition to the nation's legal tradition of prohibiting suicide.

❦

Justice Scalia, concurring.

The various opinions in this case portray quite clearly the difficult, indeed agonizing, questions that are presented by the constantly increasing power of science to keep the human body alive for longer than any reasonable person would want to inhabit it. The States have begun to grapple with these problems through legislation. I am concerned, from the tenor of today's opinions, that we are poised to confuse that enterprise as successfully as we have confused the enterprise of legislating concerning abortion—requiring it to be conducted against a background of federal constitutional imperatives that are unknown because they are being newly crafted from Term to Term. That would be a great misfortune.

While I agree with the Court's analysis today, and therefore join in its opinion, I would have preferred that we announce, clearly and promptly, that the federal courts have no business in this field; that American law has always accorded the State the power to prevent, by force if necessary, suicide—including suicide by refusing to take appropriate measures necessary to preserve one's life; that the point at which life becomes "worthless," and the point at which the means necessary to preserve it become "extraordinary" or "inappropriate," are neither set forth in the Constitution nor known to the nine Justices of this Court any better than they are known to nine people picked at random from the Kansas City telephone directory; and hence, that even when it is demonstrated by clear and convincing evidence that a patient no longer wishes certain measures to be taken to preserve her life, it is up to the citizens of Missouri to decide, through their elected representatives, whether that wish will be honored. It is quite impossible (because the Constitution says nothing about the matter) that those citizens will decide upon a line less lawful than the one we would choose; and it is unlikely (because we know no more about "life-and-death" than they do) that they will decide upon a line less reasonable.

> *The point at which the means necessary to preserve life become "extraordinary" or "inappropriate," are neither set forth in the Constitution nor known to the nine justices of this Court any better than they are known to nine people picked at random from the Kansas City telephone directory.*

The text of the Due Process Clause does not protect individuals against deprivations of liberty *simpliciter*. It protects them against deprivations of liberty "without due process of law." To determine that

such a deprivation would not occur if Nancy Cruzan were forced to take nourishment against her will, it is unnecessary to reopen the historically recurrent debate over whether "due process" includes substantive restrictions. It is at least true that no "substantive due process" claim can be maintained unless the claimant demonstrates that the State has deprived him of a right historically and traditionally protected against State interference. That cannot possibly be established here.

At common law in England, a suicide—defined as one who "deliberately puts an end to his own existence, or commits any unlawful malicious act, the consequence of which is his own death," 4 W. Blackstone, Commentaries—was criminally liable. Although the States abolished the penalties imposed by the common law (i.e., forfeiture and ignominious burial), they did so to spare the innocent family, and not to legitimize the act. Case law at the time of the Fourteenth Amendment generally held that assisting suicide was a criminal offense. . . . And most States that did not explicitly prohibit assisted suicide in 1868 recognized, when the issue arose in the 50 years following the Fourteenth Amendment's ratification, that assisted and (in some cases) attempted suicide were unlawful. Thus, "there is no significant support for the claim that a right to suicide is so rooted in our tradition that it may be deemed 'fundamental' or 'implicit in the concept of ordered liberty.'"

Petitioners rely on three distinctions to separate Nancy Cruzan's case from ordinary suicide: (1) that she is permanently incapacitated and in pain; (2) that she would bring on her death not by any affirmative act but by merely declining treatment that provides nourishment; and (3) that preventing her from effectuating her presumed wish to die requires violation of her bodily integrity. None of these suffices. Suicide was not excused even when committed "to avoid those

ills which [persons] had not the fortitude to endure." 4 Blackstone. "The life of those to whom life has become a burden—of those who are hopelessly diseased or fatally wounded—nay, even the lives of criminals condemned to death, are under the protection of the law, equally as the lives of those who are in the full tide of life's enjoyment, and anxious to continue to live." *Blackburn* v. *State*, 23 Ohio St. 146 (1873). Thus, a man who prepared a poison, and placed it within reach of his wife, "to put an end to her suffering" from a terminal illness was convicted of murder, *People* v. *Roberts*, 211 Mich. 187 (1920); the "incurable suffering of the suicide, as a legal question, could hardly affect the degree of criminality. . . ." Note, 30 Yale L.J. 408 (1921) (discussing *Roberts*). Nor would the imminence of the patient's death have affected liability. "The lives of all are equally under the protection of the law, and under that protection to their last moment. . . . [Assisted suicide] is declared by the law to be murder, irrespective of the wishes or the condition of the party to whom the poison is administered. . . ." *Blackburn*.

The second asserted distinction—suggested by the recent cases canvassed by the Court concerning the right to refuse treatment— relies on the dichotomy between action and inaction. Suicide, it is said, consists of an affirmative act to end one's life; refusing treatment is not an affirmative act "causing" death, but merely a passive acceptance of the natural process of dying. I readily acknowledge that the distinction between action and inaction has some bearing upon the legislative judgment of what ought to be prevented as suicide— though even there it would seem to me unreasonable to draw the line precisely between action and inaction, rather than between various forms of inaction. It would not make much sense to say that one may not kill oneself by walking into the sea, but may sit on the beach until submerged by the incoming tide; or that one may not intentionally lock oneself into a cold storage locker, but may refrain from coming indoors when the temperature drops below freezing. Even as a legislative matter, in other words, the intelligent line does not fall between action and inaction, but between those forms of inaction that consist of abstaining from "ordinary" care and those that consist of abstaining from "excessive" or "heroic" measures. Unlike action vs. inaction, that is not a line to be discerned by logic or legal analysis, and we should not pretend that it is.

It would not make much sense to say that one may not kill oneself by walking into the sea, but may sit on the beach until submerged by the incoming tide.

But to return to the principal point for present purposes: the irrelevance of the action-inaction distinction. Starving oneself to death is no different from putting a gun to one's temple as far as the common law definition of suicide is concerned; the cause of death in both cases is the suicide's conscious decision to "pu[t] an end to his own existence." 4 Blackstone. Of course, the common law rejected the action-inaction distinction in other contexts involving the taking of human life as well. In the prosecution of a parent for the starvation death of her infant, it was no defense that the infant's death was "caused" by no action of the parent, but by the natural process of starvation, or by the infant's natural inability to provide for itself. A physician, moreover, could be criminally liable for failure to provide care that could have extended the patient's life, even if death was immediately caused by the underlying disease that the physician failed to treat.

It is not surprising, therefore, that the early cases considering the claimed right to refuse medical treatment dismissed as specious the nice distinction between "passively submitting to death and actively seeking it. The distinction may be merely verbal, as it would be if an adult sought death by starvation instead of a drug. If the State may interrupt one mode of self-destruction, it may with equal authority interfere with the other." *John F. Kennedy Memorial Hosp.* v. *Heston*, 58 N.J. 576 (1971).

The third asserted basis of distinction—that frustrating Nancy Cruzan's wish to die in the present case requires interference with her bodily integrity—is likewise inadequate, because such interference is impermissible only if one begs the question whether her refusal to undergo the treatment on her own is suicide. It has always been lawful not only for the State, but even for private citizens, to interfere with bodily integrity to prevent a felony. That general rule has of course been applied to suicide. At common law, even a private person's use of force to prevent suicide was privileged. It is not even reasonable, much less required by the Constitution, to maintain that, although the State has the right to prevent a person from slashing his wrists, it does not have the power to apply physical force to prevent him from doing so, nor the power, should he succeed, to apply, coercively if necessary, medical measures to stop the flow of blood. The state-run hospital, I am certain, is not liable under 42 U.S.C. 1983 for violation of constitutional rights, nor the private hospital liable under general tort law, if, in a State where suicide is unlawful, it pumps out the stomach of a person who has intentionally taken an overdose of barbiturates, despite that person's wishes to the contrary.

The dissents of Justices Brennan and Stevens make a plausible case for our intervention here only by embracing—the latter explicitly and the former by implication—a political principle that the States are free to adopt, but that is demonstrably not imposed by the Constitution.

"The State," says Justice Brennan, "has no legitimate general interest in someone's life, completely abstracted from the interest of the person living that life, that could outweigh the person's choice *to avoid medical treatment*" (emphasis added). The italicized phrase sounds moderate enough, and is all that is needed to cover the present case—but the proposition cannot logically be so limited. One who accepts it must also accept, I think, that the State has no such legitimate interest that could outweigh "the person's choice to put an end to her life." Similarly, if one agrees with Justice Brennan that "the State's general interest in life must accede to Nancy Cruzan's particularized and intense interest in self-determination *in her choice of medical treatment*" (emphasis added), he must also believe that the State must accede to her "particularized and intense interest in self-determination *in her choice whether to continue living or to die*." For insofar as balancing the relative interests of the State and the individual is concerned, there is nothing distinctive about accepting death through the refusal of "medical treatment," as opposed to accepting it through the refusal of food, or through the failure to shut off the engine and get out of the car after parking in one's garage after work. Suppose that Nancy Cruzan were in precisely the condition she is in today, except that she could be fed and digest food and water without artificial assistance. How is the State's "interest" in keeping her alive thereby increased, or her interest in deciding whether she wants to continue living reduced? It seems to me, in other words, that Justice Brennan's position ultimately rests upon the proposition that it is none of the State's business if a person wants to commit suicide. Justice Stevens is explicit on the point: "Choices about death touch the core of liberty. . . . [N]ot much may be said with confidence about death unless it is said from faith, and that alone is reason enough to protect the freedom to conform choices about death to individual conscience." This is a view that some societies have held, and that our States are free to adopt if they wish. But it is not a view imposed by our constitutional traditions, in which the power of the State to prohibit suicide is unquestionable.

What I have said above is not meant to suggest that I would think it desirable, if we were sure that Nancy Cruzan wanted to die, to keep her alive by the means at issue here. I assert only that the Constitution has nothing to say about the subject. To raise up a constitutional right here, we would have to create out of nothing (for it exists neither in text nor tradition) some constitutional principle whereby, although the State may insist that an individual come in out of the cold and eat food, it may not insist that he take medicine; and although it may pump his stomach empty of poison he has ingested, it may not fill his stomach with food he has failed to ingest. Are there, then, no reasonable and humane limits that ought not to be exceeded in requiring an individual to preserve his own life? There obviously are, but they are not set forth in the Due Process Clause. What assures us that those limits will not be exceeded is the same constitutional guarantee that is the source of most of our protection—what protects us, for example, from being assessed a tax of 100% of our income above the subsistence level, from being forbidden to drive cars, or from being required to send our children to school for 10 hours a day, none of which horribles is categorically prohibited by the Constitution. Our salvation is the Equal Protection

> *What I have said above is not meant to suggest that I would think it desirable, if we were sure that Nancy Cruzan wanted to die, to keep her alive by the means at issue here. I assert only that the Constitution has nothing to say about the subject.*

Clause, which requires the democratic majority to accept for themselves and their loved ones what they impose on you and me. This Court need not, and has no authority to, inject itself into every field of human activity where irrationality and oppression may theoretically occur, and if it tries to do so, it will destroy itself.

TROXEL v. GRANVILLE (2000)

A Washington State law permitted "any person" to petition a court for visitation rights. If a court found that allowing an individual—a noncustodial parent or other relative, for instance—to have visitation rights was in "the best interests of the child," the court could authorize the visits.

In *Troxel* v. *Granville,* grandparents who were estranged from their daughter used the law to petition to gain visitation rights with their granddaughters. The mother objected to the grandparents' proposed visitation schedule. The Washington State Supreme Court said the law was unconstitutional because it violated the substantive due process right of the mother to direct the upbringing of her children.

The Supreme Court of the United States agreed that the law was invalid. A plurality of four justices, relying on a few prior Court precedents, ruled the law violated "the fundamental rights of parents to make decisions concerning the care, custody, and control of their children." Two concurring justices (including Justice Clarence Thomas) agreed with the plurality that parental rights are "fundamental" rights guaranteed by the Due Process Clause of the Fourteenth Amendment.

Justice Scalia dissented. Though clearly sympathetic to the idea that parents are free to raise their children as they see fit, he opposed extension of an unenumerated and judicially created constitutional right. Put simply, he said he does not have authority as a judge to strike down a state law that violates his sense of parental authority, but that does not violate a right contained in the Constitution of the United States.

JUSTICE SCALIA, DISSENTING.

In my view, a right of parents to direct the upbringing of their children is among the "unalienable Rights" with which the Declaration of Independence proclaims "all Men ... are endowed by their Creator." And in my view that right is also among the "othe[r] [rights] retained by the people" which the Ninth Amendment says the Constitution's enumeration of rights "shall not be construed to deny or disparage." The Declaration of Independence, however, is not a legal prescription conferring powers upon the courts; and the Constitution's refusal to "deny or disparage" other rights is far removed from affirming any one of them, and even farther removed from authorizing judges to identify what they might be, and to enforce the judges' list against laws duly enacted by the people. Consequently, while I would think it entirely compatible with the commitment to representative democracy set forth in the founding documents to argue, in legislative chambers or in electoral campaigns, that the state has *no power* to interfere with parents' authority over the rearing of their children, I do not believe that the power which the Constitution confers upon me *as a judge* entitles me to deny legal effect to laws that (in my view) infringe upon what is (in my view) that unenumerated right.

> *In my view, a right of parents to direct the upbringing of their children is among the "unalienable Rights" with which the Declaration of Independence proclaims "all Men ... are endowed by their Creator."*

Only three holdings of this Court rest in whole or in part upon a substantive constitutional right of parents to direct the upbringing of their children—two of them from an era rich in substantive due process holdings that have since been repudiated. The sheer diversity of today's opinions persuades me that the theory of unenumerated parental rights underlying these three cases has small claim to *stare decisis* protection. A legal principle that can be thought to produce such diverse outcomes in the relatively simple case before us here is not a legal principle that has induced substantial reliance. While I would not now overrule those earlier cases (that has not been urged), neither would I extend the theory upon which they rested to this new context.

Judicial vindication of "parental rights" under a Constitution that does not even mention them requires (as Justice Kennedy's opinion rightly points out) not only a judicially crafted definition of parents, but also—unless, as no one believes, the parental rights are to be absolute—judicially approved assessments of "harm to the child" and judicially defined gradations of other persons (grandparents, extended family, adoptive family in an adoption later found to be invalid, long-term guardians, etc.) who may have some claim against the wishes of the parents. If we embrace this unenumerated right, I think it obvious—whether we affirm or reverse the judgment here, or remand as Justice Stevens or Justice Kennedy would do—that we will be ushering in a new regime of judicially prescribed, and federally prescribed, family law. I have no reason to believe that federal judges will be better at this than state legislatures; and state legislatures have the great advantages of doing harm in a more circumscribed area, of being able to correct their mistakes in a flash, and of being removable by the people.

For these reasons, I would reverse the judgment below.

SCALIA'S AMERICA

~≪◦◦≫~

AFTER REVIEWING THIS COLLECTION of opinions, readers may wonder how the country would be different if Scalia's approach had prevailed in these cases. What if all of his opinions were majority opinions? What would life be like in Scalia's America?

In Scalia's America, freedom, democracy, and diversity would flourish. Freedom would be enhanced as the courts stood firm for protection of the basic liberties enumerated in the Bill of Rights. To the extent that those core freedoms had been weakened by recent Court decisions, they would be restored to their original meaning and protected against the shifting winds of public opinion. Americans would be free to criticize their politicians and government, no matter whether that criticism takes a symbolic form, such as burning an American flag, or a more traditional form, such as joining with fellow citizens to discuss the record of a candidate for political office. In addition, taxpaying Americans would have greater freedom to establish, through their elected representatives, rules governing the use of their tax dollars on federal art programs and the like.

The freedom to practice one's religion—or no religion at all—would be strengthened in Scalia's America. Courts would not view legislative efforts to accommodate religious practices with suspicion, unless the government appears to be playing favorites among the various faiths. Moreover, the Court would not disrupt popularly enacted laws that were not intentionally drawn to restrict religious practices.

All fundamental freedoms would be guaranteed by a vibrant federal government whose power was divided and balanced among three distinct branches. The judiciary would seek to interpret the law, not create it. Congress would make laws, but leave the executive free to enforce it. In following the structure set forth in the Constitution, power would be divided so that no future President, Congress, or Supreme Court could amass sufficient power to dominate the others, usurp another's authority, and deprive cherished individual liberties.

Democracy also would prosper in Scalia's America. If the Constitution is silent on an issue, that issue will be returned to the people to make democratic choices for themselves and their communities. Majority votes by citizens, rather than by nine Supreme Court justices, would determine most social policies. Indeed, Scalia's America would entrust the people to make meaningful decisions for their communities, involving important moral issues (e.g., abortion), economic issues (e.g. punitive damages), and neighborhood issues (e.g., nude dancing).

The product of enhanced freedom and revitalized democracy would be greater diversity. In Scalia's America, the diversity of the different regions of the nation would be evident as each enacted laws reflecting its values. Some states would ban homosexual marriage; others might enshrine the right to same-sex marriage in their state constitutions. Some states would impose capital punishment against all murderers; others might eliminate the death penalty altogether. The states would be free to choose, reflecting the desires of the people. This democratic policymaking and diversity of practice would stand in sharp contrast to today's Supreme Court-prescribed, one-size-fits-all standard of deciding issues.

In Scalia's America, diversity would grow as citizens of every color are treated as individuals—and equally. Any law designed to help one race by disadvantaging another would be struck down, no matter how well-intentioned. The virtue of equality would not, however, be used to eliminate the benefits of diversity. States and communities that sought to improve educational and social opportunities through single-sex organizations would be free to do so.

In Scalia's America, these expansions of freedom, democracy, and diversity would be ably protected by, among other institutions, courts that respect the rule of law. Judges charged with interpreting laws would give words their ordinary meaning. They would moor their solutions of constitutional disputes to the text of the charter and the meaning of its Framers. America would be reborn as a nation of laws and not of men.

Whether Scalia's America will ever come into being is unknowable at this point. It likely will not occur during his lifetime. However, throughout the Supreme Court's history, it sometimes happens that views—coherent, textually based, and well argued—once found in the minority, become the basis of future majority opinions. Ultimately, this result is not Scalia's to achieve; he is not likely to have a role in nominating or confirming future justices to the Supreme Court. But if future Court majorities seek to re-establish a jurisprudence that hews closer to the proper meaning of the Constitution, they will have, in Justice Scalia's opinions, an enormous intellectual foundation on which to build.

NOTES

◦⟨◦⟩◦

Introduction

1. Frost, 188 (quoting Aristotle, *The Rhetoric of Aristotle* (Lane Cooper trans., 1932).
2. *Romer* v. *Evans*, 517 U.S. 620, 653 (1996) (Scalia, J., dissenting).
3. *Pope* v. *Illinois*, 481 U.S. 497, 504 (1987) (Scalia, J., concurring).
4. *Kyles* v. *Whitley*, 514 U.S. 419, 466–467 (1995) (Scalia, J., dissenting).
5. *MCI Telecommunications* v. *AT&T*, 512 U.S. 218, 227(1994)
6. *Lamb's Chapel* v. *Center Moriches School District*, 508 U.S. 384, 398 (1993) (Scalia, J., concurring).
7. *Webster* v. *Reproductive Health Services*, 492 U.S. 490, 537 (1989) (Scalia, J., concurring).
8. *Good News Club* v. *Milford Central School*, 533 U.S. 98, 121 (2001) (Scalia, J., concurring).
9. *Morse* v. *Republican Party of Virginia*, 517 U.S. 186, 245 (1996) (Scalia, J., dissenting).
10. *Board of Commissioners, Wabaunsee County* v. *Umbehr*, 518 U.S. 668, 711 (1996) (Scalia, J., dissenting).
11. *Sosa* v. *Alvarez-Machain*, 124 S.Ct. 2739, 2776 (2004) (Scalia, J., concurring).

Chapter One: Scalia's Philosophy

1. Scalia, "The Rule of Law," 1184.
2. Ibid., 1179.

3. Schultz and Smith, 88.

4. *Maryland* v. *Craig*, 497 U.S. 836 (1990).

5. Scalia, "Originalism," 862.

6. *United States* v. *Eichman*, 496 U.S. 310 (1990).

7. *Kyollo* v. *United States*, 533 U.S. 27 (2001).

8. Scalia, *A Matter of Interpretation*, 46.

9. Scalia, "Originalism," 856.

10. Scalia, Remarks at Catholic University.

11. Starr, 25,

12. Zlotnick, 1381,

13. Scalia, *A Matter of Interpretation*, 46.

14. Ibid.

15. Ibid., 37–38.

16. United States Senate, S. Hrg. 99-1064 (statement of Sen. Kennedy).

17. Mauro.

18. Brisbin, 12.

19. Simon, 138.

20. Reid, 146 Cong. Rec., S2653.

21. Reid, 145 Cong. Rec., S1579.

22. See Chemerinksy, 392, and Zlotnick, 1416.

23. Koskela, 32.

24. Zlotnick, 1424.

25. See, e.g., 143 Cong. Rec. H5185 (daily ed. July 15, 1997) (statement of Rep. Barney Frank).

26. Mauro.

27. Schultz and Smith, xvi.

28. *Casey*, 851.

29. See, e.g., Failinger, 471.

30. *Casey*, 538, 545–546 (Blackmun, J., concurring and dissenting).

31. Schultz and Smith, 209.

32. Ibid., xiii.

Chapter Two: Interpreting Laws

1. *Smith* v. *United States*, 508 U.S. 223 (1993).

2. *Wisconsin Public Intervenor* v. *Mortier*, 501 U.S. 597, 621 (1991) (Scalia, J., concurring in the judgment).

3. *Conroy* v. *Aniskoff,* 507 U.S. 511, 519 (1993) (Scalia, J., concurring in the judgment).

4. Ibid.

5. *Nixon* v. *Missouri Municipal League,* 124 S. Ct. 1555, 1566 (Scalia, J., concurring in the judgment).

CHAPTER THREE: SEPARATION OF POWERS

1. Clark, 754.

2. Fox and McAllister, 244-245.

3. *Mistretta v. United States,* 488 U.S. 361 (1989).

4. Schultz and Smith, 89.

5. *Plaut v. Spendthrift Farm,* 514 U.S. 211, 239 (1995).

CHAPTER FOUR: RACE

1. *Bolling* v. *Sharpe,* 347 U.S. 497 (1954).

2. *Fullilove* v. *Klutznick,* 448 U.S. 448, 507) (1980) (Marshall, J., concurring).

CHAPTER FIVE: ABORTION

1. *Griswold* v. *Connecticut,* 381 U.S. 479 (1965).

2. *Eisenstadt* v. *Baird,* 405 U.S. 438 (1972).

3. *Hodgson* v. *Minnesota,* 497 U.S. 417 (1990).

4. Ibid., 480 (Scalia, J., concurring and dissenting)

5. *Akron* v. *Akron Center for Reproductive Health,* 462 U.S. 416, 458 (1983) (O'Connor, J., dissenting).

CHAPTER SIX: DEATH PENALTY

1. *Furman* v. *Georgia,* 408 U.S. 238 (1972).

2. *Rhodes* v. *Chapman,* 452 U.S. 337, 346 (1981), quoting *Trop* v. *Dulles,* 356 U.S. 86, 101 (1958) (plurality opinion).

3. *Thompson* v. *Oklahoma,* 487 U.S. 815, 859 (1988).(Scalia, J., dissenting).

CHAPTER SEVEN: RELIGIOUS FREEDOM

1. *Everson* v. *Board of Education,* 330 U.S. 1 (1947).

2. Ibid., 15

3. See, e.g., Carter, 109.

4. Sullivan, 449.

5. *Goldman* v. *Weinberger,* 475 U.S. 503 (1986).

6. *Sherberg* v. *Verner,* 374 U.S. 398 (1963).

7. *Employment Division of Oregon* v. *Smith*, 494 U.S. 872, 890 (1990).
8. *Board of Education of Kiryas Joel* v. *Grumet*, 512 U.S. 687 (1994) (Scalia, J., dissenting) (quoting *Zorach* v. *Clauson*, 343 U.S. 306 (1952)).
9. *Durham v. United States*, 94 U.S. App. D.C. 228 (1954).

CHAPTER EIGHT: GENDER EQUALITY

1. *Craig* v. *Boren*, 429 U.S. 190 (1976).
2. *Rostker* v. *Goldberg*, 453 U.S. 57 (1981).
3. *Michael M.* v. *Superior Court of Sonoma County*, 450 U.S. 464 (1981).

CHAPTER NINE: FREE SPEECH

1. Term comes from Justice Oliver Wendell Holmes in *Abrams* v. *United States* 250 U.S. 616, 630 (1919) (Holmes, J., dissenting).
2. *McConnell* v. *Federal Election Commission*, 124 S.Ct. 619 (2003) (Thomas, J., concurring and dissenting).
3. 503 U.S. 703 (2000).
4. Ibid., 742 (Scalia, J., dissenting).
5. Ibid., 749.
6. Ibid., 764.
7. *Austin* v. *Michigan Chamber of Commerce*, 494 U.S. 652, 692 (1990) (Scalia, J., dissenting).
8. Public Law 107-155 (2002).

CHAPTER TEN: NON-SPEECH AND UN-FREE SPEECH

1. *Barnes* v. *Glen Theater, Inc.*, 501 U.S. 560 (1991) and *City of Erie* v. *Pap's A.M.*, 529 U.S. 277 (2000).

CHAPTER ELEVEN: HOMOSEXUALITY

1. *Bowers* v. *Hardwick*, 478 U.S. 186, 191 (1986).
2. 116 U.S. 620 (1996).
3. Ibid., 637 (Scalia, J., dissenting).

CHAPTER TWELVE: OTHER "RIGHTS"

1. *Chicago v. Morales*, 527 U.S. 41, 85 (1999) (Scalia, J., dissenting).
2. *United States* v. *Carlton*, 512 U.S. 26, 40 (1994) (Scalia, J., concurring in judgment).
3. Ibid., 41–42.

BIBLIOGRAPHY

Barron, Jerome A., and C. Thomas Dienes. *Constitutional Law*, 6ᵗʰ ed. West Group, 2003.

Bork, Robert H. *The Tempting of America: The Political Seduction of the Law*. The Free Press, 1990.

Brisbin, Jr., Richard A. *Justice Antonin Scalia and the Conservative Revival*. The Johns Hopkins University Press, 1997.

Burton, Shawn. "Justice Scalia's Methodological Approach to Judicial Decision-Making: Political Actor or Strategic Institutionalist?" *University of Toledo Law Review* 34 (Spring 2003): 575.

Bybee, Jay S. "Printz, The Unitary Executive, and the Fire in the Trash Can: Has Justice Scalia Picked the Court's Pocket?" *Notre Dame Law Review* 77 (November 2001): 269.

Carter, Stephen L. *The Culture of Disbelief: How American Law and Politics Trivialize Religious Devotion*. Basic Books, 1993.

Clark, Bradford R. "The Constitutional Structure and the Jurisprudence of Justice Scalia." *St. Louis Law Journal* 47 (Spring 2003): 753.

Chemerinsky, Erwin. "The Jurisprudence of Justice Scalia: A Critical Appraisal." *Hawaii Law Review* 22 (Summer 2000): 385.

Elsasser, Glen. "No Contest: Top Court's Top Fighter is Scalia, Verbal Combat is Conservative's Forte." *Chicago Tribune*, May 27, 1997.

Eskridge, Jr., William N. "The New Textualism." *UCLA Law Review* 37 (April 1990): 621.

Failinger, Marie A. "Not Mere Rhetoric: On Wasting or Claiming Your Legacy, Justice Scalia." *University of Toledo Law Review* 34 (Spring 2003): 425.

Fox, Autumn, and Stephen R. McAllister. "An Eagle Soaring: The Jurisprudence of Justice Antonin Scalia." *Campbell Law Review* 19 (Spring 1997): 223.

Frank, Barney. Statement. *Congressional Record* 143, daily ed. (July 15, 1997): H 5185.

Friedman, Lawrence M. *American Law: An Introduction*. 2nd ed. W.W. Norton & Company, 1988.

Frost, Michael. "Justice Scalia's Rhetoric of Dissent: A Greco-Roman Analysis of Scalia's Advocacy in the VMI Case." *Kentucky Law Review* 91 (2002 / 2003): 167.

Gerhardt, Michael J. "A Tale of Two Textualists: A Critical Comparison of Justices Black and Scalia." *Boston University Law Review* 74 (January 1994): 25.

Hall, Kermit L., ed. *The Oxford Guide to United States Supreme Court Decisions*. Oxford University Press, 1999.

Kannar, George. "The Constitutional Catechism of Antonin Scalia." *Yale Law Journal* 99 (April 1990): 1297.

Karkkainen, Bradley C. "'Plain Meaning': Justice Scalia's Jurisprudence of Strict Statutory Construction." *Harvard Journal of Law & Public Policy* 17 (Spring 1994). 401.

Koby, Michael H. "The Supreme Court's Declining Reliance on Legislative History: The Impact of Justice Scalia's Critique." *Harvard Journal on Legis.* 36 (Summer 1999): 369.

Koskela, Alice. "Scalia Shows Textualists Have a Sense of Humor." *Advocate* (Idaho) 43 (October 2000): 31.

Marquand, Robert. "High Court's Colorful Man in Black." *The Christian Science Monitor*, March 3, 1998.

Mauro, Tony. "High Court Adjourns for the Summer Intact." *Legal Times*, July 9, 1990, 10.

Public Law 107–155 (2002).

Reid, Harry. Statement. *Congressional Record* 145, daily ed. (February 12, 1999): S 1579.

Reid, Harry. Statement. *Congressional Record* 146, daily ed. (April 13, 2000): S 2653.

Scalia, Antonin. *A Matter of Interpretation: Federal Courts and the Law.* Edited by Amy Grutman. Princeton U. Press, 1997.

Scalia, Antonin. Remarks at the Catholic University of America, Washington, D.C., October 18, 1996. http://www.courttv.com/archive/legaldocs/rights/scalia.html.

Scalia, Antonin. "The Rule of Law as a Law of Rules." *University of Chicago Law Review* 56 (Fall 1989): 1175.

Scalia, Antonin. "Originalism: The Lesser Evil." *University of Cincinnati Law Review.* 57(1989): 849.

Schultz, David A., and Christopher E. Smith. *The Jurisprudential Vision of Justice Antonin Scalia.* Rowman & Littlefield Publishers, Inc., 1996.

Simon, James F. *The Center Holds: The Power Struggle Inside the Rehnquist Court.* Simon & Schuster, 1995.

Smith, Christopher E., and Madhavi McCall. "Justice Scalia's Influence on Criminal Justice." *University of Toledo Law Review* 34 (Spring 2003): 535.

Starr, Kenneth W. *First Among Equals: The Supreme Court in American Life.* Warner Books, 2002.

Sunstein, Cass R. "Justice Scalia's Democratic Formalism." *Yale Law Journal.* 107 (November 1997): 529.

Sullivan, Kathleen M. "Justice Scalia and the Religion Clauses." *Hawaii Law Review* 22 (Summer 2000): 449.

U.S. Congress. Senate. Committee on the Judiciary. *Nomination of Judge Antonin Scalia to be Associate Justice of the Supreme Court of the U.S.: Hearing 99-1064 before the Committee on the Judiciary.* 99th Congress, 2nd sess., 1986.

Zlotnick, David M. "Justice Scalia and His Critics: An Exploration of Scalia's Fidelity to His Constitutional Methodology." *Emory Law Journal* 48 (Fall 1999): 1377.

CASES

Adarand Constructors, Inc. v. *Pena,* 515 U.S. 200 (1995).

Agostini v. *Felton,* 521 U.S. 203 (1997).

Akron v. *Akron Center for Reprod. Health,* 462 U.S. 416 (1983).

Atkins v. *Virginia,* 535 U.S. 304 (2002).

Austin v. *Michigan Chamber of Commerce,* 494 U.S. 652 (1990).

Barnes v. *Glen Theater, Inc.,* 501 U.S. 560 (1991).

Bd. of Comm'r, Wabaunsee County v. *Umbehr,* 518 U.S. 668 (1996).

Bd. of Educ. of Kiryas Joel v. *Grumet,* 512 U.S. 687 (1994).

Bolling v. *Sharpe,* 347 U.S. 497 (1954).

Bowers v. *Hardwick,* 478 U.S. 186 (1986).

Buckley v. *Valeo,* 424 U.S. 1 (1976).

Callins v. *Collins,* 510 U.S. 1141 (1994).

Chicago v. *Morales,* 527 U.S. 41 (1999).

City of Erie v. *Pap's A.M.,* 529 U.S. 277 (2000).

Comm. for Public Educ. and Religious Liberty v. *Regan,* 444 U.S. 646 (1980).

Conroy v. *Aniskoff*, 507 U.S. 511 (1993).

Craig v. *Boren*, 429 U.S. 190 (1976).

Cruzan v. *Dir., Mo. Dep't. of Health*, 497 U.S. 261 (1990).

Durham v. *United States*, 94 U.S. App. D.C. 228 (1954).

Eisenstadt v. *Baird*, 405 U.S. 438 (1972).

Employment Division of Oregon v. *Smith*, 494 U.S. 872 (1990).

Fullilove v. *Klutznick*, 448 U.S. 448 (1980).

Furman v. *Georgia*, 408 U.S. 238 (1972).

Goldman v. *Weinberger*, 475 U.S. 503 (1986).

Good News Club v. *Milford Central School*, 533 U.S. 98 (2001).

Gratz v. *Bollinger*, 123 S. Ct. 2411 (2003).

Griswold v. *Connecticut*, 381 U.S. 479 (1965).

Grutter v. *Bollinger*, 123 S. Ct. 2325 (2003).

Hill v. *Colorado*, 503 U.S. 703 (2000).

Hodgson v. *Minnesota*, 497 U.S. 417 (1990).

Korematsu v. *United States*, 323 U.S. 214 (1944).

Kyollo v. *United States*, 533 U.S. 27 (2001).

Lamb's Chapel v. *Center Moriches School District*, 508 U.S. 384 (1993).

Lawrence v. *Texas*, 123 S. Ct. 2472 (2003).

Lee v. *Weisman*, 505 U.S. 577 (1992).

Lemon v. *Kurtzman*, 403 U.S. 602 (1971).

Marbury v. *Madison*, 5 U.S. 137 (1803).

Martin v. *PGA Tour, Inc.*, 532 U.S. 661 (1991).

Maryland v. *Craig*, 497 U.S. 836 (1990).

McConnell v. *FEC*, 124 S. Ct. 619 (2003).

MCI Telecomm. v. *AT&T*, 512 U.S. 218 (1994).

Michael M. v. *Superior Court of Sonoma County*, 450 U.S. 464 (1981).

Mistretta v. *United States*, 488 U.S. 361 (1989).

Morrison v. *Olsen*, 487 U.S. 654 (1988).

Morse v. *Republican Party of Virginia*, 517 U.S. 186 (1996).

National Endowment for the Arts v. *Finley*, 524 U.S. 569 (1998).

Penry v. *Lynaugh*, 492 U.S. 302 (1989).

Planned Parenthood of Southeastern Pennsylvania v. *Casey*, 505 U.S. 833 (1992).

Plaut v. *Spendthrift Farm*, 514 U.S. 211 (1995).

Pope v. *Illinois*, 481 U.S. 497 (1987).

Rhodes v. *Chapman*, 452 U.S. 337 (1981).

Richmond v. *J.A. Croson Co.*, 488 U.S. 469 (1989).

Roe v. *Wade*, 410 U.S. 113 (1973).

Romer v. *Evans*, 116 U.S. 1620 (1996).

Rostker v. *Goldberg*, 453 U.S. 57 (1981).

Scott v. *Sanford (Dred Scott)*, 60 U.S. 393 (1956).

Sherbert v. *Verner*, 374 U.S. 398 (1963).

Smith v. *United States*, 508 U.S. 223 (1993).

Stenberg v. *Carhart*, 530 U.S. 914 (2000).

Thompson v. *Oklahoma*, 487 U.S. 815 (1988).

Troxel v. *Granville*, 530 U.S. 57 (2000).

United States v. *Carlton*, 512 U.S. 26 (1994).

United States v. *Eichman*, 496 U.S. 310 (1990).

United States v. *Va.*, 518 U.S. 515 (1996).

Wallace v. *Jaffree*, 472 U.S. 38 (1985).

Webster v. *Reproductive Health Services*, 492 U.S. 490 (1989).

Wisconsin Public Intervenor v. *Mortier*, 501 U.S. 597 (1991).

Zelman v. *Simmons-Harris*, 536 U.S. 639 (2002).

Zorach v. *Clauson*, 343 U.S. 306 (1952).

ACKNOWLEDGMENTS

I AM GRATEFUL FOR THE TIME, talents, and efforts of some respected friends and colleagues. Of my reviewers, I want to highlight the contributions of Dana Nelson, for his excellent suggestions on organization, and Paul D. Clement, Esq., for his substantive input and overall support for this project. I sincerely hope that forty or so years from now someone will be putting together a collection of Paul's Supreme Court opinions.

Neil Bradley, Robert Charrow, Esq., David Cirasuolo, Matthew DeMazza, John J. O'Brien, Esq., and John F. Ring, Esq. all reviewed drafts and provided constructive criticism and encouragement. David Lopez is an inspiring friend who provided invaluable guidance to me.

I also want to acknowledge the research assistance and administrative support of Gee Gee Bacote, Jared Dunkin, and Christine Thomas. My warm wishes extend to the team at Regnery, especially Rowena Itchon, for their shared vision.

On a personal note, I want to thank my mother for her rugged individualism and her love of words. Both took root in her "mistake." Special thanks go to my father for his unfailing support for this and every other endeavor I have undertaken.

And then there are my girls: my wife, Kerrie, and our daughter, Kiley. Thanks, Kerrie, for holding down the fort and allowing me to pursue this goal. To Kiley, I hope you one day appreciate the writings of Justice Scalia half as much as you do those of Doctor Seuss.

Last—and most—thanks be to God for all of the blessings He bestowed on me during the course of this project.

INDEX